Psychological Perspectives on Human Diversity in America

Master Lectures in Psychology

Psychological Perspectives on Human Diversity in America

Master Lecturers

Linda Garnets

James M. Jones

Douglas Kimmel

Stanley Sue

Carol Tavris

Edited by
Jacqueline D. Goodchilds

AMERICAN PSYCHOLOGICAL ASSOCIATION
WASHINGTON, DC

Second printing November 1993
Third printing November 1995

Published by the
American Psychological Association
750 First Street, NE
Washington, DC 20002

Copies may be ordered from
APA Order Department
P.O. Box 2710
Hyattsville, MD 20784

Typeset in Cheltenham by Harper Graphics, Waldorf, MD

Printer: Braun-Brumfield, Inc., Ann Arbor, MI
Technical editor and production coordinator: Valerie Montenegro

Library of Congress Cataloging-in-Publication Data

Psychological perspectives on human diversity in America/master lecturers, Linda Garnets . . . [et al.]; edited by Jacqueline D. Goodchilds.
    p. cm.—(The Master Lectures)
    Lectures presented at the 1990 APA Convention in Boston.
    Includes bibliographical references.
    ISBN 1-55798-122-1 (acid-free paper)
    1. Difference (Psychology) 2. Sex differences (Psychology) 3. Homosexuality—Psychological aspects. 4. Race—Psychological aspects. 5. Ethnopsychology. I. Garnets, Linda. II. Goodchilds, Jacqueline D. (Jacqueline Desire), 1926– . III. American Psychological Association. Convention (1990 : Boston, Mass.) IV. Series.
    BF697.P759   1991
    155.8'2'0973—dc20   91-20477
                                            CIP

Printed in the United States of America

CONTENTS

PREFACE

For a close to unconscionably long time, much as we psychologists took the white rat as an apt exemplar for behavior, we took the white male college student as exemplar for human behavior. We acknowledge that perspective today as a limited one, but what to do about it? Let us hope this book will assist us all to move a bit toward a more inclusive view of individual and interpersonal human behavior. I can personally and do gratefully attest to the fact that all contributors to this book are exceedingly knowledgeable about their topics and worked diligently, thoughtfully, and very hard to assemble our discipline's current understanding of those topics and to consider the implications that can and should be drawn therefrom.

This volume undoubtedly represents a step or possibly leap forward, but lest we too loudly laud our accomplishment, some words of caution are in order. First, consider how we conceptualize perspective and diversity. In these pages the authors repeatedly remind us that race, ethnicity, gender, and sexual orientation are dimensions, not categories of human experience, requiring Cartesian rather than Aristotelian modes of thinking, if you will. Yet in science and in practice we easily and often forget and ignore that inconvenient but vital reality.

Second, in the multidimensional space of human behavior, note that this book discusses four dimensions only. Why and how does it happen to be these and not others? An obvious answer is the limitations of time and space: There is room for at most five per theme. For this volume, it was necessary to break with custom and solicit a two-for-one arrangement, thus providing five contributors for four topics. The four topics were selected as major aspects of diversity about which psychology does have something to say and which affect members of our society in important ways. Yes, there are others of major impact in the here and now. Regarding the "now," we guiltlessly acknowledge that our discipline is generally ahistorical. As to the "here," there are among the many missing dimensions (e.g., physical appearance, forms of "impairment," chronological/biological age, regional and urban/rural differences) two in particular whose absence is a matter of some concern in this context: These are notably (a) religion/religiosity and (b) social class or, as we sometimes glibly term it, socioeconomic status. Psychologists quite appropriately include these topics in our purview, but they are largely and more thoroughly in the domain of our sister discipline of sociology. We thought of reaching across the sacrosanct disciplinary boundaries for a fifth chapter but did not ultimately do so.

And finally and again about the "here" aspect, this volume reports the state of our science in reference to the American experience. We thus remain within and do not attempt to cross major cultural boundaries, an admittedly parochial stance. But stay tuned: this time the United States and Canada, next time the world.

For each annual convention of the American Psychological Association (APA), the Continuing Education Committee in consultation with other segments of governance selects a major theme, specific topics within that theme, and the four or five individual psychologists who will prepare and present what are known as the Master Lectures. As shortly thereafter as is humanly possible, the lectures are assembled and published in the book format you now have before you. It is with special pleasure that as the member of the committee most closely identified with this particular theme—at the time I was president of the Society for the Psychological Study of Social Issues (Division 9)—I happily commend to you the Master Lectures from the Boston APA convention, with the sincere expectation that the material herein will both inform and expand the boundaries of your efforts in psychological science and in the practice of that science.

JACQUELINE D. GOODCHILDS

JAMES M. JONES

PSYCHOLOGICAL MODELS OF RACE: WHAT HAVE THEY BEEN AND WHAT SHOULD THEY BE?

J ames M. Jones has written extensively in the area of race relations over the past 20 years. After earning a BA from Oberlin College in 1963 and an MA from Temple University in 1967, Jones received a PhD in experimental social psychology from Yale University in 1970. He took his first faculty position at Harvard University, where he developed a number of new courses such as "The Social Psychology of Afro-American History," "Black Culture," and "Black Lives: A Psycho-Biographical Approach."

In 1972, Jones's book *Prejudice and Racism* (Addison-Wesley) was published and continues to be one of the most comprehensive treatments of the relationships between prejudice, group conflict, and racism. Jones continued his dissertation research on the psychology of humor during a sabbatical year from 1973–74, when he studied the calypso humor in Trinidad under a Guggenheim Fellowship. Upon his return from Trinidad, Jones began to pull together his writings on race, sports, and humor, and incorporate his growing awareness of the important element of culture to develop his concept of *TRIOS*. TRIOS describes five general psychosocial variables that are pointedly implicated in racial and cultural comparisons. They are Time, Rhythm, Improvisation, Oral expression, and Spirituality. He expanded these ideas in recent articles published in Dovidio and Gaertner's *Prejudice, Discrimination and Racism* (Academic Press, 1986), and Katz and Taylor's *Toward the Elimination of Racism* (Plenum, 1988).

Jones has recently been a strong advocate for the inclusion in psychology textbooks of more systematic material on ethnic minority populations. He is currently writing an introductory psychology textbook with Spencer Rathus that will incorporate ethnic minority content throughout the text. Jones is professor of psychology and Director of the Minority Fellowship Program at the University of Delaware and Interim Executive Director for Public Interest at the American Psychological Association (APA).

JAMES M. JONES

PSYCHOLOGICAL MODELS OF RACE: WHAT HAVE THEY BEEN AND WHAT SHOULD THEY BE?

Introduction

R ace has always been a complex and controversial subject in this society. It has been a matter of legal, political, economic, social, and psychological meaning throughout the relatively brief history of the United States. It has defined who shall enjoy the rights and privileges of citizenship and to what degree and in what ways. It has served to alienate, oppress, disadvantage, and outrage us. It has humiliated, embarrassed, and exposed us. It has been misunderstood, misused, and abused; at the same time, it has been a source of pride, a condition of accomplishment, perseverance, resilience, and creativity.

Race has been one of the recurring and critical themes of psychology from the beginnings of the science in 1892. The legacy of psychology with respect to race is a decidedly mixed one. It cannot be said that the concern of psychology with matters of race has produced the greatest accomplishments of our discipline, yet we have made some contributions that stand out. In the pages that follow, I will highlight some of the more interesting studies done over the past 90 years; draw out the implications of this work for our understanding of race relations; and point out some of the consequences of these studies for members of minority racial groups and members of the current majority population in this society. I will note some possible implications for psychological practice, assessment, and research in the decade ahead.

It should be noted at the outset that race has been a subject largely defined in terms of Black and White. Occasionally Asian Americans and American Indians are considered in the analysis of race effects, but more frequently that analysis is along lines of cultural effects. Hispanic issues are rarely conceived in terms of race but more commonly ethnicity with its range of cultural and linguistic issues. In an attempt to follow some of the empirical and conceptual themes in psychology, I have chosen to focus largely but not exclusively on the results of research and arguments regarding Blacks and, for comparative purposes, Whites. Many, but certainly not all, of the conclusions we draw from such an analysis have relevance for the other racial groups.

This chapter is organized into four sections. The first reviews some perspectives and lines of reasoning on race from early in this century. Definitions, basic conceptual orientations, and illustrative examples of research are presented. The second section addresses the question of the biological basis of race and the evidence for "a race difference," and why it is or is not important to pursue this line of enquiry. The third reviews the evidence for continuing bias of Whites against Blacks—understood as the analysis of prejudice, racism, and discrimination—and proposes how that might affect the social and psychological responses of Blacks to interracial interactions. In the fourth section, selected areas of theory and research are considered, and some of the psychotherapy implications for clinical practice are explored. This will include the studies designed to assess "racial differences" and to understand foundations of behavior among members of racial groups.

Race Definitions and Concepts—Origins in Psychology

According to Bloom (1971), race is

> A major segment of a species originally occupying since the first dispersal of mankind a large geographically unified and distinct region touching on the territory of other races only by relatively narrow corridors. Within such a region, each race acquired its distinctive genetic attributes with its visible appearance and its invisible biological properties, through selective forces and all aspects of environment including culture. (p. 16)

Although this formal definition describes a biological construct genetically transmitted, it allows for the influence of environment on the race concept itself. This environmental or social influence is made more explicit in the definition offered in the recent report of the National Research Councils Committee on the Status of Black Americans (Jaynes and Williams, 1989). They observe that "the meaning of race is a matter of social interpretation, however, not a fact of biology or genetics" (p. 376).

The social definition is echoed by sociologist Pierre vanden Berghe (1967), who defines race thus:

> The human group that defines itself, and/or is defined by other groups as different by virtue of innate or immutable characteristics. These physical characteristics are in turn assumed to be intrinsically related to moral, intellectual and other non-physical attributes or abilities. A race, therefore, is a group that is *socially defined on the basis of physical criteria.* (italics added)

A more sociological definition comes from Banton (1983):

> "Race" relations are distinguished not by the biological significance of phenotypical features but by the social use of those features as signs identifying group membership and the roles people are expected to play. (p. 77)

Omi and Winant (1986) offer a similarly sociohistorical definition:

> Race is indeed a pre-eminently *sociohistorical* concept. Racial categories and the meaning of race are given concrete expression by the specific social relations and historical context in which they are embedded. Racial meanings have varied tremendously over time and between societies. (p. 60; italics added)

Race, then, refers to a group of people who share biological features that come to signify group membership and the social meaning such membership has in the society at large. Race becomes the basis for expectation regarding social roles, performance levels, values, and norms and mores for group and nongroup members and in-group members alike. Since there is a compelling tendency to categorize individuals into groups, and since the phenotypical racial factors are easily detected, race is one of the most salient grounds for social categorization.

There is substantial research evidence to support the notion that group members show a systematic bias in favor of members of their own group (cf. Brewer, 1979). Indeed, *racism* is defined by *Webster's New Collegiate Dictionary* (1977) as "a belief that race is the primary determinant of human traits and capacities and that racial differences produce an inherent superiority of a particular race" (p. 704).

Thus race defines what is considered important about human beings, and further, provides a means by which relative value and capacity is judged. The idea that these attributes inhere in people blurs the basis for racial differences. Social categorization based on race and the resultant discrimination against persons so categorized derives from the basic premise of racial superiority. That this negative categorization has also been associated with various degrees of geographical isolation, as in reservations for American Indians, internment camps and urban communities for Asian Americans, and urban and rural ghettos for Blacks, makes the significance of race compelling for our discipline.

In spite of the fact that as recently as 1970, a Louisiana statute designated anyone with as much as 1/32 "Negro blood" as Black, and although several psychologists continue to assert that racial differences in IQ reflect genetic differences that cannot be explained by environmental factors (cf. Jensen, 1985; Rushton, 1988), for the most part, psychology has approached race as a social concept. The meaning of race, by and large, has been exemplified by research that focuses on (a) how Whites have regarded members of other races as reflected in studies of prejudice, discrimination, and racism, and (b) how racial groups, primarily Blacks, have reacted to this perception and the disadvantages they have been subjected to over many years.

What is important is that the sociocultural meaning of race is attached to rather vague presumptions of biological differences. It is the social valuation that matters. Given here are several excerpts from comments and judgments made by Whites in several different positions of authority.

A progressive politician from California, Chester Powell, offered his "bottom line" on race in 1909:

> . . . social separateness seems to be imposed by the very law of nature. [An educated Japanese] would not be a welcomed suitor for the hand of any American's daughter . . . an Italian of the commonest standing and qualities would be a more welcomed suitor than the finest gentleman of Japan. So the line is biological, and we draw it at the biological point—at the propagation of the species." (Daniels, 1968, p. 49)

Abraham Lincoln offered the following "defense" of his position on race:

> I am not, nor ever have been, in favor of bringing about in any way the social and political equality of the white and black races; I am not, nor ever have been, in favor of making voters or jurors of Negroes, nor qualifying them to hold office. . . . I will say in addition to this that there is a physical difference between the white and

black races which I believe will ever forbid the two races living together on terms of social and political equality. And inasmuch as they cannot so live, while they do remain together, there must be the position of superior and inferior, and I as much as any other man am in favor of having the superior position assigned to the white race. (Nicolay & Hay, 1894, pp. 369, 370, 457, 458)

Psychologist Floyd Allport had these comments on the race question in 1924:

> The vast differences in cultural adaptation between primitive and civilized races are to be ascribed as much to "social inheritance" and environmental factors as to innate difference in capacity. It is fairly well established, however, that the intelligence of the white race is of a more versatile and complex order than that of the black race. It is probably superior also to that of the red or yellow races. . . .
> This discrepancy in mental ability is not great enough to account for the problem which centers about the American negro, or to fully explain the ostracism to which he is subjected. . . . The heart of the negro question is to be reached, not in the sphere of intelligence or temperament, but of sociality . . . growing up in an environment of poverty and ignorance, where stealth and depredation are often the accepted means of livelihood, he has had no opportunity for developing socialized traits . . . [Thus] The whole trouble has been that the moral side of his education was not begun soon enough. He becomes literate and learns the skilled trades; but the deeper foundations of earlier character training are lacking. . . . We need not so much colleges for members of the colored race as homes in which they can be properly reared." (pp. 386–387)

Kardiner and Ovesy (1951) describe the deprivation model in stark and uncompromising terms in their *Mark of Oppression*:

> The Negro, in contrast to the white, is a more unhappy person; he has a harder environment to live in, and the internal stress is greater. By "unhappy" we mean he enjoys less, he suffers more. There is not one personality trait of the Negro the source of which cannot be traced to his difficult living conditions. *There are no exceptions to this rule.* The final result is a wretched internal life. (p. 81, emphasis added)

Taken together, these quotes suggest a tone or tenor that, over a sweep of history and circumstance, reflects a basic attitude or belief that, irrespective of the biological facts, Blacks as a racial group are less capable and deserving and valuable than Whites.

Empirical studies attempted to show the basis of Black inferiority from IQ to temperament. Ferguson (1916) published *The Psychology of the Negro: An Experimental Study*, from which he concluded that Blacks lacked capacity for abstract thought, but were very adept at sensory and motor tasks. This led him to propose that Blacks should be trained for manual labor where such skills could be put to best use.

Crane (1923) sought to test the idea that a failure of inhibition was responsible for the ". . . impulsiveness, improvidence and immorality which the negro everywhere manifests" (p. 10). Crane hypothesized that acts of inhibition required three things: (1) a drive that needed to be inhibited; (2) an intellectual understanding of the merit of inhibiting this drive in favor of a more distant goal; and (3) the ability to substitute an alternative behavior that is incompatible with the original drive. It is this substitution that represents the volitional act of inhibition. It is this act that Crane believed Blacks were less capable of than Whites; this failure, therefore, was responsible for the negative behavior, according to his hypothesis.

Crane set up a guillotine situation in which a heavy block of wood fell toward the subject's hand, which was placed on a block below. Subjects were told the block would stop before it hit them and therefore not to move their hand. Crane expected that Black subjects would be less capable of resisting the temptation to move the hand than White subjects, thus demonstrating his "failure of inhibition" hypothesis.

His results showed that Black subjects did indeed make larger, more vigorous movements on the first trial, but on all subsequent trials, they made no movement at all. Whites, on the other hand, made smaller but clear movements on the first trial, and they continued making these movements well into the experiment on subsequent trials. Thus, ". . . the Negro group shows, on the whole, a very much lower Flinch Product rating than the White group." (p. 75)

Crane had some difficulty in accounting for this result based on the hypothesized nature of the racial differences. He rationalized it by suggesting that the Black subjects got their concern out of the way on the first trial and that this helped them adapt earlier. Crane mused that if Whites had done that, they would have mastered it earlier as well. Crane clearly was scurrying to salvage his hypothesis and concluded interestingly that "In a way, the more naive performances seem to accomplish more successfully the task set by the experimenter in his directions to the subject" (p. 75). Despite all of the accounts and the elaborate conception of this test, when the results violated his expectation, Crane reinterpreted the entire situation so as to leave intact his basic belief that Whites are superior in this way to Blacks. It is an excellent illustration of what Boykin (1979) calls the "law of personal presuppositions": "You will rarely find a research-scholar concluding anything in his or her research that is inconsistent, contradictory, or threatening to his or her own self-definition, self-sustenance, and value system" (p. 88).

Although race is a biological concept, its major significance in this society is social. For example, why should members of Shoal Creek Country Club in Alabama refuse to allow a person willing to pay a $35,000 membership fee to play golf just because he is Black? On what biological basis is this policy founded? Quite obviously, none.

Nevertheless, there is some presumption, in many instances, that phenotypical biological differences are associated with other differences in temperament, values, moral judgments, and the like. It is this assumption that probably fuels the most significant aspect of the meaning of race. For example, Linneaus (cited in Guthrie, 1976, p. 32) categorized the races by both physical and behavioral traits as follows:

Homo Americanus	Reddish, choleric, erect, tenacious, contented, free; ruled by custom
Homo Europaeus	White, ruddy, muscular, stern, haughty, stingy; ruled by opinion
Homo Asiaticus	Yellow, melancholic, inflexible, light, inventive; ruled by rites
Homo Afer	Black, phlegmatic, indulgent, cunning, slow, negligent; ruled by caprice

Thus taxonomies that link cultural and geographical as well as racial dimensions are joined with phenotypical traits such as skin color, along with psychological characteristics and locus of control. It is this congeries of concepts, attitudes, and beliefs that make understanding a concept like race so difficult.

Psychology has purveyed over the years part of the scientific argument for racial differences, which as noted by Abraham Lincoln, have only one profile—White superiority and Black inferiority. The question psychologists raise seems to be "Are Blacks inferior because of their genes or their environment?" Is there not a conception of human capacity and value that disrupts this historical equation?

Traditional psychological perspectives on race have been dominated by three concerns: (a) Black–White differences; (b) the effects of discrimination, poverty, and disadvantage on Black attitudes, performance, and personality; and (c) factors that promote prejudice in Whites and ways to alleviate or eliminate it.

One of the profound consequences of these notions and reactions to the race concept is that Blacks in particular, and other minority racial and ethnic groups more generally, have developed a level of distrust of Whites that continues to be a subject of concern in interpersonal and intergroup relations. For psychology, that formal interpersonal situation known as the psychotherapeutic relationship has suffered a great deal because of the racial problems noted above. For social interaction, group relations, and organizational performance, the negative consequences have been far-reaching and not easily ameliorated.

More pointedly, Blacks and other minority racial and ethnic groups share distrust of psychology as a discipline that purports to understand human behavior. This distrust of psychology stems in part from the apparent inability of traditional approaches to discern bases of strength, resilience, and capacity and competence in these racial groups. The so-called deficit model of human behavior tends to dominate the discipline and serves to alienate those psychologists and would-be psychologists from minority racial and ethnic groups from full participation in the discipline. The emergence of race-based psychologies (cf. Martinez, 1986; R. Jones, 1980; and Ramirez, 1983) share a critical reevaluation of the Eurocentric and Anglo perspective on human behavior. One of the important aspects of a consideration of race is the response of psychologists from minority ethnic and racial groups to the persistently negative implications of traditional race concepts in psychology.

Is There a "Race Difference"? Biological Approaches to Race

Are there significant differences among the races, and if so, what are they? In spite of the difficulty in defining race as shown in the previous section, and the tendency for race to take on a sociopolitical meaning with self-serving biases operating, psychologists have been greatly concerned with establishing the extent and nature of racial differences in psychological performance.

Crane (1923) noted that two race-relevant questions could be asked. The first—"Is there a difference between the races?"—is relatively simple and is answerable by observing systematic differences between samples drawn from Black and White populations. This is the kind of study Crane did, and it is most typical of race-comparative research by psychologists. The second question—"Is there a race difference?"—is much more difficult to answer. According to Crane, the answer to this question requires ". . . demonstrating that the difference is an innate psychological one, characteristic of and due to the fact of race, and race alone, and its experimental determination must necessarily involve the testing of two groups of subjects—black and white—who have been living under *like environmental and cultural conditions!*" (p. 73, italics in original).

For the most part, attempts to show a race difference have focused on the measurement of intelligence or IQ. Not only has this controversy centered around racial differences, but it has also been directed at the degree of heritability of IQ. If one believes that racial differences in IQ are proven and that IQ is highly heritable, then one is inclined to conclude or at least infer that Blacks are genetically inferior. This set of circumstances makes the issue of racial differences of profound concern.

The King's Library

ulat   l as an inbred, geographically isolated pop-
natu   e by its physical features. The geographical
majc   it to note because it has been one of the
biolc   . One of the major characteristics of human
know   er, all races possess all of the blood types
a grou   oportion of any single type found among
all so   e a race. Type O is most common among
ample   solute percentages may vary. So, for ex-
Congo   % A, 6% B, and 68% O. Pygmies of the
Rose &   e 23% A, 22% B and 55% O (Lewontin,
genetic   nother index, about 85% of all human
racial g   d other proteins occurs *within* a local
group n   accounted for by differences based on
            ose, & Kamin, 1984).

Wh   e species to which all humans on the
planet b   view a race as a subspecies, capable
of breed   her subspecies but rarely doing so.
Zuckerma   geographic isolation has for the most
part been   tural, and religious factors that maintain separ   groups. Thus race may best be understood   hat differ principally in cultural, political, and   far less extent in biological ways.

We als   has been a fact of life in the United
States for m   ixing leads to the "mulatto hypothesis," whicl   l rise directly with the amount of
Caucasian "   . Using skin color as the basis for
racial classii   nerally quite inconsistent, leading
noted anthro   ovits (1958) to conclude that no
evidence exi   pothesis, whether the amount of
Caucasian blc   by inspection or ascertained from ge-
nealogies or anthropometric measurement.

The American Association for the Advancement of Science (AAAS) sponsored a symposium on *Science and the Concept of Race* (cf. Mead, Dobzhansky, Tobach, & Light, 1968), which concluded that the significant cross-breeding around the world between persons of African origin and other groups made it extremely difficult and probably not useful to make claims for racial differences. One of the participants (Scott, 1968) noted that

> From a biological viewpoint the term race has become so encumbered with superfluous and contradictory meanings, erroneous concepts, and emotional reactions that it has almost completely lost its utility. . . . The term should be replaced with the concept of population. It is hoped that the understanding of the biological nature of populations will eventually lead to the abandonment of the term race. . . . (p. 59)

Thus race is not a useful concept because by definition, the requirements for a pure racial designation are rarely met. Then what do studies of "a race difference" tell us? I submit that we can know very little about parametric differences that can be traced to race alone. On the other hand, there are numerous studies that show differences between people who belong by social definition to different racial groups. We will look more closely at some of this work in the fourth section of this paper.

Making sense out of race difference research because of the definitional and conceptual problems is not the only difficulty. There is also the fundamental problem that variability among members of the species is greater within subspecies (i.e., racial groups) than for the species as a whole. Zuckerman (1990) reports a study by Latter (1980) that analyzed 18 genetic systems, including blood serum, enzymes, and serum proteins, in 40 populations within 16 subgroups around the world. He analyzed the variability within and between populations and found that the greatest amount of variation, 84%, was accounted for by the genetic diversity among individuals *within* the same tribe or nation. Only 10% was accounted for by racial groupings and 6% by geographical regions. As Zuckerman concludes from his review, the evidence is compelling that racial groups are much more alike than they are different.

A final problem concerns the sample requirements for a test of the difference hypothesis. We have noted that a strong test for a race difference would compare two groups that differ on nothing but race. As we know, race makes a difference in myriad ways in this society and has for several centuries. Even with consistent findings of IQ differences in the range of 15 points on the Stanford-Binet between Blacks and Whites, on what basis do we conclude that this difference is "racial"? For the most part, these racial difference studies are correlational in nature and always leave open the possibilities of other variables influencing the obtained result. With the combinations of genetic admixtures through cross-breeding over several centuries, geographical intermixing through migration and limited but persistent integration, and cultural variations *within* racial groups, that elusive psychological or even biological explanation seems still to be quite remote.

My conclusion from this brief overview is that attempting to show a race difference that is posited as a biological fact is of little utility. What would probably be of much greater value is the exploration of sources of variability *within* racial groups. Exploring sources of in-group variability would have the twin virtues of reducing the tendency to exaggerate racial differences and of discovering more about the full range of behaviors exemplified by members of racial groups. This argues for a diminution of race-comparative research and more exploratory hypothesis-generating research aimed at uncovering variables that help explain sources of within-group variability in behavior.

Given these caveats, I will briefly mention some of the major contemporary trends in studies proposing a biological basis for race differences. One provocative approach comes from Richard Herrnstein (1989), who accepts the basic notion of the heritability of IQ and worries that women with higher IQs (as estimated by educational level) are having fewer offspring. The result, according to Herrnstein, would be lowering of the population IQ.

The effect of lowered IQ, by Herrnstein's analysis, is a potential lowering of worker productivity, particularly in those jobs that require a greater degree of cognitive complexity. Herrnstein points out that IQ scores correlate about .5 with productivity for the work force as a whole, thus accounting for an "astonishing" 25% of the variance. Perhaps 25% of the variance is a psychometric tour de force, but one must wonder of what the other 75% consists. Might we do well to concentrate on locating the missing three fourths?

Debates about racial differences in IQ are most associated with Arthur Jensen's work (Jensen, 1969). A recent article (Jensen, 1985) makes a very strong case for the g factor in IQ tests. That is the notion of Charles Spearman (1927) that variation in Black–White differences on various tests could be traced directly to the amount of general abstract reasoning g required by the tests. The more the g required, the greater would be the Black–White differences because the fundamental race difference was in general mental ability. Jensen reviewed a number of large-scale studies of various tests and used various factor analytic techniques to pull out those common loadings associated with g. He found consistent evidence that the correlation between a test's g loading and the average Black–White difference on the test is positive and significant.

Having accepted this relationship, he describes the principle components of g. Using a series of complex and simple mental tasks, he finds that speed of information processing, particularly for complex tasks, produces reliable Black–White differences that are associated with the g loadings noted earlier. Thus, Jensen proposes that speed of information processing is the specific g component that predicts Black–White differences in test performance and educational attainment.

The real bottom line issue concerns the sociopolitical implications of this research and the conclusions drawn therefrom. The proponents of g theory argue that because g predicts performance that is relevant to job productivity, failure to use tests as the principal measure of suitability for a job will undermine the quality of the work force. Programs that substitute other considerations such as "group representation" are, by this reasoning, misguided.

Another effort to pose biological interpretations on putative racial differences comes from Philippe Rushton (1988) and Rushton and Bogaert (1987). Rushton describes what he calls "differential K theory" to explain differences among Mongoloid, Caucasoid, and Negroid races. He contrasts two basic reproductive strategies ranging from r, characterized as high egg output and no parental care to K, described by low egg production and maximum parental care. Oysters producing 500 million eggs a year reflect an *r*-strategy, and great apes producing one offspring every 5 to 6 years the *K*-strategy.

Rushton extrapolates his *r/K* theory to humans, proposing that "races" can be distinguished by their *r/K* strategies where *r*-types would have more offspring, high infant mortality, early sexual reproduction, shorter life, rapid maturation. *K* strategists would be just the opposite.

Rushton's theory suggests that Orientals are most *K*-like, followed by Caucasians, and then Negroids. An example of the kind of data he produces is the observation that Black Americans have shorter gestation periods. By week 39, 51% of Black babies have been born, contrasted with only 33% of White babies. He cites other statistics showing motoric precocity for Black babies, earlier sexual interest and activity for Black adolescents, and higher death rates for Blacks than the other two groups. This kind of rambling observation is carried further to social organization, where it is alleged that Blacks have higher divorce rate, child abuse, and delinquency as indicators of lower social organization predicted by differential *K* theory.

Brain size, presumed by Rushton to be related to intelligence—an idea that almost no one currently endorses— is suggested to vary in the order proposed for other variables (see Gould, 1981). Very effective critiques of this notion have been presented. Zuckerman and Brody (1988) criticize Rushton on four basic grounds: (a) there is no conceptual rationale that serves to unite IQ scores, penis size, cranial size, personality, dancing styles, arrest records, twinning rate, and sexual practices in the fostering of fertility; (b) socioeconomic status is correlated with each of the variables with which race is supposedly correlated—hence the data offered to support the race theory could as easily reveal a social variable like socioeconomic status (SES) as the main cause; and (c) there is no statistical analysis to document any part of this conjecture. In short, the theory and the argument on its behalf fail the most basic tests of scientific rigor.

Finally, two interesting studies test the biological and social effects on IQ by looking at transracial adoptions. In the first, Scarr and Weinberg (1983) conducted a transracial adoption study designed to test the hypothesis that Black and interracial children reared by White families perform on IQ and school achievement tests as well as other adoptees because they are reared in the culture of the tests and schools. The subjects were 130 socially defined Black children and 143 biological children of adoptive parents in 101 families. Children varied in age so that children ages 4–7 were given Stanford Binet, children ages 8–16 the WISC, and older children and adults the WAIS. Table 1 gives comparisons of biological and unrelated parent–child IQ correlations.

These results show two things. First, there is clear evidence of a relationship of biology to IQ scores. The IQ correlations between parents and their biological offspring was on the average higher ($r = .36$) than the correlations between parents and unrelated children ($r = .20$). Sec-

Table 1
**Comparisons of Biological and Unrelated Parent–Child IQ Correlations
in 101 Transracial Adoptive Families**

Parent–child relationship type	N (pairs)	r
Parents–unrelated children		
Adoptive mother–adoptive child	174	.21
Natural mother–own child of adoptive family	217	.15
Adoptive father–adopted child	170	.27
Natural father–own child of adoptive family	86	.19
Parents–biological children		
Adoptive mother–own child	141	.34
Natural mother–adopted child	135	.33
Adoptive father–own child	142	.39
Natural father–adopted child	46	.43

Note. Natural parents of adoptive children's IQ was based on educational level, *not* IQ scores. From "The Minnesota Adoption Studies: Genetic Differences and Malleability" by S. Scarr and R. Weinberg, 1983, *Child Development, 54*, p. 262. Copyright 1983 by University of Chicago Press. Reprinted by permission.

ond, there is also evidence of a clear, strong family or context effect. The correlation of the IQs of parents of adoptive children with the biological offspring of the adoptive parents is relatively low ($r = .16$). The correlations of IQs of adoptive parents with their adoptive children, however, is significantly higher ($r = .24$). This study, then, provides evidence for both biological and environmental effects on IQ. In addition, IQ correlations among biological siblings was about .42 and among biologically unrelated adoptive siblings *in the same family* was .44! This suggests that the family effect for children of differing biological characteristics is exceedingly high.

While the Scarr and Weinberg study implies that environmental effects on IQ are significant, Elsie Moore (1986) evaluated family socialization effects directly. She gave the WISC to 46 socially defined Black children, half of whom were adopted by Black families and half of whom were adopted by White families. All had been adopted by age 2. Results showed a significantly higher WISC score for the transracially adopted children than for the traditionally adopted children—117 versus 104.

In a second phase, conducted in the children's homes, Moore observed strategies employed by the mothers to help their children perform well on a cognitively complex block design task from the Wechsler Bellevue Scale. Moore found that White mothers tended to release tensions through joking, laughing, and so on, give more positive evaluations of their child's performance (e.g., "You're good at this"), give more generalized hints to help in problem solving, and show more enthusiasm in the form of cheers and applause. Black mothers, by contrast, tended to release tension in more negative ways such as scowling or frowning, give more negative evaluations of their child's performance (e.g., "You know that doesn't look right"), give specific instructions rather than general hints for problem solving, and generally use expression of displeasure at the child's performance ("You could do better than this if you really tried").

The significant differences in IQ in the absence of any biological relationship between children and adoptive parents makes the patterns of interaction of great interest. The pattern of observed differences is provocative and in need of follow-up. It seems to suggest differences in child-rearing beliefs, teaching styles, and affective expression between Black and White parents. The question we must ask is "Why these differences?" Since these two sets of adoptive parents were similar in SES (though not identical because they differed both in paternal education levels and overall socioeconomic index), there is a temptation to look to ethnic and racial variations for the answers. It appears that the Black mothers were less generous in their praise, affective support, and encouragement. This kind of observation demands more systematic research. Follow-up interviews might reveal the foundation of their attitudes about parenting, teaching, and socialization that gives rise to these behavioral differences. There may well be real and persistent differences in attitudes, norms, and beliefs that translate to behavioral differences. If these differences have systematic effects on academic performance, this would be important to know.

To carry these environmental effects even further, Plomin and Daniels (1987) evaluated the question "Why are children in the same family so different?" They argue that three factors determine whether there are differences between children: (a) biology, (b) nonshared environmental effects, and (c) shared environmental effects. The first is simply how much variance can be accounted for by genes. The second is how much variance is accounted for by the fact that the children are influenced by different environmental events; and the third is effect of shared environments. They conclude that nonshared environmental effects are responsible for differences in personality, temperament and IQ (after childhood). This means that even though parents may think they are imparting similar values, attitudes, and standards to their children and are providing them with generally similar experiences, what will affect their children most is what they experience uniquely, not what they share with their sibling.

If that is the case in general for biological siblings, how much of the difference in characteristics of Blacks and Whites might be attributed to their "nonshared environments"? As we seek to test varieties of racial differences, it seems quite obvious that substantial racial differences would be likely on the basis of the nonshared environmental effects. The most consistent pattern of such a nonshared effect might well be the phenomenon of racism and its differential impact on Blacks and Whites.

Conclusion

The concept of race as a way to characterize differences is fraught with problems. The criteria for determining what Crane calls "a race difference" are not met by the work done to date for several reasons, including: (a) difficulty with the concept and definition; (b) the history of genetic cross-breeding; (c) greater within-race variability than between-race difference; and (d) noncomparability of racial samples when comparative research is conducted.

There is evidence of racial differences (socially defined), however, in IQ and other test performance. Evidence suggests that some of these differences are linked to characteristics that are heritable, and some are attributable to socialization and cultural variations.

The research that is most needed now concerns the development of (a) better understanding of the sources of within race variability and (b) the mediators of socialization and cultural effects on IQ and other cognitive test performance.

IQ is often equated with intelligence: "The term 'intelligence' should be reserved for the rather specific meaning I have assigned to it, namely, the general factor common to standard tests of intelligence" (Jensen, 1969, p. 19).[1] If we adopt a biological approach to intelligence, it can be understood as human adaptation to the environment that increases the likelihood of reproductive success—that is, surviving and thriving. Given dramatically different ecological circumstances and their correspondingly different adaptational demands, what we see as racial differences may be better understood as variations in adaptational requirements. Therefore, a more interesting task would be to ascertain the forms of intelligence that derive from ecological circumstances and adaptational strategies and opportunities. Intellectual and information processing is certainly important, but so too are various forms of social perception, functioning, and sensitivity. Rather than continue to force our research into race-comparative models that have the inevitable consequence of proposing value-based interpretations on any differences discovered, it would serve us well to focus on those conditions to which we adapt, how we adapt, and the consequences of certain adaptations for subsequent behavioral patterns and outcomes.

Nonshared environmental effects suggest that racial differences that we do detect may well be due to the nonshared environments of Blacks and Whites. The most obvious element of the nonshared environments is the differential impact of race itself on the experiences of Blacks and Whites.

---

[1]However, Jensen went on to say that this operationalization of intelligence was very narrow and did not address a variety of other attributes related to mental and other abilities. Thus, I believe, Jensen leaves open the notion of multiple intelligences, or capacities, as argued by people like Gardner (1983) and Sternberg (1985).

Social and Psychological Responses to Race—White Reactions to Blacks

White Attitudes Toward Blacks

As we have seen, race is best understood as a socially meaningful concept that signifies group membership with sociopolitical consequences. For the purposes of taxation, African slaves were defined as ⅗ the value of a single White person. Thus Black people, whether slaves or not, were devalued by the laws of the land. Supreme Court Justice Roger B. Taney, writing the opinion in the Dred Scott case of 1857, affirmed the notion that a Negro had no rights a White man was bound to respect by ruling that though not a slave, Dred Scott was nevertheless, *because of his race*, not a citizen of Missouri and therefore not entitled to bring suit in a federal court. And in 1896, *Plessy v. Ferguson* established racial separation as the law of the land.

These official acts of government helped to establish a negative value on Blacks, the results of which were continued denigration and socialized disrespect. We have seen some of the examples of this from the words of psychologists who sought "scientifically" to establish the basis of the deficiencies that would rationalize these negative assessments. Early studies of White perceptions of Blacks revealed patterns of negativity.

Bogardus (1925) developed a "social distance" measure of racial attitudes. He considered Dutch people, Spaniards, Jews, Norwegians, and Negroes to be races. His data show that 88.2% of Whites would not accept Negroes into their neighborhood, 61.3% would not want to work with Negroes, and only slightly more than half would even accept Negroes as citizens.

Subsequent studies of White perceptions toward Blacks explored the theme of attitudes through an assessment of stereotyping—the generalizations of social traits to all members of a racial group. Katz and Braly (1935) studied the tendency of Princeton men to ascribe stereotypes to several racial groups. Blacks were characterized as superstitious, lazy, happy-go-lucky, ignorant, and musical. A replication of this study by Gilbert in 1951 found the same attributes, except that *happy-go-lucky* was replaced by *pleasure-loving*. A replication by Karlins, Coffman, and Walters (1967) found that both *happy-go-lucky* and *pleasure-loving* were included in the stereotypes, *musical* and *lazy* remained, and *ostentatious* was added. Subjects were asked to assign values to the traits with $+2$ being positive and -2 being negative. While the content of the racial stereotypes hardly changed over the 30 years, the value attached to the traits went from being quite negative ($-.67$), to neutral ($+.07$).

Social psychologists have been studying these changes in White attitudes and behaviors toward Blacks for many years. The overt racial hostility has tended to subside, and surveys of White attitudes have shown consistent improvement over the years. Yet social psychologists have very cleverly developed paradigms that show continued animosity towards Blacks; this work belies the survey data suggesting moderation in racial attitudes. I will review three models of this research.

Dovidio, Evans, and Tyler (1986) sought to test the idea that stereotypes, rather than being simply emotionally charged biased perception, represented cognitive structures that are employed in making judgments about people. If this is so, then people who maintain a stereotypical bias would find it easier to process information about a person who superficially fits that bias. This was indicated by the speed with which a subject could perform certain judgments involving social information.

Subjects, White male and female college students, were shown two slides in order. The first slide contained the words *white, black* or *house*, and the second slide showed one of 16 adjectives, 8 of which described people and 8 of which did not. The task for half the subjects was to determine if the second word "could ever be true" of the group named in the first slide, and for the other half of the subjects, to determine if the second word "is always false" for that group. The adjective-traits were constructed so that they were *stereotypical* of either Blacks or Whites and were either positive or negative instances of such stereotypes. For example, Black stereotypes were "musical" and "sensitive" (positive), "lazy" and "imitative" (negative). White stereotypes were "ambitious" and "practical" (positive), "conventional" and "stubborn" (negative).

Results showed that overall, subjects responded most quickly to positive traits. As shown in Table 2, this was most pronounced when *White* was the prime word, and the traits were positive and White ste-

Table 2
Mean Reaction Times in Milliseconds to Adjective Traits Under Black and White Priming Conditions

Adjective trait types	Prime categories	
	White	Black
Positive stereotype		
White	777	918
Black	888	820
Negative stereotype		
White	949	994
Black	1118	954

Note. From "Racial Stereotypes: The Contents of Their Cognitive Representations" by J. Dovidio, N. Evans, and R. Tyler, 1986, *Journal of Experimental Social Psychology, 22*, p. 30. Copyright 1986 by Academic Press. Adapted by permission.

reotypic (for example, ambitious, practical). They responded most slowly when *White* was the prime to negative traits associated with Blacks (lazy and imitative). In short, White positive stereotypes about Whites were the easiest to process. They also responded more quickly to a Black stereotype word after a Black prime than after a White prime. These data show that Whites do indeed carry with them a stereotype of both Blacks and Whites, that the stereotype of Whites is more positive than that of Blacks, and that it affects the way in which they process related social information.

Irwin Katz and his colleagues have developed a model of racial ambivalence to describe White attitudes toward Blacks (Katz, 1981). He suggests that White attitudes reflect a basic ambivalence based on conflict between American cultural values of humanitarianism and egalitarianism and the Protestant work ethic. The former values embrace principles of racial equality and regard the negative circumstances of Blacks as indicative of unfair disadvantage. The latter values, on the other hand, perceive equality principles as a violation of the equity aspect of the Protestant ethic. This violation occurs because, by this reasoning, Blacks have poor work habits, which lead to their disadvantage and justify their disadvantage. The basic tenet of this theory is that the two orientations are independent. That is, a person can hold both humanitarian and egalitarian and Protestant ethic values at the same time and, depending on which is salient, trigger the attitude associated with it.

Katz and Hass (1988) conducted two experiments to show the validity of this reasoning. Subjects in the first study filled out a set of questions that measured their attitudes toward Black Americans and the extent to which they endorsed the principles of the Protestant Ethic (PE) and the Humanitarianism–Egalitarianism (HE) values. Table 3 gives examples of these items.

It was expected and found (see Figure 1) that a high score on the PE scale would be associated with higher anti-Black sentiments ($r = +.40$), and a high score on the HE scale would be associated with Pro-Black sentiments ($r = +.46$). PE did not correlate with pro-Black sentiment ($r = -.14$) nor did HE correlate with anti-Black sentiment ($r = -.28$).

In a second study, White subjects filled out a racial attitude scale after being *primed* by Humanitarian–Egalitarian or Protestant Ethic values. The priming effect was manipulated by having subjects fill out either the HE scale or the PE scale prior to filling out the racial attitudes scale. In a control condition, the HE and PE scales were filled out *after* the racial attitude scales. The authors sought to determine if priming subjects in humanitarian–egalitarian ideals would lead to a more positive attitude toward Blacks, and if priming them with the PE scale would lead to a more negative attitude. Table 4 shows that the results confirmed this prediction. That is, when subjects filled out the HE scale first, they gave more pro-Black responses on the attitude scale. When they filled

Table 3

Items From the Anti/Pro-Black Attitude Scales and the Humanitarian/Protestant Ethic Value Scales

Pro-Black

1. Black people do not have the same employment opportunities that Whites do.
2. It's surprising that Black people do as well as they do, considering all the obstacles they face.
3. Too many Blacks still lose out on jobs and promotions because of their skin color.
4. Most big corporations in America are really interested in treating their Black and White employees equally.[*]
5. Most Blacks are no longer discriminated against.[*]
6. Blacks have more to offer than they have been allowed to show.
7. The typical urban ghetto public school is not as good as it should be to provide equal opportunities for Blacks.
8. This country would be better off if it were more willing to assimilate the good things in Black culture.
9. Sometimes Black job seekers should be given special consideration in hiring.
10. Many Whites show a real lack of understanding of the problems that Blacks face.

Anti-Black

1. The root cause of most of the social and economic ills of Blacks is the weakness and instability of the Black family.
2. Although there are exceptions, Black urban neighborhoods don't seem to have strong community organization or leadership.
3. On the whole, Black people don't stress education and training.
4. Many Black teenagers don't respect themselves or anyone else.
5. Blacks don't seem to use opportunities to own and operate little shops and businesses.
6. Very few Black people are just looking for a free ride.[*]
7. Black children would do better in school if their parents had better attitudes about learning.
8. Blacks should take the jobs that are available and then work their way up to better jobs.
9. One of the biggest problems for a lot of Blacks is their lack of self-respect.
10. Most Blacks have the drive and determination to get ahead.[*]

Protestant Ethic

1. Most people spend too much time in unprofitable amusements.
2. Our society would have fewer problems if people had less leisure time.
3. Money acquired easily is usually spent unwisely.
4. Most people who don't succeed in life are just plain lazy.
5. Anyone who is willing and able to work hard has a good chance of succeeding.
6. People who fail at a job have usually not tried hard enough.
7. Life would have very little meaning if we never had to suffer.
8. The person who can approach an unpleasant task with enthusiasm is the person who gets ahead.
9. If people work hard enough they are likely to make a good life for themselves.
10. I feel uneasy when there is little work for me to do.
11. A distaste for hard work usually reflects a weakness of character.

Humanitarianism–Egaliarianism

1. One should be kind to all people.
2. One should find ways to help others less fortunate than oneself.
3. A person should be concerned about the well-being of others.
4. There should be equality for everyone—because we are all human beings.
5. Those who are unable to provide for their basic needs should be helped by others.
6. A good society is one in which people feel responsible for one another.
7. Everyone should have an equal chance and an equal say in most things.
8. Acting to protect the rights and interests of other members of the community is a major obligation for all persons.
9. In dealing with criminals the courts should recognize that many are victims of circumstances.
10. Prosperous nations have a moral obligation to share some of their wealth with poor nations.

[*] Item scored in reverse.

Note. From "Racial Ambivalence and American Value Conflict: Correlational and Priming Studies of Dual Cognitive Structures" by I. Katz and R. G. Hass, 1988, *Journal of Personality and Social Psychology, 55*, p. 905. Copyright 1988 by the American Psychological Association. Reprinted by permission.

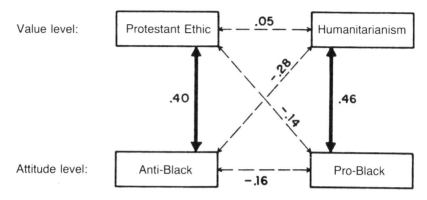

Figure 1. Pooled product–moment correlations between value and attitude scores. From "Racial Ambivalence and American Value Conflict: Correlational and Priming Studies of Dual Cognitive Structures" by I. Katz and R. Hass, 1988, *Journal of Personality and Social Psychology, 55*, p. 898. Copyright 1988 by the American Psychological Association. Reprinted by permission.

out the PE scale first, they gave more anti-Black responses. This finding suggests that racial attitudes are not static, but heavily influenced by the ideological or value context in which they are assessed or activated.

Finally, Rogers and Prentice-Dunn (1981) conducted a study in which they had White subjects deliver shock to Black or White confederates in a biofeedback paradigm. The biofeedback "victims" were either Black or White and in one condition, were overheard by the subject

Table 4
Effect of Value Scale Priming on Racial Attitude Scores

Measured attitude	Priming condition		
	HE Scale ($n = 19$)	PE Scale ($n = 20$)	Control ($n = 20$)
Pro-Black			
M	36.79	32.25	33.10
SD	4.13	11.56	6.94
Anti-Black			
M	27.79	34.05	27.70
SD	8.54	7.83	11.05

Note. The higher the score, the more extreme the attitude. HE = Humanitarianism–Egalitarianism; PE = Protestant Ethic. From "Racial Ambivalence and American Value Conflict: Correlational and Priming Studies of Dual Cognitive Structures" by I. Katz and R. G. Hass, 1988, *Journal of Personality and Social Psychology, 55*, p. 899. Copyright 1988 by the American Psychological Association. Reprinted by permission.

saying derogatory things about the subject. In the other condition, no such derogatory comments were heard. The amount of shock delivered to the confederate measured subjects' level of aggression. Results are depicted in Figure 2 and show that when they are *not* angered, Whites showed *less* aggression towards Blacks than Whites. But, when they had been angered, they showed *more* aggression toward Blacks than Whites. Again, context effects can shift not only attitudes but also behaviors from positive to negative with so slight a twist of circumstance.

If we put these studies together, a very ominous pattern emerges. Whites continue to hold negative attitudes toward Blacks in spite of the emerging norms that suggest this is no longer appropriate. This becomes clear when we remove some of the inhibition of social desirability, as in studies of priming that permit assessment of attitudes through subtle means like reaction times, or when we provide an ostensibly appropriate excuse for negative behavior, with the continuation of behaviors widely

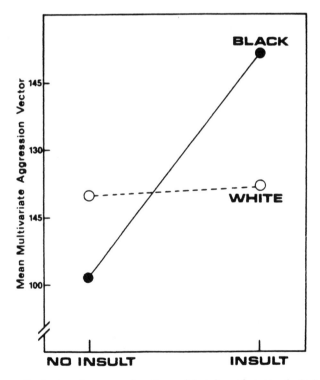

Figure 2. Aggression as a function of insult and race of victim. From "Deindividuation and Anger-Mediated Interracial Aggression: Unmasking Regressive Racism" by R. Rogers and S. Prentice-Dunn, 1981, *Journal of Personality and Social Psychology, 41*, p. 68. Copyright 1981 by the American Psychological Association. Reprinted by permission.

believed to belong to an earlier time as a result. The improvement in race relations over the years may come down to only an ambivalence on matters of race, an ambivalence that is easily provoked into more virulent racial antipathy as we have seen, for example, on college campuses in recent years. Problems of prejudice and racism persist, in other words.

So is it surprising that Blacks who have reacted historically with mistrust continue to be skeptical of the motives and intentions of Whites? The racial ambivalence of Whites as proposed by Katz and his colleagues is also an element of the attitudes held about Whites by Blacks. It also may be reflected in the attitudes that Blacks hold about themselves.

Some Institutional Consequences of Racial Attitudes

What difference does it make what attitude Whites have toward Blacks? There is solid evidence that suggests negative or ambivalent racial attitudes have significant implications for Black Americans. I offer two empirical examples that suggest how significant this could be.

Word, Zanna, and Cooper (1974) tested the role of self-fulfilling prophecy as a mediator of interracial interaction. Simply put, it is believed that the attitudes and actions of one person may influence the behavior of the other in a dyadic interaction such that the other's behavior confirms the unstated expectation of the first person. The well-known Pygmalion Effect of Rosenthal and Jacobson (1966) is one of the best examples. With respect to race, this implies that negative expectations held by Whites may induce behavior by Blacks that confirms that expectation. The test of this idea was conducted in two related experiments.

Experiment 1 required young White Princeton undergraduates to interview high school students to determine if they wished them to join their team for a decision-making task. The high school students were confederates of the experimenter and included both Black and White students. Each subject interviewed three students. The first was White and was termed a "warm-up." The second and third were Black or White respectively, as determined by a prearranged counterbalanced order. The interviews lasted a total of about 45 minutes. Measures taken during the interviews included physical distance between subject and interviewee; forward lean in 10-degree units; eye contact; and shoulder orientation as indicated by deviation from parallel. These measures were taken collectively to indicate the degree of "immediacy," defined by Mehrabian (1969) as ". . . the extent to which communication behaviors enhance closeness to and nonverbal interaction with another . . . greater immediacy is due to increasing degrees of physical proximity and/or increasing perceptual availability of the communicator to the addressee" (p. 203).

Table 5
Mean Interaction Behavior as a Function of Race of Job Applicant:
Experiment 1

Behavior	Relia-bility	Blacks	Whites	t^b	p
Total immediacy[a]	—	−.11	.38	2.79	<.02
Distance	.90	62.29 inches	58.43 inches	2.36	<.05
Forward lean	.68	−8.76 degrees	−6.12 degrees	1.09	n.s.
Eye contact	.80	62.71%	61.46%	<1	n.s.
Shoulder orientation	.60	22.46 degrees	23.08 degrees	<1	n.s.
Related behaviors					
Interview length	—	9.42 min.	12.77 min.	3.22	<.01
Speech error rate	.88	3.54 errors/min.	2.37 errors/min.	2.43	<.05

Note. From "The Nonverbal Mediation of Self-Fulfilling Prophecies in Interracial Interaction" by C. Word, M. Zanna, and J. Cooper, 1974, *Journal of Experimental Social Psychology, 10,* p. 114. Copyright 1974 by Academic Press. Reprinted by permission.
[a]See text for weighting formula, from Mehrabian (1969).
[b]*t* test for correlated samples was employed.

Results illustrated in Table 5 show that a total immediacy score was significantly lower for Black than White interviewees. In addition, interview length was shorter and speech errors were higher.

Using this pattern of nonverbally mediated interactions as a differential model for Black versus White interactions, a second experiment was conducted in which Princeton men served as job applicants being interviewed for a job in career services. These subjects, all of whom were White, were interviewed by confederates who were themselves White and were trained to behave in the manner associated with the Black or White interviewee profile from the first study. That is, subjects were now interviewed *as if* they were White or Black. Following these interviewed, videotapes of the subjects' responses to the interviews were given to independent judges to rate. In addition, subjects rated their own mood and interviewer friendliness and adequacy. These ratings are shown in Table 6.

Results support the predictions that those in the nonimmediate condition were judged to be less competent and to have responded with less immediate behaviors themselves (greater distance and more speech errors).

The results of this study show that subjects who were treated in a subtly negative way actually behaved in objectively verifiable ways that

Table 6
Mean Applicant Responses Under Two Conditions of Interviewer
Immediacy: Experiment 2

Response	Relia-bility	Non-immediate	Immediate	F	P
Applicant performance					
Rated performance	.66	1.44	2.22	7.96	<.01
Rated demeanor	.86	1.62	3.02	16.46	<.001
Immediacy behaviors					
Distance	—	72.73 inches	56.93 inches	9.19	<.01
Speech error rate	.74	5.01 errors/min.	3.33 errors/min.	3.40	<.10
Self reported mood and attitudes					
Mood	—	3.77	5.97	1.34	n.s.
Interviewer friendliness	—	4.33	6.60	22.91	<.001
Interviewer adequacy	—	−1.07	1.53	8.64	<.01

Note. From "The Nonverbal Mediation of Self-Fulfilling Prophecies in Interracial Interaction" by C. Word, M. Zanna, and J. Cooper, 1974, *Journal of Experimental Social Psychology, 10*, p. 118. Copyright 1974 by Academic Press. Reprinted by permission.

confirmed their inadequacy. They were less qualified for the job! If this can be demonstrated with respect to White subjects, what is the overall implication for Blacks and other designated racial and ethnic groups (e.g., those with speech differences) when they interview with someone who holds such ambivalent racial attitudes? This pattern perhaps describes some of the negative conditions that reinforce racial mistrust and support the notion of institutional racism.

A second study is even more practical. Henderson (1979) collected personality data from 115 policemen in Cleveland, Ohio. Measures included the Edwards Personal Preference Schedule (EPPS) and the Cattell 16PF. Henderson also had performance ratings by both superior officers and peers. Table 7 shows the correlations between personality standing and performance ratings for Black and White policemen. A White policeman is evaluated favorably when he is outgoing, freethinking, and heterosexual. A Black policeman with these attributes is more inclined to get a negative performance evaluation. Conversely, a Black policeman who is deferent, orderly, nondominant, and nonaggressive is evaluated favorably, whereas these same attributes in a White policeman have no bearing or a negative bearing on his performance ratings. Mean aggregate data showed that the personality profiles of Black and White policemen

Table 7

Correlations of Several Personality Factors with Superior-Officer and Peer Ratings of Black and White Patrol Officers

	Whites (N = 75)			Blacks (N = 40)		
	Officer	Peer	Mean[a]	Officer	Peer	Mean[a]
EPPS scales						
Deference	−.02	−.08	44	.23	.19	47
Order	−.11	−.05	44	.46	.43	44
Autonomy	−.07	−.03	44	.37	.30	49
Affiliation	.00	.06	41	.27	.21	32
Dominance	.00	.08	58	−.28	−.20	57
Abasement	.03	−.09	35	.05	.15	31
Endurance	−.13	−.20	49	.31	.23	43
Heterosexuality	.12	.11	74	−.55	−.45	72
Aggression	.00	.01	53	−.13	−.02	56
16 PF scales						
Outgoing, easygoing	.19	.14	5.6	−.25	−.22	5.5
Enthusiastic, happy-go-lucky	.00	.01	6.0	−.17	−.11	5.4
Liberal, free thinking	.21	.28	5.0	−.04	−.10	6.1
Self-sufficient, resourceful	.02	−.02	5.4	−.19	−.13	5.5

Note. From "Criterion-Related Validity of Personality and Aptitude Scales: A Comparison of Validation Results Under Voluntary and Actual Test Conditions" by N. D. Henderson. In *Police Selection and Evaluation: Issues and Techniques* (p. 190) edited by C. Spielberger, 1979. Westport, CT: Greenwood Publishers Group. Reprinted by permission.
[a]EPPS based on percentile scores (general population mean = 50); 16 PF based on sten scores (general population mean = 5.5).

did not differ at all. What differed is what they meant to their superiors. Over time, if one were to use these criteria for selection purposes, what would happen? The Blacks selected and promoted within the force would be retiring and unassertive, and the Whites would be strong and forceful. What would the attitudes of the White policemen toward their Black colleagues be? There are some intriguing "catch-22" implications to such a hypothetical situation.

Thus Blacks are treated and understood differently from Whites. Again we must observe the pattern of differential experience in this society as a result of race. Negative attitudes persist in spite of a lessening of some more overtly hostile expressions. These negative attitudes, however, are not far below the surface and come into play very easily in ways that we often do not suspect. The victims, though, do suspect. They experience the negativity and react to it. That reaction may in some cases have deleterious effects on their attitudes and performance.

Returning to our earlier discussion, we consider the following: How can one compare a sample of Whites and Blacks and conclude that they are different in specifiable ways and that the difference is due to race? When one controls for SES, does one have comparability? SAT scores for Whites who come from families earning less than $10,000 per year are higher than for Blacks who come from families earning over $50,000 per year. There are many complex psychosocial dynamics in that 75% of unexplained variance mentioned earlier. The simple point is that race is an extremely complex factor with regard to psychological responses to a variety of important situations. To adequately understand this phenomenon, we must go well beyond simple biological conceptions, or race-comparative analysis. The dynamic interplay of psychological, biological, and social forces demands a multilevel analysis and understanding of race-related phenomena.

Selected Studies of Race Differences and Related Race Effects

Considerations of race have led to a preoccupation with differences between races as we have seen. The biological arguments for difference suggest a hardwired cortical level difference that is transmitted genetically and manifested in cognitive activities of the sort measured by tests of mental abilities. There remains substantial debate about all aspects of these ideas. There is also a substantial interest in softwired racial differences that, lacking any attempt at biological explanation, require some sort of sociocultural interpretation. The races are different, it is assumed, and research programs seek to document both the ways in which they are different and the reasons for the differences.

For the most part, research into racial differences is rather atheoretical. The most common approach is to take an idea, a measurement instrument, or a finding in the literature, and see if Blacks differ from Whites, if American Indians differ from Anglo-Americans, or if Asians differ from Hispanics and Blacks and Anglo-Americans, and so forth. It is important to note that if one claims a racial difference, the strong form of that claim is that they differ because of something about their racial character exclusive of all other desiderata. Trying to determine what variables distinguish races "uniquely" is not an easy matter, as we have seen. Biology seems on its face to be the most straightforward such distinction, but it is faulty as well.

We have seen that variability within race is greater than differences across races. Therefore, even when racial differences are uncovered, the realistic prospect is that they account for far less of the variability than do differences within either of the racial groups being studied. Moreover, studies of racial difference reported in the literature rarely have samples that qualify as representative of within-race diversity.

Against this complex picture of race, we may ask the following question: What do studies of racial difference mean? For the most part, I suggest that virtually all studies of racial differences are hypothesis-generating or seek to demonstrate effects or relationships we believe to exist. This is fine and a service to psychology to expand the knowledge base of human characteristics and behavioral potential. But a review of all the published studies in APA journals and some selected other journals such as *Child Development, Journal of Experimental Social Psychology*, and *Journal of Research in Personality*, reveals very little systematic knowledge accumulation. For the most part, studies are one-shot questions such as the following: Will Blacks and Whites be different on this variable or characteristic? As noted earlier, these studies are typically atheoretical.

Race is inextricably bound up in cultural effects. The world is different for a Black, Chicano, Puerto Rican, or American Indian from what it is for a White or Anglo-American, as we have seen. The world is different when one speaks a language other than English, or speaks it with an accent, or has traditions that are different from those most commonly described in our society. Thus, the study of race differences has become an attempt to catalogue the array of ways people differ as a result of their location in society, their history, and their cumulative interactions within their group and between themselves and members of other groups.

No unified theory of these kinds of sociocultural or historical effects exists, although we do often develop generalized notions that are used to "explain" findings. Father absence, for example, explained every form of Black performance from test scores to free-throw accuracy in basketball players. Since we do not have a grand theory about race, I propose to look at some selected findings of research that explores some racial differences or race effects and to extrapolate from them in order to determine what understanding might be gained of aspects of clinical issues.

The psychotherapeutic situation has been of great interest for psychologists. As a context in which dyadic communication and interaction take place with a presumed level of trust and mutuality, much attention is paid to racial differences between therapist and client. Racial differences are among the most commonly explored. How does research on race effects relate to the therapeutic situation?

As we have seen, mistrust is one of the legacies of race relations in this society. Terrell and his associates (Terrell, Terrell, & Taylor, 1981; Terrell & Terrell, 1984; Watkins & Terrell, 1988; and Watkins, Terrell, Miller, & Terrell, 1989) have developed a Cultural Mistrust Inventory (CMI), designed to measure the degree to which Blacks mistrust Whites in a variety of situations. Sentiments such as "It is best for Blacks to be on their guard when among Whites," "Whites will say one thing and do another," or "A Black person can usually trust his or her White co-workers" are typical items from the CMI.

Scores on this inventory have been related to several interesting variables. One study proposed that cultural mistrust might have the effect of lowering motivation to cooperate or perform in situations managed or controlled by Whites. The authors (Terrell, Terrell, & Taylor, 1981) reasoned that IQ test scores could be influenced by the extent to which one were willing to perform for a White experimenter when level of mistrust was high. One hundred Black college students who had scored high or low on the CMI were administered the WAIS by a Black or White graduate student. It was hypothesized and found that subjects who scored high on the CMI and who were tested by a White examiner had the poorest scores on the WAIS. The WAIS scores for those who tested high on the CMI were 95.6 and 86.4 when tested by Black and White examiners, respectively. The WAIS scores for those who tested low on the CMI were 91.7 and 97.8 when tested by Black and White examiners, respectively.

Could it be true that Black subjects who feel mistrust of Whites would either consciously or unconsciously sabotage their performance? Is it a self-handicapping strategy that prevents evaluation? Are there instances in which feelings of mistrust may increase motivation to perform? Is it a risk factor for poor therapeutic outcome? While this study raises some interesting possibilities, it is distinguished more by the questions it raises than the answers it provides.

Terrell and his colleagues have explored the relationship of cultural mistrust to therapeutic outcome in a series of studies of counselor preference. Terrell and Terrell (1984) looked at termination rates of Black clients at a community mental health center as a function of race of counselor and cultural mistrust. After intake interviews and completion of all agency forms, including the Cultural Mistrust Inventory, 135 Black clients were randomly assigned to a Black or White counselor. Premature termination was defined by a failure to return for the second or any subsequent sessions. Twenty-five percent of the clients assigned to a Black counselor failed to return, while 43% of those assigned to White counselors failed to return. CMI scores for the premature terminators were higher ($M = 94.3$) than those for clients continuing in treatment ($M = 75.1$). Furthermore, although CMI scores were not significantly different as a function of counselor race overall, they were significantly lower for those clients who continued in treatment with White as compared to Black counselors. It seems that cultural mistrust is perhaps most indicative of a Black client's willingness to enter and remain in treatment with a White counselor. The level of mistrust is associated with significantly different patterns of behavior and performance for Blacks in situations that involve interracial interaction and some elements of assessment.

Watkins, Terrell, Miller, and Terrell (1989) looked at the expectations of Black college students for counselor effectiveness as a function of CMI scores and race of counselor. Subjects who were a nonclient population of Black students at a northeast University filled out the Counselor Effectiveness Rating Scale (CERS), which measures counselor credibility, and the Personal Problem Inventory (PPI), which asks subjects to rate the extent to which a counselor might be able to help them with certain typical problems of college students (dating, studying, finances, etc.). In this analogue study, identical credentials of the counselor were presented to all subjects, except that half of them were told that the counselor was White and half were told that he was Black. An analysis of the credibility measure revealed an interaction showing that highly mistrustful subjects thought that the White counselor was less credible. It was also found that for four problem areas—general anxiety, shyness, dating difficulties, and feelings of inferiority—highly mistrustful subjects thought that the White counselor would be significantly less able to help. In addition, regardless of the counselor's race, highly mistrustful subjects felt that the counselor would not be able to help with sexual function problems.

Not only is there evidence for the negative consequences of cultural mistrust for the therapy or counseling situation, but the negative expectations may be problem-specific and carry a strong self-fulfilling prophecy as well. Needless to say, the historical circumstances of race relations contribute to this pattern of mistrust and its consequences for the cross-racial therapy situation. To what extent are so many of the racial differences observed based on this salient and persistent mistrust effect? Might it be a worthwhile enterprise to begin to assess how levels of mistrust operate in the therapy situation and ways in which our practice can operate to reduce its negative influences?

Similar results have been obtained when using *acculturation* as the concept. Acculturation may be seen as the reciprocal of cultural mistrust. The more acculturated a person is, the less cultural mistrust they would be expected to have. Atkinson and Gim (1989) gave the Suinn-Lew Asian Self-Identity Acculturation Scale, and the Attitudes toward Seeking Professional Psychological Help Scale to 557 Asian-American students, including Chinese, Japanese, and Korean Americans. The most highly acculturated students were (a) most likely to recognize personal need for professional psychological help, (b) most tolerant of stigma associated with psychological help, and (c) most open to discussing their problems with a psychologist.

With American Indians, the concept of *bicultural competence* seems to be another aspect of the acculturation theme (LaFromboise, 1982; LaFromboise & Rowe, 1983). Skills to which bicultural competence give rise include: ". . . communication skills to enhance self-determination, coping skills to resist the pressure to acculturate or give up one's Indian identity, and discrimination skills to determine the appropriateness of assertive behavior in Indian and non-Indian cultures" (LaFromboise & Rowe, 1983, p. 592). Schinke, Botvin, Trimble, Orlandi, Gilchrist, and Locklear (1988) suggest that acculturation to Anglo-American norms, styles, and values can be stressful to American Indians and could be in part responsible for problems of substance abuse. One hundred thirty seven American Indians were divided into two groups: an experimental group that underwent training in bicultural competence skills and a control group that received no training. Results supported the notion that such skills training could improve knowledge of problems associated with substance abuse and self-reported reduction in use of alcohol, tobacco, and drugs.

Some further guidance is provided by Stanley Sue and Nolan Zane (1987), who suggest that although race or ethnic effects in therapy are real, they operate at a more distal level. What really shapes therapy outcomes is the therapy process itself or proximal influences. Two factors that influence therapy outcome are *credibility* and *giving*. Credibility can be ascribed or achieved. In the Terrell et al. work, race is an ascribed characteristic that is defined by skin color and *assumed* belief and value characteristics. However, Sue and Zane suggest that credibility can also be achieved. How to achieve credibility is perhaps one of the most important areas for development of the clinical context. In the face of the powerful effects of mistrust, it may well be one of the most important subjects for training and research in the area of interracial therapy dynamics.

The bicultural or acculturation model is also applicable to Blacks. William Cross proposed a model of Black identity development (Cross, 1979). His model takes as a starting point a condition he calls "deracination," or a status where race is rejected as a self-relevant categorization. A statement typically endorsed in this stage is "I often say: Why should I be judged by my race?" This does mean that one is not conscious or race, for in this model, race consciousness coincides with internalization of a mainstream anti-Black bias. The phase of identity development characterized by the statement "I sometimes feel that Black people are inferior to White people" is labeled *pre-encounter* in anticipation of an event that challenges the prevailing viewpoint.

A critical event initiates the stage labeled *encounter* and usually comes in a form that draws attention to one's own racial categorization and the societal bias against the group. The encounter then awakens a deep racial identification, causing the person to immerse himself or herself in activities relevant to Blacks. A typical sentiment of this phase is "My emotions are like an exciting 'sea of Blackness,' and it is such a wonderful feeling, it makes me want to shout to the world, 'I'm Black and I'm proud.' " Then, after the heady experience of Black immersion, the person begins to feel the need for more balance, and emerges from this state searching for something more. This third stage, then, immersion/emersion, gives rise to a more balanced perspective on oneself as a racial being whose Blackness has positive features but not all-inclusive ones.

Persons achieve a state in which the new found Blackness is integrated with other aspects of the person so that group and self-referents are more manageable. This new *internalization* is characterized by endorsing statements such as "I feel like I'm living my Blackness rather than trying to prove it to someone." This internalization maintains the sense of personal identity, while adopting a *commitment* to the group. This final stage, then, has two parts: internalization and internalization with commitment.

Parham and Helms (1981; 1985; Helms, 1986) have developed the Racial Identity Attitude Scale (RIAS) to measure the stages of the Cross model. The RIAS is a 30-item attitude scale that measures subject responses on a 5-point Likert scale. The items operationalize the dimensions of the Cross model. Studies have shown the scale to have fairly good reliability (about .71) and to make interesting connections between racial identity and counseling outcomes. Pomales, Claiborn, and LaFromboise (1986) found, for example, that students scoring high on the encounter stage preferred the culturally sensitive counselor. Bradby and Helms (1985) found that internalization and encounter attitudes were positively related to client satisfaction, but pre-encounter attitudes predicted the total number of sessions the client attended. Parham and Helms (1985) showed that both pre-encounter and immersion attitudes (pro-White–anti-Black and pro-Black–anti-White, respectively) were associated with distress and feelings of inferiority. Emerging Black identity as measured by encounter attitudes was associated with self-actualization and a reduction in feelings of inferiority and anxiety.

Taken together, these studies suggest the feasibility of (a) developing a model of Black identity with the different levels or stages and (b) developing and effectively using a scale to assess the model. There are many interesting questions arising from this kind of work that relate to the dynamics by which one develops personal identity structures, and the behavioral and psychosocial consequences of their pattern and content. This is particularly important for the therapeutic situation in which the mistrust variable continues to be important but is surrounded by conflicting motives and needs at different stages of self-awareness. This work suggests strongly that one needs to have some understanding of where the client is in his or her personal identity development in order to understand what may be the most salient needs and strategies to employ.

Assessment raises another general set of problems for understanding race differences. Just as with IQ tests, there are often charges of bias in the assessments instruments that leads to improper diagnoses or characterizations of racial groups. The MMPI is perhaps most widely studied, and although many argue for the need of new race norms, recent re-norming seems to have produced an instrument that is representative and useful.

TRIOS—A Model of Adaptation

In my own analysis of Black culture, I have proposed a five-part model of cultural evolution labeled *TRIOS*. TRIOS is an acronym standing for five dimensions of human experience: Time, Rhythm, Improvisation, Oral expression and Spirituality. The concepts emerged from an analysis of racial differences in sports performance (Jones & Hochner, 1973), African religion and philosophy (Jones, 1972; Mbiti, 1970), Trinidadian culture (Jones & Liverpool, 1976), and psychotherapy with Black clients (Jones & Block, 1984).

These five dimensions reflect basic ways in which individuals and cultures orient themselves to living. They refer to how we experience and organize life, make decisions, arrive at beliefs, and derive meaning. TRIOS is important because along these dimensions of human experience, we will find divergences between the Euro-American and Afro-American perspective. The culture in which we live has evolved from the Euro-American perspective, but both have interacted and necessarily share in the fabric of contemporary culture. The matter is in part one of emphasis and preference.

TRIOS stands as a set of conceptualized dimensions of human perception and experience organized as a clustered "culture/personality" orientation and is depicted in Figure 3. In considering the question of cultural differences, the dimensions of TRIOS are represented as two poles of possibility. On one extreme is the materialistic, future-oriented, iconographic, individualistic profile of the hard-working, narrowly driven high achiever. On the other extreme is the spiritual, present-oriented, orally expressive, socially responsive profile of the gregarious, flexible, easy-going, affectively driven person. These idealized polarities form the dialectical basis of cultural and personality synthesis.

There are a number of implications of the TRIOS concepts for the psychotherapy situation. For a more detailed review of these ideas, see Jones and Block, 1984). I will now give a brief overview of some ways in which the TRIOS concept may have implications for the psychotherapy situation.

Time. There are several implications of the time concept for psychotherapy. First, surface aspects of time would suggest that the interpretation of behavior in the context of time, such as punctuality, may not have comparable meaning for Black clients. That is, the temporal units themselves may mean something different to Black clients so that time-based notions of resistance may be less applicable. Second, if nonlinear time experiences are not fit into a temporal behavioral se-

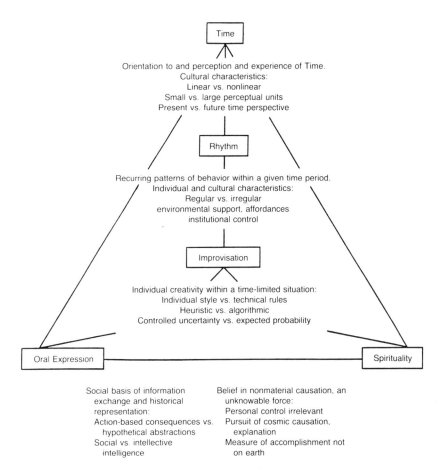

Figure 3. TRIOS: A model of Black cultural adaptation with psychotherapeutic implications. From "Racism in Black and White: A Bicultural Model of Reaction and Evolution," by J. M. Jones. In *Eliminating Racism: Profiles in Controversy* (p. 122), edited by P. A. Katz and D. A. Taylor, 1988. New York: Plenum. Copyright 1988 by Plenum Publishing. Reprinted by permission.

quence, some of the analytic processes of therapy may prove less useful. For example, the implications of the past in understanding the present, and the important role of the present as a means of understanding, predicting, and controlling the future may not have ready applicability. Third, judgments of success and failure in life and the therapeutic situation itself may be different. Therapeutic success may depend on outcomes over a shorter time frame, one that can be assimilated to an "expanded present" rather than a hypothetical future.

Rhythm. As here conceived, rhythm has implications for the precipitation of mental illness and the modes of therapy that may offer some relief. The ebb and flow of conversation follows rhythmic patterns, and the therapy situation itself may constitute a behavioral and conversational arrhythmia for Black clients. The compatibility of rhythms has strong implications for the perceptions of empathy as well. A therapist's ability to tune in to a patient's thoughts and feelings is directly related to successful therapy outcome. A mismatch of expectations between client and therapist—as, for example, when a client expects more direction and the therapist expects more "insight"—may undermine synchrony and damage the therapeutic relationship.

Improvisation. There are several implications of improvisation for the therapy situation. First, the etiology of mental illness itself may rest in important ways on the improvisation. To the extent that institutional structures maintain rigid standards of performance that inhibit improvisational behavior strategies and problem-solving tendencies, goal attainment is thwarted. If improvisation is a learned style of achievement and the institutions conspire to eliminate it, a behavioral vacuum may occur with potential mental health and behavioral consequences. A second implication comes from the therapy situation itself. Improvisation is a singular style. This singularity leads to a "do-it-yourself" orientation; hence a client may expect to create his or her own solutions rather than respond to what may come from the therapist. Even if this seems contraindicated by the therapist, ownership is important. Third, the therapy situation itself is not conducive to an improvisational style and therefore may result in relatively lower rates of participation.

Oral expression. Oral means of self-expression and cultural communication place a premium on lived experience. Thus authenticity may derive more from the presumption or demonstration of relevant experience than from formal education as represented by degrees, licenses, and so forth. This relates to the Sue and Zane (1987) concept of credibility. Because oral expression tends to be less abstract (with the exception of forms such as fables, metaphors, and proverbs), words devoid of action and meaning in an action context may be rejected. Thus the therapy situation may need to be more behavior-based or "action oriented" than conceptual and thought-oriented.

Spirituality. To the extent that therapy is seen as a context for increasing or restoring personal control and efficacy in clients, certain adjustments may need to be made when dealing with clients who are highly spiritual. For example, it is possible that discrepancies between personal and social causation and traditional spiritual beliefs may lead to a tendency to externalize causes of problems, leading to a perception of denial. In fact, such externalizing may well represent a belief system rather than a personal evasive problem-solving strategy.

These ideas are certainly not proven by empirical data. They are offered, rather, as an example of some possible implications of this model for the therapy situation. It is entirely possible that understanding the cultural dimensions of race will enable psychologists to better prepare themselves and their students for crosscultural therapy.

Conclusions

Race is a concept laden with emotional, sociopolitical, conceptual, and pragmatic ambiguities. It has elicited fear, moral indignation, and doubt among people in their daily lives. Psychology and psychologists have helped ameliorate these difficult circumstances in many instances and exacerbated them in others.

Race has always held major significance for its biological implications. Yet as we have seen, there is not very much sound scientific support for uniqueness among races. Furthermore, race has always included a strong geographical component, which makes biological aspects more plausible on the surface. However, in contemporary society, the geographical boundaries implied in a strict race concept do not readily apply. Moreover, the geographical isolation not only impacts the biology through inbreeding but also establishes characteristic patterns of cultural evolution that become in many respects indistinguishable from the presumed biological elements of racial designation.

McDougall (1921) illustrates the conjoining of biology, geography, and culture when assayed to distinguish the "races" of Europe. His analysis lead to a hierarchy of races headed by the "Nordic" races of Scandinavia, followed by the "Alpine" races of middle Europe, with the "Mediterranean" races of southern Europe bringing up the rear. The Nordics were individualistic, self-contained, intellective, future-oriented, introverted, and curious. The Mediterraneans were the opposite (sociable, extroverted, emotional, present-oriented, etc.) in all of these characteristics. To show how central a racial criterion was to his assessments, McDougall hailed the emerging IQ tests as wonderful advancements in "mental anthropology." Many of these same individual and cultural characteristics are associated with different racial and ethnic groups today.

There are some important implications of this basic orientation to race that I have explored in the preceding pages. I will now review the essential points that have been emphasized.

First, race is a biological concept whose significance is social. It has become the basis for differential experiences of members of this society and hence has merged with cultural influences to create substantial nonshared environments for Blacks and Whites. These nonshared environments or experiences create circumstances in which racial differences are perpetuated. The interpersonal and institutional effects described in this paper illustrate some of the ways in which race operates. Racism, prejudice, and discrimination are core ingredients of the social significance of race. They operate subtly to create the largely nonshared environment that perpetuates the distrust and mistrust of Whites and of the institutions that they control.

Second, within-group variation is substantial and needs to be taken into account when discussing or responding to racial issues. When we talk about Blacks as a group based on a sample of some specified people, we run the risk of misrepresenting true population effects. The biological basis of race tends to assume that members of a so-called race are to a large degree "all alike." In fact, as we have seen, within-group variation, according to biological criteria, is greater than between-group differences. What may seem to confirm the within group similarity is typically phenotypic attributes such as skin color, hair texture, and facial features. Even here, however, there are substantial variations within groups. The net result is that racial groups—Blacks in particular—are categorized, stereotyped, and, on the basis of cultural standards, devalued. Recognizing larger in-group variation is one way of reducing some of the negative consequences of racial bias.

Third, what the biological studies of racial differences show most clearly, I believe, is that there are persistent environmental effects that modulate biological templates for behavior. They further show that while there may be systematic effects, there is a large amount of variance that race leaves unexplained. They suggest to me that persistent attempts to demonstrate racial differences, although an acceptable enterprise, is not likely to yield the most important new information about human behavior. Models of human functioning such as represented by the TRIOS ideas hold promise by asking different questions and demanding different methodologies for their exploration.

Fourth, psychotherapy situations are strongly influenced by issues of trust. Because race is so fundamentally implicated in trust, there is a need for research to better understand how this can be addressed and for training to put the knowledge gained into practice. Credibility is a key ingredient in therapy, and race effects tend to undermine it. However, credibility is not automatic for same-race client–therapist dyads, nor is it impossible to achieve for different race dyads. Understanding dimensions of culture, levels of expectation, and ways in which gifts of practical utility can be made early in the interaction will likely serve to reduce the problems inherent in the cross-race dyad situation.

Fifth, assessment devices should look not only at evidences of pathology and illness but also at forms of adaptation to problems posed by race as signals for the kind of mental health intervention that has the best prospects for success. Measures of acculturation, mistrust and identity show great promise as means of assessing adaptation levels to the racial elements that affect everyday adjustments as well as life stage processes. Both the research in these areas and the applications to the therapy situation are needed.

In closing, I must make note of the growing tensions in our society that reflect race and ethnicity considerations. More generally, the question of "diversity," the general theme of these Master Lectures, is one which seems to have generated two heads of steam: one that extols the virtue and natural evolution of diversity in this society and the world community; and a second that seems to reject diversity as a code word for expanded rights of out-groups and a concomitant "lowering of quality" in institutions. The second viewpoint is seen by many as the new conservatism, and the former viewpoint is branded as "radical" by others.

It is my view that an understanding of social relationships, the consequences of institutional values and practices on minority group members, and the subtle biases that creep into everyday parlance and actions is a starting point for addressing these important dynamics in contemporary society. The analysis of race effects contained in the present chapter is intended to add to this perspective.

References

Allport, F. (1924). *Social psychology*. New York: Houghton Mifflin.

Atkinson, D. R., & Gim, R. H. (1989). Asian-American cultural identity and attitudes toward mental health services. *Journal of Counseling Psychology, 36,* 209–212.

Banton, M. (1983). *Racial and ethnic competition*. Cambridge, England: Cambridge University Press.

Bloom, L. (1971). *The social psychology of race relations*. Cambridge, MA: Schenkman Publishing.

Bogardus, E. (1928). *Immigration and race relations*. Boston, MA: D.C. Heath.

Boykin, A. W. (1979). Black psychology and the research process: Keeping the baby but throwing out the bath water. In A. W. Boykin, A. J. Anderson, & J. F. Yates (Eds.), *Research directions of Black psychologists* (pp. 85–106). New York: Russell Sage Foundation.

Bradby, D., & Helms, J. E. (1985). Black racial identity attitudes and White therapist cultural sensitivity in cross-racial therapy dyads: An exploratory study. In J. Helms (Ed.), *Black and White racial identity: Theory, research and practice* (pp. 165–176). New York: Greenwood Press.

Brewer, M. B. (1979). In-group bias in the minimal intergroup situation: A cognitive–motivational analysis. *Psychological Bulletin, 86,* 307–324.

Crane, A. L. (1923). Race differences in inhibition: A psychological study of the comparative characteristics of the Negro and the White man as measured by certain tests, with special reference to the problem of volition. *Archives of Psychology, 63,* 9–84.

Cross, W. E. (1979). The Negro-to-Black conversion experience: An empirical analysis. In A. W. Boykin, A. J. Anderson, & J. F. Yates (Eds.), *Research directions of Black psychologists* (pp. 107–130). New York: Russell Sage Foundation.

Daniels, R. (1968). *The politics of prejudice*. New York: Atheneum.

Dovidio, J., Evans, N., & Tyler, R. (1986). Racial stereotypes: The contents of their cognitive representations. *Journal of Experimental Social Psychology, 22*, 22–37.

Ferguson, G. O. (1916). *The psychology of the Negro: An experimental study*. New York: The Science Press.

Gardner, H. (1983). *Frames of mind: The theory of multiple intelligences*. New York: Basic Books.

Gilbert, G. M. (1951). Stereotype persistence and change among college students. *Journal of Abnormal and Social Psychology, 46*, 245–254.

Gould, S. J. (1981). *The mismeasure of man*. New York: W. W. Norton.

Guthrie, R. V. (1976). *Even the rat was white*. New York: Harper and Row.

Helms, J. (1986). Expanding racial identity theory to cover counseling process. *Journal of Counseling Psychology, 33*, 62–64.

Henderson, N. D. (1979). Criterion-related validity of personality and aptitude scales: A comparison of validation results under voluntary and actual test conditions. In C. Spielberger (Ed.), *Police selection and evaluation: Issues and techniques* (pp. 179–195). Westport, CT: Greenwood Publishers Group.

Herrnstein, R. J. (1989, May). IQ and falling birth rates. *The Atlantic Monthly*, pp. 73–79.

Herskovitz, M. (1958). *The myth of the Negro past*. Boston: Beacon Press.

Jaynes, G. D., & Williams, R. M. (Eds.). (1989). *A common destiny: Blacks and American society*. Washington, DC: National Academy Press.

Jensen, A. R. (1969). How much can we boost IQ and scholastic achievement? *Harvard Educational Review, 39*, 1–123.

Jensen, A. R. (1985). The nature of the Black–White difference on various psychometric tests: Spearman's hypothesis. *The Behavioral and Brain Sciences, 8*, 193–263.

Jones, J. M. (1972). *Prejudice and racism*. Reading, MA: Addison-Wesley.

Jones, J. M. (1988). Racism in Black and White: A bicultural model of reaction and evolution. In P. A. Katz & D. A. Taylor (Eds.), *Eliminating racism: Profiles in controversy* (pp. 117–136). New York: Plenum Press.

Jones, J. M., & Block, C. B. (1984). Black cultural perspectives: The *Clinical Psychologist, 37*, 58–62.

Jones, J. M., & Hochner, A. R. (1973). Racial differences in sports activities: A look at the self-paced versus reactive hypothesis. *Journal of Personality and Social Psychology, 27*, 86–95.

Jones, J. M., & Liverpool, H. (1976). Calypso humour in Trinidad. In A. Chapman & H. Foot (Eds.), *Humour: Theory and research*, (pp. 259–286). London: John Wiley, Ltd.

Jones, R. L. (1980). *Black psychology: Second edition*. New York: Harper and Row.

Kardiner, A., & Ovesy, L. (1951). *The mark of oppression*. New York: W. W. Norton.

Karlins, M., Coffman, T. L., & Walters, G. (1967). On the fading of social stereotypes: Studies in three generations of college students. *Journal of Personality and Social Psychology, 13*, 1–16.

Katz, D., & Braly, K. (1935). Racial stereotypes of one hundred college students. *Journal of Abnormal and Social Psychology, 28*, 280–290.

Katz, I. (1981). *Stigma: A social psychological analysis*. Hillsdale, NJ: Erlbaum.

Katz, I., & Hass, R. G. (1988). Racial ambivalence and American value conflict: Correlational and priming studies of dual cognitive structures. *Journal of Personality and Social Psychology, 55*, 893–905.

LaFromboise, T. (1982). *Assertion training with American Indians: Cultural/behavioral issues for trainers*. Las Cruces, NM: New Mexico State University.

LaFromboise, T., & Rowe, W. (1983). Skills training for bicultural competence: Rationale and application. *Journal of Counseling Psychology, 30*, 589–595.

Latter, B. D. H. (1980). Genetic differences within and between populations of the major human subgroups. *The American Naturalist, 116*, 220–237.

Lewontin, R. C., Rose, S., & Kamin, L. J. (1984). *Not in our genes: Biology, ideology and human nature*. New York: Pantheon Books.

Martinez, J. L. (Ed.). (1986). *Chicano psychology*. Orlando, FL: Academic Press.

Mbiti, J. (1970). *African philosophy and religions*. New York: Doubleday.

McDougall, W. (1921). *Is America safe for democracy?* New York: Charles Scribner's Sons.

Mead, M., Dobzhansky, T., Tobach, E., & Light, R. (Eds.). (1968). *Science and the concept of race*. New York: Columbia University Press.

Mehrabian, A. (1969). Some referents and measures of nonverbal behavior. *Behavior Research Methods and Instrumentation, 1*, 203–207.

Moore, E. (1986). Family socialization and the IQ test performance of traditionally and transracially adopted Black children. *Developmental Psychology, 22*, 317–326.

Nicolay, J. G., & Hay, J. (Eds.). (1894). *Abraham Lincoln, complete works*. New York: The Century Company.

Omi, M., & Winant, H. (1986). *Racial formation in the United States: From the 1960's to the 1980's*. New York: Bantam Books.

Parham, T. A., & Helms, J. E. (1981). The influence of Black students' racial identity on preference for counselor's race. *Journal of Counseling Psychology, 28*, 250–257.

Parham, T. A., & Helms, J. E. (1985). Relation of racial identity attitudes to self-actualization and affective states of Black students. *Journal of Counseling Psychology, 32*, 431–440.

Plomin, R., & Daniels, D. (1987). Why are children in the same family so different from one another? *The Behavioral and Brain Sciences, 10*, 1–60.

Pomales, J., Claiborn, C. D. & LaFromboise, T. D. (1986). Efforts of Black students' racial identity on perceptions of White counselors varying in cultural sensitivity. *Journal of Counseling Psychology, 33*(1), 57–61.

Ramirez, M. (1983). *Psychology of the Americas: Mestizo perspectives on personality and mental health*. New York: Pergamon Press.

Rogers, R., & Prentice-Dunn, S. (1981). Deindividuation and anger-mediated interracial aggression: Unmasking regressive racism. *Journal of Personality and Social Psychology, 41*, 63–73.

Rosenthal, R. R., & Jacobson, L. F. (1968). Teacher expectations for the disadvantaged. *Scientific American, 4*, 19–23.

Rushton, J. P., & Bogaert, A. F. (1987). Race differences in sexual behavior: Testing an evolutionary hypothesis. *Journal of Research in Personality, 21*, 529–551.

Rushton, J. P. (1988). Race differences in behaviour: A review and evolutionary analysis. *Personality and Individual Differences, 9*, 1009–1024.

Scarr, S., & Weinberg, R. (1983). The Minnesota adoption studies: Genetic differences and malleability. *Child Development, 54*, 260–267.

Schinke, S. P., Botvin, G., Trimble, J., Orlandi, M., Gilchrist, L., & Locklear, V. (1988). Preventing substance abuse among American-Indian adolescents: A bicultural competence skills approach. *Journal of Counseling Psychology, 35*, 87–90.

Scott, J. P. (1968). Race as a concept. In M. Mead, T. Dobzhansky, E. Tobach, & R. Light (Eds.), *Science and the concept of race* (pp. 59–64). New York: Columbia University Press.

Spearman, C. W. (1927). *The abilities of man.* New York: Macmillan.

Sternberg, R. (1985). *Beyond IQ: A triarchic theory of human intelligence.* New York: Cambridge University Press.

Sue, S., & Zane, N. (1987). The role of culture and cultural techniques in psychotherapy: A critique and reformulation. *American Psychologist, 42,* 37–45.

Terrell, T., & Terrell, S. (1984). Race of counselor, client sex, cultural mistrust level, and premature termination from counseling among Black clients. *Journal of Counseling Psychology, 31,* 371–375.

Terrell, F., Terrell, S., & Taylor, J. (1981). Effects of race of examiner and cultural mistrust on the WAIS performance of Black students. *Journal of Counseling Psychology, 49,* 750–751.

vanden Berghe, P. (1967). *Race and racism: A comparative perspective.* New York: John Wiley.

Watkins, C. E., & Terrell, F. (1988). Mistrust level and its effects on counseling expectations in Black client–White counselor relationships: An analogue study. *Journal of Counseling Psychology, 35,* 194–197.

Watkins, C. E., Terrell, F., Miller, F., & Terrell, S. (1989). Cultural mistrust and its effects on expectational variables in Black client–White counselor relationships. *Journal of Counseling Psychology, 36,* 447–450.

Webster's New Collegiate Dictionary. (1977). Springfield, MA: G. & C. Merriam Company.

Word, C., Zanna, M. P., & Cooper, J. (1974). The nonverbal mediation of self-fulfilling prophecies in interracial interaction. *Journal of Experimental Social Psychology, 10,* 109–120.

Zuckerman, M. (1990). Some dubious premises in research and theory on racial differences. *American Psychologist, 45,* 1297–1303.

Zuckerman, M., & Brody, N. (1988). Oysters, rabbits and people: A critique of "race differences in behavior" by J. P. Rushton. *Personality and Individual Differences, 9,* 1025–1033.

STANLEY SUE

ETHNICITY AND CULTURE IN PSYCHOLOGICAL RESEARCH AND PRACTICE

S tanley Sue is professor of psychology at the University of California, Los Angeles, and Director of the National Research Center on Asian American Health, a research center funded by the National Institute of Mental Health (NIMH). He received a BS degree from the University of Oregon in 1966 and a PhD degree from the University of California, Los Angeles (UCLA) in 1971. Prior to his professorship at UCLA, he served for ten years on the psychology faculty at the University of Washington, and from 1980–1981 he was Director of Clinical–Community Psychology Training at the National Asian American Psychology Training Center in San Francisco, an APA-approved internship program.

His research has been devoted primarily to the study of the adjustment of, and delivery of mental health services to, culturally diverse groups, especially Asian Americans. His work documented the effects of culture on conceptions of mental health, help-seeking behaviors, and means to provide culturally appropriate forms of treatment. The National Research Center on Asian American Mental Health, which he directs, is engaged in research on assessing the prevalence of mental health problems, on determining the factors that predict positive treatment outcomes, and on the effectiveness of the mental health system for Asian Americans. Sue is also conducting research on the factors that predict educational achievements among Asian Americans.

Sue has been involved in various professional affairs and organizations. He has served as Chair of the APA Board of Convention Affairs, as member of the APA Board of Social and Ethical Responsibility in Psychology, and founder and Executive Secretary of the Asian American Psychological Association. He is currently the President of the Division of Clinical and Community Psychology for the International Association of Applied Psychology, and President-elect of the Society for the Psychological Study of Social Issues (APA Division 9). Sue has held appointments on the editorial boards of such journals as *American Psychologist, American Journal of Community Psychology, Journal of Community Psychology*, and *Hispanic Journal of Behavioral Sciences*. For the past 5 years, he has regularly taught in mainland China and is Visiting Professor of Psychology at South China Normal University in Guangzhou.

In recognition of his work, Sue received the American Psychological Association's 1986 Award for Distinguished Contributions to Psychology in the Public Interest; 1989 Award for Distinguished Contributions to Clinical Psychology from the Los Angeles County Society of Clinical Psychologists; 1990 Distinguished Contributions Award from the Asian American Psychological Association; and 1990 Award for Distinguished Contributions Through Research from the Society for the Psychological Study of Ethnic Minority Issues (APA Division 45).

STANLEY SUE

ETHNICITY AND CULTURE IN PSYCHOLOGICAL RESEARCH AND PRACTICE

H odgkinson (1983) has indicated that in the future, the motive for working with, and knowing about, different ethnic groups such as American Indians, Asian Americans, Blacks, and Latinos will not be political liberalism or obligation. Rather, the motive will be enlightened self-interest. His belief reflects the fact that our society is becoming increasingly multiethnic and that the self-interest of all will be served by developing skills and competencies in working with diverse populations. For psychologists, the tasks are to better understand ethnic groups, form appropriate conceptualizations of behavior that are applicable to diverse groups, and promote the welfare of all human beings through education and teaching and psychological interventions. These tasks are neither simple nor new, but there is a special sense of importance in addressing them because of population changes and the continuing discrepancies in well-being between various groups.

This chapter is addressed to a general audience of psychologists and students, especially practitioners, who are interested in ethnicity and who want to begin the important task of integrating ethnic minority issues in teaching, research, and practice. It provides me with the opportunity to elaborate on some of my ideas on ethnic minority issues and to integrate the work of other scholars. Several areas are covered. First, a brief description of the status of different ethnic groups (primarily American Indians, Asian Americans, Blacks, and Latinos) is presented in order to illustrate contemporary issues of concern. Second, the concepts of culture, ethnicity, and minority group status are introduced. Third, these concepts are used to examine acculturation, personality development, mental health, and mental health services. Fourth, recommendations for teaching, research, and practice are given. Finally, value conflicts that are pertinent to the understanding of ethnic minority groups are presented. Although it is not possible to review all of the literature in these areas, I shall use the research literature to highlight important issues.

Status of Ethnic Minority Groups

The increasing diversity of the American population is apparent from population statistics. There has been a sizable growth in the proportion of ethnic minority group populations from 1980–1990, and an even larger proportion of ethnic minority groups is projected for the year 2000. The 1990 population of American Indians/Eskimos/Aleuts (2 million), Asians (7.3 million), Blacks (30 million), and Latinos (22.4 million) represented growth rates of, respectively, 38%, 108%, and 13%, 53% from the figures in 1980 (Andersen, 1991). In contrast, the 1990 White population of about 200 million reflected a growth rate of only 11% during this period of time. Early in the 21st century, one third of the United States population will be members of an ethnic minority group (Jones, 1990).

In addition to population changes, ethnic group differences exist on indicators of well-being. For example, certain ethnic minority groups exhibit lower levels of educational attainments, income, occupational mobility, and life expectancy and higher rates of poverty and crime than the national average (see California State Department of Education, 1986; *The 1990 Almanac*, 1990). The findings are not new in that social scientists as well as the general public are aware of these problems. They have had the effect of stimulating research into and theory construction of the causes of status differences and means of intervening to promote the welfare of various groups. While much research has been devoted to understanding "deficits" among ethnic minority groups, more recently—perhaps in the past decade—greater emphasis has been placed on research regarding competencies and regarding between- and within-ethnic-group differences. Snowden (1984) has been critical of the overemphasis on research demonstrating the negative aspects of family life, extensive psychopathology, and low academic achievements of Blacks. Indeed, he argues that to fully understand the status of Blacks, personal competencies and family and community resources must also be examined. Another important trend in attempting to understand ethnic minority groups is the focus on between- and within-group differences. Generalizations concerning majority–minority status are often inappropriate because ethnic groups vary on many characteristics. For example, in a study of clients in the mental health system in Seattle, O'Sullivan, Peterson, Cox, and Kirkeby (1989) found that American Indians, Asian Americans, Blacks, and Latinos exhibited significant differences in demographic backgrounds, rates of utilization, and levels of psychopathology. In such a situation, gross categories such as ethnic minority group versus Whites fail to have much meaning. Even when one group is discussed, there are major within-group differences. This is particularly apparent in the case of American Indians, who represent some 511 federally recognized tribes (LaFromboise, 1988) and Asian Americans, who have many distinct languages and backgrounds (e.g., Chinese, Filipinos, Japanese, Koreans, and Southeast Asians).

The following major questions underlie the examination of the status of ethnic minority groups:

1. What accounts for the differences in characteristics between ethnic minority groups?

2. What are the respective contributions of culture, individual and institutional prejudice, and discrimination to status differences?

3. How can we best intervene to promote the welfare of all groups?

4. To what extent are widely used research strategies, theories, and intervention strategies invalid or ineffective with ethnic minority populations?

In turn, these questions have led to concrete issues of contention, ones that have generated quite a bit of controversy and affect, as illustrated in the following terms: *Affirmative action* in recruitment, hiring, and promotions; *cultural bias* in theory, research, and practice; *deficit model*; and *racism*.

Key Concepts

Before proceeding further, it would be wise to identify the groups I shall be discussing and the central concepts in this chapter. My discussion has relevance particularly for the groups traditionally considered ethnic minorities—namely, American Indians, Asian Americans, Blacks, and Latinos. As I shall indicate, these groups are defined by their cultural characteristics, ethnic identity, and minority group status. In turn, concepts or features are important because they have bearing on research, theory, and practice. Although other groups may indeed be included within the boundaries of my definitions, these four have been the focus of my research.

Culture

The concept of culture has been defined by social scientists in many different ways. Kroeber and Kluckhohn (1952) suggested that culture is the patterns of behaviors transmitted by symbols that represent the distinctive achievements of human groups; culture can also be seen as the set of rules and norms that promote stability and harmony within a society (Gibbs & Huang, 1989); Banks (1987) defines culture as the behavior patterns, symbols, institutions, values, and human products of a society. Although it is possible to find hundreds of different definitions of culture, most of them point to several features: (a) the products of a society or group such as behavioral patterns, knowledge, attitudes, values, and achievements; (b) the means for transmitting products through norms, rules, institutions, communication patterns, and socialization practices; and (c) the variability that exists between groups and societies.

The importance of culture has been noted by many investigators, especially those involved in cross-cultural research. Triandis and Brislin (1984) argue that cross-cultural research can aid the development of psychological theory. By testing one's theory in different societies, the relevance and validity of the theory for human beings (and not simply for one's own culture) can be established. They also cite as benefits of cross-cultural research the fact that investigators can increase the range of variables studied. For example, assume that a researcher is interested in the relationship between the age of weaning and personality development. Because different cultures vary in the age of weaning, the investigator benefits from having a wider age range to study. Similarly, cultures can be found to differ in variables that for ethical or practical reasons are difficult to manipulate as independent variables (e.g., the effects of certain human values on helping behaviors).

Despite the need to more fully integrate culture and cross-cultural considerations into our research, theory, and practice, progress has been slow. Culture and cultural influences are often unrecognized or unappreciated. For example, some years ago I attended a counseling workshop in which cross-cultural experts from throughout the world were invited to attend (Sue, 1983). The format of the workshop was for each participant to present his or her paper, after which a discussant would provide a critique. The first two papers generated some lively and heated discussion. Soon afterward, several of the participants from Asian countries indicated some reluctance to present their papers. They argued that formal presentation of the papers was unnecessary and that much more could be accomplished by an informal exchange of ideas. The participants then debated the merits of formal versus informal presentations and concluded that formal presentations would be made optional. This minor crisis over the format failed to reveal initially an underlying cultural difference. We later found out that some of the participants from the Asian countries were apprehensive over the possibility that after their formal paper presentation, discussants might strongly criticize their papers in public, something that occurred in the first two presentations. Such a situation might cause much embarrassment. The irony of the situation was that the group of cross-cultural experts failed to see a cultural bias in the format of the workshop. In our society, paper presentations at workshops often generate critical and public comments. Such is not the case in other societies, in which major controversies are often negotiated prior to formal, public presentations.

Why is there a failure to recognize or appreciate cultural factors? Albert (1988) has examined several factors that can lead to the neglect of cultural variables. They include the lack of contact and experience with other cultures; the need to simplify rather than complicate perceptions within a cultural context; fears stereotyping others because of cultural backgrounds; ethnocentric bias; and equating diversity with elitism. As noted later, these factors are often at the root of much emotional conflict within and between individuals.

Ethnicity

Properly speaking, ethnicity can broadly refer to a religious, racial, national, or cultural group (Gordon, 1978). For the purposes of this chapter, ethnicity is used as a social–psychological sense of "peoplehood" in which members of a group share a unique social and cultural heritage that is transmitted from one generation to another. Since culture is a defining characteristic, individuals in a particular ethnic group may share common behavioral patterns, attitudes, and values. Members also feel a consciousness of kind and an interdependence of fate with others in the group (Banks, 1987). Thus American Indians, Asian Americans, Blacks, and Latinos may share with other members of their group beliefs about their fate or common struggles in American society.

That ethnicity is an important concept is undeniable. Psychologists have examined, for example, ethnic groups themselves or the institutions, individuals, or societal conditions that affect ethnic groups in the following areas: social behaviors, communication styles, attitudes, beliefs, attributions, and achievements; child-rearing practices, family structure, sex roles, and community characteristics; ethnic identity, self-esteem, and self-hatred; deviance, mental health, crime, adjustment, violence, and socioeconomic status; acculturation and assimilation; prejudice, discrimination, racism, and stereotyping; prevention, treatment, and intervention. These studies have often raised a great deal of controversy and issues regarding the validity and adequacy of theoretical paradigms, measurement instruments, and research strategies have been questioned. Given the wide range of topics pertinent to ethnic minority groups, I shall be selective in presenting some of the issues and research findings. It should be noted that Blacks and Latinos have been the groups studied the most. Much less work has been devoted to American Indians and Asian Americans.

Another important point to recognize is that members of ethnic groups exhibit a great deal of heterogeneity. Given this heterogeneity, are presentations of group characteristics necessarily stereotypic? Here, it is important to distinguish between the purposes of communication. At one level, when between-group comparisons are made, generalizations about group characteristics may be needed. For ethnicity and culture to have meaning, between-group differences in values and traits may have to be highlighted. Inkeles & Levinson (1969) introduced the notion of *modal personality* to describe different ethnic groups. While members of a particular group may exhibit heterogeneity, the modal (i.e., average) characteristics of groups may show meaningful differences that are important to consider when between-group comparisons are made. For example, Asians and Whites may exhibit differences on certain measures of individualism. These differences provide the context for understanding ethnic groups. However, the context or modal patterns must not be confused with the characteristics of individual members of a group who may or may not possess the modal patterns associated with the group. Otherwise, individuals are stereotyped according to their culture. At another level of communication, we may wish to emphasize within group heterogeneity. Not all White Americans are individualistic, even though they may as a group be higher on individualism than members of other groups. By understanding the purpose of communication and by recognizing these levels of communication, stereotyping can be minimized.

Minority Group Status

Recently, objections have been expressed over the term *minority* within the phrase *ethnic minority group*. (Similar objections have been raised for the terms used for specific groups, as noted in the June 1990 issue of *Focus* [*American Psychological Association, 1990*]. For example, *African Americans* is increasingly used to refer to *Blacks*. The latter term appears in this chapter to maintain consistency with the term used in other chapters.) *Minority* has historically been associated with notions of inferiority and deficits. Furthermore, the concept of minority implies that there is a majority, and one could argue that there is no real ethnic majority group in the United States (Whites can be conceived as including many different ethnic groups) or in the world. My use of the term is intentional. Rather than to imply that ethnic minority groups should be viewed as inferior or deficient, I want to convey the fact that minority status has an impact on the groups. Thus the situation of American Indians, Asian Americans, Blacks, and Latinos is not solely a function of their own cultures. Rather, historical and contemporary forms of prejudice and discrimination have also been experienced. For example, alcohol abuse among American Indians cannot be fully understood by references to cultural differences. Patterns of exploitation have also accompanied their history. In other words, to fully understand these groups, culture and minority group status must both be analyzed. Mi-

nority group status is used as a general concept to convey ethnic relationships in which some groups have experienced prejudice and discrimination. It is this status that distinguishes cross-cultural research,
in which different cultural groups are examined, from ethnic minority
research, in which cultural differences *and* ethnic relations are critical
considerations.

Obviously, the effects of culture and minority status can be easily
confounded. Over time, cultural values of a group may change as a result
of ethnic relations. The main point is that the two effects are pertinent
to the understanding of ethnic minority groups.

Personality and Identity

While cognizant of intragroup variability, social scientists have found
that ethnic groups often exhibit different personality characteristics
because of cultural influences (Price-Williams, 1985). For example, different ethnic groups have been found to vary on characteristics such as
self-disclosure, assertiveness, cooperativeness, shyness, individualism,
interpersonal styles, and introversion. Coupled with this emphasis on
cultural influences on personality has been recognition that for ethnic
minorities, the social context (i.e., minority status in society) for the
groups is also an important determinant of personality (Rogoff & Morelli,
1989).

Because of minority–majority group relations, investigators have
been interested in defining and conceptualizing the identity of ethnic
minority groups, finding means to measure and assess identity, discovering correlates of identity, and studying the factors that influence identity. One of the most widely investigated areas has been self-esteem and
identity. In 1957, James Baldwin wrote: "I can conceive of no Negro
native to this country who has not, by the age of puberty, been irrepa-
rably scarred by the conditions of his life. The wonder is not that so
many are ruined but that so many survive" (p. 71). At that time, Baldwin
was reflecting on a widely held belief about the detrimental consequences of racism and about difficulties that ethnic minority individuals
have in achieving self-esteem. The pioneering work of Clark and Clark
(1947) empirically demonstrated Black children's negative evaluations
of Blackness and the tendency among many of the children to identify
themselves as being White. Over time, the notion that Blacks develop
self-hatred and negative self-images has been criticized (Banks, 1984).
Methodological and conceptual problems have hindered studies of self-
identity. Moreover, it seems highly likely that changes in group identity
have occurred from the early investigations by the Clarks, because of
the civil rights and the "black-is-beautiful' movements.

Whereas past research was targeted to the potential deficits that
ethnic minorities have in developing self-esteem and adaptive person-

alities, the current trend in ethnic minority research is to focus on: (a) individual differences in identity development, (b) the processes of acculturation and assimilation, and (c) positive aspects of ethnicity and culture. In terms of individual differences, numerous conceptual schemes, typologies, stages of identity development, and measures have been proposed by researchers to investigate the self-identification process (e.g., Atkinson, Morten, & Sue, 1979; Cross, 1978; Parham & Helms, 1981). These researchers demonstrate the within-group variability that exists and take into account different reactions (e.g., rebellion, acquiescence, and separatism) to cultural and societal influences. The individual differences are used to predict other behaviors ranging from adjustment to preferences for the ethnicity of therapists. A related trend has been to study the processes of acculturation (learning the rules, role behaviors, values, and attitudes of another cultural group) and assimilation (the amalgamation of one group into another). Although these processes have been the focus of research for decades (see Allport, 1954), attempts have been made to more rigorously define and measure these processes and their correlates among different ethnic groups (see Berry, Trimble, & Olmedo, 1986; Padilla, 1987; Suinn, Richard-Figuerod, Lew, & Vigil, 1985). In the process, important questions have been raised that still have not been resolved. In acculturation, which ethnic cultural values tend to be extinguished and which are maintained over time? What elements of the majority cultural group tend to be adopted? Is cultural identity simply the sum of elements of the two cultures, or do the cultures interact to create quite distinct personality traits? What is meant by bicultural or multicultural adaptation?

Finally, studies of the strengths and resources that exist in ethnic communities have increased. For example, rather than examining the "tangle of pathology" often associated with Black families, Wilson (1989) has investigated the role of extended family members among Blacks. He found evidence that single parents as well as their children were affected positively by the presence of grandmothers who provided assistance on household tasks, emotional support, and child care. The effects of churches, families, folk healers, etc., on adaptation have also been examined as resources (Comas-Diaz, 1988; Hsu, 1985; Padilla & Salgado De Snyder, 1985; Trimble & LaFromboise, 1985). Interest in the strengths found in ethnic minority communities has led to a reconsideration of the position that ethnic groups are deficient and also to a wider range of prevention and intervention strategies to enhance well-being.

Prevalence of Mental Health Problems

With respect to mental health, the traditional assumption has been that ethnic minority groups have high rates of deviance because of stressors such as prejudice and discrimination and cultural conflicts. Kramer,

Rosen, and Willis (1973) went so far as to say that "Racist practices undoubtedly are key factors—perhaps the most important ones—in producing mental disorders in Blacks and other underprivileged groups. . . . (p. 355). American Indians were believed to be prone to alcoholism and suicide; Latinos were depicted as being lazy, laden with crime, and undependable; Blacks were viewed as having antisocial personality patterns and drug addiction; and despite the popular stereotype of adjustment, Asian Americans were characterized as being passive and unassertive.

The empirical evidence with respect to the nature and prevalence of mental disorders among ethnic minority groups is equivocal. Investigations based on the data collected from the Epidemiological Catchment Area Study, which surveyed large-community samples at five sites in the United States, have been inconclusive. For the most part, Blacks have not been found to vary much from Whites in the prevalence of depression and other psychiatric disorders (Somervell, Leaf, Weissman, Blazer, & Bruce, 1989; Neighbors, 1984). In a well-designed national survey of Blacks, Jackson, Neighbors, & Gurin (1986) found that over 63% of the respondents indicated that they had experienced a serious personal problem in their lives. Since the survey did not specifically assess rates of psychiatric disorders, it is difficult to relate this finding with those from other groups. In the case of Mexican Americans, few ethnic differences were found with Whites in the prevalence of DSM-III disorders (Burnam et al., 1987). Major epidemiological prevalence studies have not been conducted for American Indians and Asian Americans. Some investigators believe that American Indians and Alaska Natives experience high rates of mental disorders, especially those associated with social stress. Overall rates of alcoholism and drug abuse appear high, although the prevalence varies considerably from tribe to tribe (LaFramboise, 1988; Manson, 1986). In the case of Asian Americans, no prevalence studies exist. Westermeyer, Vang, and Neider (1983) have found that Indochinese refugees experienced the highest one-year incidence rate of psychiatric disorders ever recorded among any group of adults. Some investigations of mental health services point to the fact that Asian Americans underutilize services but exhibit more severe disturbances than other groups. They suggest that many Asian Americans with milder personal problems avoid using services. Therefore, prevalence rates based on analyses of treated cases may seriously underestimate the extent of mental disorders in this population (Abe & Zane, 1990).

The inability to draw conclusions more firmly concerning the prevalence of mental disorders among ethnic minority groups is understandable for several reasons (see Jones & Korchin, 1982; Neighbors, 1984). First, as mentioned previously, few studies have focused on these groups. Second, difficulties have been found in sampling from a large enough population base. Third, and related to the second point, is that the groups are quite heterogeneous, so that unless an adequate sample is found, findings from particular groups may not be representative. The different ethnic groups are also likely to differ from each other, making generalizations invalid. Fourth, methodological problems, especially in finding cross-culturally valid research strategies and measures, have hindered the ability to draw conclusions. While these problems cannot tell us what the prevalence rates are, there is simply no evidence that the rates are lower than those found for White Americans.

The discussion concerning the rates of mental disorders naturally leads into the controversies over assessment, measurement, and diagnosis.

Assessment and Evaluation

Clinical psychologists as well as researchers have become increasingly aware of limitations in the assessment tools used to evaluate the psychological status of ethnic minority groups. These limitations are particularly apparent when assessment instruments have not been standardized or validated on these groups and when the ethnic individuals are markedly different from mainstream Americans (Brislin, Lonner, & Thorndike, 1973). Yet, assessment must proceed. The clinician who encounters a culturally dissimilar client is often required to make an evaluation of the client; researchers interested in cross-cultural comparisons must frequently use psychological tests; and mental health planners or administrators need to evaluate the well-being of all Americans.

Neighbors, Jackson, Campbell, and Williams (1989) suggest that diagnosticians or clinicians may make two kinds of errors. The first involves the diagnostician's incorrect assumption that Blacks and Whites are naturally different, so that similar symptoms exhibited by both groups are judged to be nonequivalent. That is, ethnic differences in the manifestations of psychopathology are believed to exist when this is not the case. The second error is the opposite of the first in that ethnic minorities may not actually exhibit the same symptoms for a particular disorder and yet the diagnostician assumes that all individuals must show the same symptoms for the disorder. Underlying the error is the belief that there are universal criteria for disorders and that groups can be evaluated in a similar fashion. This second error has been criticized the most. Rogler, Malgady, and Rodriguez (1989) argue that evaluations and norms based on White populations are often inappropriately applied to Latinos. As an example, they indicate that in Puerto Rican culture, beliefs in spiritualism are common. Therefore, certain items on assessment measures (e.g., the item, "Evil spirits possess me at times," on the MMPI) may be inappropriately judged to be pathological, according to

White norms. In an interesting and insightful analysis of clinical judgement, Lopez (1989) concluded that bias can occur in opposite directions. Underpathologizing is apparent when clinicians minimize the psychopathology among ethnic minority groups. For example, Ridley (1984) notes that when symptoms of persecution seen in a Black client are automatically assumed to be caused by prejudice and discrimination, the clinician may be underpathologizing. On the other hand, overpathologizing can occur when symptoms of persecution are judged to be signs of a paranoid delusion rather than a reality-based response to a hostile environment.

The cultural background of the clinician can influence the evaluations of clients. In an interesting study, Li-Repac (1980) had five White and five Chinese American therapists rate Chinese and White clients during a videotaped interview. White clinicians rated Chinese clients with less favorable adjectives than did Chinese clinicians. However, in the case of White clients, the Chinese rather than the White clinicians used less favorable adjectives as descriptors. The results indicate that ratings and assessment may be influenced by cultural factors.

Because assessment relies heavily on verbal communication and proficiency in English, limited language facility among clients is a difficult problem for clinicians. Many immigrants and refugees speak very little or no English. Language difficulties increase the risk that assessment procedures that depend on verbal or written communication will be inaccurate. With the severe shortage of bilingual therapists, reliance on interpreters increases. The typical one-to-one interview procedure becomes one of three dyads, increasing the risk of communication errors. Although interpreters are often described as highly motivated and involved, one mental health professional feels that "Generally, their motives are generous, and the 'little' changes and embellishments that they bring into the translation are made with the most laudable intent" (Tung, 1985, p. 8). Unfortunately, these "changes" can distort information and interfere with the assessment process.

Additional problems occur because the bilingual interpreter must translate the questions into a language that may not contain corresponding words or concepts. The meaning of certain behaviors is not always preserved in translations, especially culture-specific idioms (Rogler, Malgady, & Rodriguez, 1989). Interpreters may also be influenced by the cultural norms and values to which they adhere and may hesitate to reveal certain symptoms that might be viewed negatively by the community. They report reluctance to ask about sexual matters, financial background, material considered to be disrespectful to the client, and information related to suicide or homicidal thoughts.

In one study (Marcos, 1979), distortions of the interpretive process were recorded on audiotapes with Chinese- and Spanish-speaking interpreters. Distortions were found involving omissions, substitutions, condensation, and change of focus. Interpreters whose family members were being interviewed frequently minimized psychopathology and often answered questions before asking the patient. Macros suggests that to reduce interpreter distortions, the clinician and interpreter should discuss the goals of the evaluation, the areas to be assessed, and sensitive topics that may have to be examined. In addition, the interpreter's level of competence in both languages and attitudes toward the patient and interview should be explored. Pre-interview practice, to demonstrate the need to be accurate in translating all information, is also needed.

Given the problems in assessment involving the meaning of symptom expression among different cultural groups, how can we proceed? Later, I shall offer some suggestions for evaluation. For the time being, an important point to keep in mind is that most investigators emphasize the lack of research and the need to conduct further research in discovering biases and the factors that influence bias (Lopez, 1989; Neighbors et al., 1989; Rogler, Malgady, & Rodriguez, 1989).

Mental Health Services

An important issue in mental health is the adequacy of services for members of ethnic minority groups. If one reviews the literature, the most frequently cited problem in the provision of mental health services to ethnic minority groups concerns cultural and linguistic mismatches between clients and therapists and the detrimental effects that mismatches often have on therapy outcomes (see Comas-Diaz & Griffith, 1988; Dudley & Rawlins, 1985). Ethnic minority clients may have difficulties in finding therapists who are bilingual or bicultural, or both, who can communicate and can understand the values, lifestyles, and backgrounds of American Indians (Attneave, 1985; Trimble & LaFromboise, 1985), Asian Americans (Leong, 1986; D. W. Sue & D. Sue, 1985), Blacks (Jenkins, 1985; Snowden, 1982), and Latinos (Acosta, 1984; Casas, 1985; Munoz, 1982; LeVine & Padilla, 1980). As we have seen, cultural differences can affect assessment. These differences can also affect the development of therapist–client rapport, alliance, and effectiveness.

Because of the history of ethnic and race relations, therapists may also hold stereotypes or biases concerning ethnic minority clients. Kenneth Clark (1972) argues that the mental health profession has not been immune to the forces of racism in society and that racism may be reflected in processes such as diagnosis, assessment, and treatment. Jones and Seagull (1977) discussed these biases in terms of countertransference on the part of the therapist. Using less psychodynamic terminology, others have simply referred to the stimulus value of ethnic clients to therapists. Since the stimulus values of individuals are frequently influenced by societal values, ethnic clients may be victims of stereotypes. It should be mentioned that ethnic minority clients may also have biases concerning the therapist, and that transference/countertransference phenomena occur regardless of the ethnicity of therapists or clients. In any event, the general assumption is that biases per se are likely to be detrimental to the therapeutic process. The consensus among the investigators cited above is that ethnic minority clients have a more difficult time than White clients achieving good outcomes from treatment because of mismatches and therapist biases in treatment.

Is there evidence that ethnic minority clients fare worse than White clients in the mental health system? Some investigators have cited the problems ethnic clients experience, including differential or discriminatory forms of treatment (Yamamoto, James, & Palley, 1968), therapist preferences for client characteristics that place ethnic minorities at a disadvantage (Schofield, 1964), underutilization of services on the part of some ethnic groups (Snowden & Cheung, 1990), high premature termination rates, and ineffectiveness of traditional mental health services for ethnic minority clients (President's Commission on Mental Health, 1978). In an earlier study (Sue, 1977), I examined nearly 14,000 clients in the mental health system in the Seattle area, particularly the status of ethnic minority clients. The findings were disturbing. Ethnic clients were found to vary in utilization patterns and to terminate treatment permaturely. Asian Americans and Latinos severely underutilized, whereas Blacks and American Indians overutilized services in comparison to their respective populations. All ethnic minority groups tended to drop out of treatment very quickly, with about half of them terminating from treatment after one session compared to the 30% dropout rate for Whites. Ethnicity was a significant predictor of premature termination even after other client demographic variables (e.g., social class, gender, and age) and treatment variables (e.g., type of treatment received and personnel rendering treatment) were controlled.

Of course, the study was conducted about one-and-one-half decades ago. To what extent have improvements been made in the mental health system, and have the improvements, if any, increased the effectiveness of the mental health system for ethnic minority groups? One study has recently tried to link changes in the mental health system to utilization and premature termination patterns of ethnic minority clients. O'Sullivan et al. (1989) studied the status and situation of ethnic clients in the Seattle mental health system, a decade after the study by Sue (1977). They noted that the system had made special efforts to hire ethnic providers, create ethnic-specific services, and establish innovative and culturally consistent treatment modalities. Using some of the same variables reported in the earlier study, they found that the situation had improved considerably. Ethnic minority groups for the most part were no longer underutilizing services; their dropout rates had been reduced and were not much different from those of Whites. O'Sullivan and his colleagues attributed the changes to the increasing cultural responsiveness of the system to underserved populations. In an earlier study, Wu and Windle (1980) raised this possibility when they found that the number of ethnic personnel at a mental health agency is directly related to Black and Asian client utilization of services.

The work of O'Sullivan and his colleagues is certainly encouraging in that perhaps our mental health systems have become more effective and culturally appropriate for diverse groups. Some of our own research (Sue, Fujino, Hu, Takeuchi, & Zane, 1990) supports the findings of O'Sullivan et al. (1989) with respect to dropout rates but not to utilization rates. Our study was based on thousands of Asian American, Black, Mexican American, and White clients seen in the Los Angeles County Mental Health System from 1983–1988. It was intended to examine utilization rates, dropout rates (after one session), and treatment outcomes (using pre- and post-treatment Global Assessment Scale scores). Furthermore, we wanted to find out if therapist–client matches in ethnicity and language would be associated with dropping out and treatment outcomes. Results indicated that Asian Americans and Mexican Americans tend to underutilize services in comparison with their populations, while Blacks tend to overutilize services. Moreover, dropout rates for ethnic clients were higher (in the case of Blacks) and lower (in the case of Asian Americans) than for Whites. Interestingly, in general, Asian Americans fared better when they saw a therapist who was matched ethnically and linguistically. Similar effects were found for Mexican Americans. However, ethnic matches were not significantly related to outcomes for Blacks and Whites. We do not know why matching is related to outcomes for some groups but not others, but it would be erroneous to simply conclude that ethnicity of the therapist is unimportant for Blacks. The disturbing finding is that Blacks were the least likely of any group to show positive treatment outcomes. Furthermore, the importance of ethnic match may depend heavily on the ethnic–cultural identity of clients, since a great deal of within-group heterogeneity exists. For some clients in the same ethnic minority group, match may be quite important. We do know that ethnic or language matches do not ensure *cultural* matches, which may be of major importance.

The emphasis on individual differences implicitly recognizes the complexity of the match issue. For some clients, mismatches may be beneficial. Tyler, Sussewell, and Williams-McCoy (1985) have developed the Ethnic Validity Model in an attempt to specify the advantages and disadvantages that can occur in matches and mismatches. In this model, individuals have a conception of a reference group and of validity within that group. Ethnic validity for different groups may converge, diverge, or conflict. Convergence refers to patterns of interaction in which some or all of the criteria for well-being transcend culture, race, and ethnicity. Divergence is a situation in which the patterns of well-being are unique and reflect cultural or racial differences. Conflict occurs when the patterns in various groups not only differ but also clash. Ideally, the tasks are to enrich convergence (e.g., the commonalities) and divergence (e.g., pluralism) and to reduce conflict. The therapy encounter may serve to accomplish these tasks. Therapists and clients who match ethnically and culturally may relate well to one another and share experiences and perspectives. However, matches may not be conducive to transcending cultural biases and limitations. In mismatches, the advantage is that clients and therapists can learn about cultural diversity and confront conflicting validities. Problems can occur when cultural differences cannot be surmounted, and the capacity to communicate is limited.

Recommendations for Teaching, Research, and Practice

In this chapter, I have reviewed some of the current research and have highlighted the problems with respect to ethnic diversity encountered in psychology. We can also see how progress is being make—albeit slowly—in addressing ethnic minority issues. Now I would like to offer some suggestions for enhancing ethnic diversity. The suggestions are primarily based on my experiences in the field. They will cover teaching, research, and practice. Finally, I would like to discuss general value conflicts that occur. In my opinion, much of the controversies in ethnic minority group issues occur because of these conflicts, and it is critical to understand the nature of the conflicts if we are to address these issues.

Teaching

Given the fact that we live in a multiethnic society, the teaching of diversity and ethnicity is essential. Many universities, such as Stanford, now require as part of the undergraduate curriculum a course on ethnicity and different cultural groups. The teaching of cultural diversity must also be a part of the education and training of psychologists. But how can this be accomplished?

One of the most important publications on the teaching of psychology with respect to sociocultural and gender issues was edited by Bronstein and Quina (1988). This publication deals with the means by which ethnic and gender issues can be integrated into psychology courses or be taught as separate courses (e.g., a course on ethnic minority mental health). Contributors to the publication illustrate how sociocultural and gender contents can be included in introductory, abnormal, developmental, social, personality, experimental, psychobiology, history, and health psychology courses, at the undergraduate as well as the graduate level. Implicit in this edited volume is the need for integrating diversity content into existing courses as well as for separate courses on ethnicity.

As to having separate courses on ethnicity or culture, there are advantages and disadvantages. Such courses would enable intensive coverage of ethnic issues and provide a gestalt for students. Not many changes in the curriculum would be necessary, and faculty would tend to have little objection to having an instructor for the course. However, unless the courses are a required part of the curriculum, few students (usually those who are already knowledgeable or interested) may take them, perhaps isolating the courses from the rest of the curriculum. Furthermore, difficulties may be found in finding an adequate instructor; or if ethnic instructors are found, they may be stereotyped as having expertise only on ethnic minority issues.

Perhaps the most difficult task is the integration of sociocultural content into existing psychology courses. Such integration would allow students to see the relevance of ethnicity and culture in various areas of psychology and all students would be exposed to the material. Considerable resistance may be present to the incorporation of ethnic issues in all courses. First, faculty may oppose such efforts. Some may perceive the integration as a violation of their academic freedom and right to teach courses in the manner that they see fit. Other faculty may feel unqualified to address ethnic minority concerns. Second, a few students may also oppose coverage of sociocultural issues in courses. At some graduate programs which have tried to institute greater curriculum emphasis on ethnic minority groups, students have protested the effort, arguing that the emphasis might draw them away from the "usual" contents in their courses and that students should not be required to learn sociocultural issues. Third, some faculty believe that not enough is known about ethnic issues and these issues may not be relevant for certain courses in areas such as psychobiology and physiological psychology. Fourth, courses dealing with ethnic minority issues can create tension because the issue are often controversial, and instructors need to be skilled in dealing with this tension.

To overcome some of these problems, several things can be done. The most important is to consider ethnic and cultural issues important and essential to psychology. Funding agencies, the American Psychological Association (APA) as well as the APA Accreditation Program, government agencies, mental health facilities, and universities can have a major effect in facilitating matters by emphasizing the need for education and training on ethnic minority affairs. Furthermore, incentives can be provided to faculty for offering ethnic content in their courses. For example, it would be helpful to allow faculty interested in teaching ethnicity release time to develop a curriculum or course resources. At UCLA a project sponsored by the Ford Foundation allowed faculty the opportunity to take a seminar on the teaching of topics relating to gender, ethnicity, and ethnic women in various psychology courses. The course focused on teaching strategies, curriculum development, and issues arising from the incorporation of the course materials. Faculty were given release time or summer salary supplements. Other incentives such as funds to attract guest speakers or to develop a videotape library for use in courses may also be valuable. The hiring of faculty who have expertise in ethnicity should be of high priority. The main point is that it is possible to find ways of overcoming resistance to the teaching of ethnicity and culture, and that creative and innovative strategies should be found.

Research

Earlier, I mentioned the growing interest in conducting research that examines intragroup differences and resources and strengths among ethnic minority communities. I would now like to offer some recommendations for research strategies that can help to minimize cultural bias. Three approaches can be used in research designs: (a) point, (b) linear, and (c) parallel (Zane & Sue, 1986). Point research refers to isolated group comparisons on one construct or set of constructs derived from one culture. The empirical focus is from one reference point that logically can be derived from only one culture. We have seen how ethnic minorities have been compared to Whites in areas such as self-concept and ethnic identity, psychopathology, and personality. When found, cultural differences can be considered to indicate that ethnic individuals actually differ from Whites on the given dimension.

Researchers have exercised caution in accepting the simple notion that observed differences reflect actual differences according to an assumed construct. For example, Gynther (1972) found that Blacks consistently scored higher than Whites on several pathological scales of the MMPI. However, he notes that these results do not necessarily reflect a greater degree of maladjustment on the part of Blacks, because conceptual equivalence of many MMPI items across cultures does not exist (although the recently revised MMPI-2 version has not yet been examined for cross-cultural appropriateness, it is purportedly more culturally responsive). Although valuable in generating a large array of rival hypotheses, the information yield of such research is limited. This is because, given the monocultural approach using monocultural measures, alternative explanations based on cultural differences in values and behaviors are always post hoc.

In response to these problems, a linear research model has developed. Linear research involves a sequence of studies aimed at systematically testing the set of hypotheses predicted by the theory underlying the single construct of interest. Like point research, this construct is usually developed from a single perspective. However, rather than one isolated study, there are two or more empirical points of reference on which to compare cultural groups. If the pattern of cultural differences (or similarities) manifests according to the construct's theory, the construct is considered to be a universal that allows for meaningful cultural comparisons.

As an illustration, let us examine studies conducted by Dohrenwend and Dohrenwend (1969), who were interested in determining if certain ethnic groups differed in psychopathology. After administering the Midtown 22-item symptom questionnaire, they did find ethnic differences: Puerto Ricans scored higher in psychological disturbance than did Jewish, Irish, or Black respondents in New York City. But how did they know if the Puerto Ricans were actually more disturbed or if the findings were simply an artifact of the measure? To test whether the higher score among Puerto Ricans indicated higher actual rates of disorders, patients matched in types of psychiatric disorders from each ethnic group were administered the same questionnaires. Because patients were matched on type and presumable severity of disorders, one would expect no differences in symptom scores. However, Puerto Ricans again scored higher. Dohrenwend and Dohrenwend concluded that the higher scores for Puerto Ricans probably reflects a response set or a cultural means of expressing distress on the questionnaire rather than actual rates of disturbance.

Although an improvement on point research, linear approaches have a major drawback. Even if multiple comparisons demonstrate that a construct developed from one cultural perspective is applicable in another culture, the question still remains as to whether a construct developed from an alternative perspective can better explain the phenomena under study. In other words, linear studies do not actually balance ethnic perspectives in research. They simply test the adequacy of one perspective in the absence of the other. Almost all linear research has focused on the cross-cultural applicability of constructs derived from our Western viewpoint. Aside from perpetuating the dominance of the Western viewpoint, such cultural contrasts often mask important individual differences within a cultural group.

To represent accurately ethnic minority perspectives, research must develop separate but interrelated ways of conceptualizing the behavioral phenomena of interest, one based on a Western conceptualization, the other reflecting an ethnic minority interpretation. Essentially, parallel designs consist of two linear approaches, each based on an alternative cultural viewpoint. In parallel research, it is incumbent upon the researcher to develop a priori two sets of descriptive and explanatory variables. Too often misinterpretations of ethnic minority behavior occur due to a lack of a proper conceptual framework. We simply have failed to develop innovative conceptual "tools" that one can more appropriately apply to ethnic minority groups. By requiring the concurrent examination of different cultural explanations, the parallel approach fosters divergent thinking—the type of reasoning needed to develop solutions to address adequately the paradoxes involved in ethnic minority problems.

The development of competing constructs based on differing cultural vantage points allows one to determine the overlapping and non-overlapping effects of different cultures. In previous research, when cultural differences did appear, it frequently was not clear if such differences actually existed or if the construct of interest was differentially applied to the two cultural groups. In the parallel approach, the salience of a construct is empirically tested by comparing it with another equally plausible explanatory concept developed from the ethnic group's host culture. Thus, we should greatly expand the employment of parallel research studies.

Assessment

Skepticism has been voiced over assessment because of possible biases in the nosological systems; in the use of cognitive, personality, and psychopathology measures; and in making clinical inferences. Despite the skepticism, psychologists are frequently required to make evaluations in schools, mental health agencies, and courtrooms. What procedures can be used in such circumstances? Although issues of reliability and validity are involved, perhaps it is wise to distinguish two aspects. The first deals with assessment procedures in general. The second includes special procedures that may be necessary with ethnic groups.

In any assessment task, the first step is to specify what characteristic one is interested in measuring—the referral question. The second step is to select the most appropriate inventory or test. Although factors such as the ease of administration, cost, and degree of expertise required are often considered, reliability and validity of the measure for the characteristic of interest are the most important factors. Test manuals should include information on reliability and validity as well as norms and samples upon which the norms are based. Of course, many assessment tools have not been adequately developed for different ethnic minority populations. With ethnic minority populations, the following guidelines are important to consider:

1. See if the test or assessment instrument has been standardized and normed on the particular ethnic minority group of the client.

2. If the test has not been standardized and normed on the group, use caution in interpreting the results.

3. Use multiple measures or multimethod procedures to see if tests provide convergent results.

4. Try to understand the cultural background of the client in order to place test results in a proper context.

5. Enlist the aid of consultants who are familiar with the client's background and culture.

6. Use tests that can be linguistically understood by clients.

7. If one is unsure of the validity of tests for a particular ethnic client, use the findings as hypotheses for further testing rather than as conclusive evidence.

Since many assessment tools have not been used extensively with ethnic minority populations, these guidelines are important to follow.

Treatment

How can clinicians engage in more effective forms of treatment with ethnic minority clients? Traditionally, researchers and practitioners have advocated two strategies—one concerning the necessity for therapists to know the culture and background of clients and the other concerning the use of specific techniques to use with ethnic minority clients. Both strategies have not been very effective. While few individuals would quarrel with the importance of cultural knowledge, such knowledge has not directly led to an increased understanding of how to conduct psychotherapy. Several other questions can be raised. How much cultural knowledge is necessary? Isn't it impossible to fully know the cultures of all diverse groups in the United States? If one studies the cultural background of a client, isn't there the danger of stereotyping the client? Will knowing the culture of a client lead to insight into how to conduct psychotherapy? That is, given knowledge of client's culture, what should therapists do? Inability to address these questions fully led some investigators to question whether cultural knowledge was a sufficient condition for conducting effective psychotherapy.

In response to the need for more concrete suggestions on how to conduct therapy, some clinicians attempted to devise what was considered culturally consistent forms of intervention. For example, Asian Americans tend to prefer psychotherapists who provide structure, guidance, and direction rather than nondirectedness in interactions (Kim, 1985). Clinicians were advised to be directive with Asian Americans. Similar suggestions were made for other minority group clients. For Latinos, some clinicians felt that therapists should focus on reframing problems as medical ones in order to reduce client resistance; for Blacks, action-oriented and externally focused rather than intrapsychic approaches were recommended (see Sue & Zane, 1987). However, these recommendations also raised questions. Is it possible for therapists to change their therapeutic orientations in working with ethnic clients? For instance, a psychoanalytic therapist might find it very difficult to become more action-oriented when working with a Black client. By using a specific approach—one presumably based on the culture of the client—how does one deal with intragroup variability, as ethnic minority clients may show a great deal of individual differences? Is there a single, culturally consistent form of treatment for each ethnic group? Given the inability to address these questions fully, I believe we should investigate therapeutic processes rather than simply argue for cultural knowledge or culturally specific forms of treatment. The two processes that appear to be critical, at least in the initial treatment sessions, are credibility and gift giving (i.e., seeing that the client receives a benefit early in the treatment process).

Credibility. At least two factors are important in enhancing credibility: ascribed status and achieved status. Ascribed status is one's position or role assigned by others or by cultural norm. In some cultures, the young are subordinate to elders, women defer to men, and those who are naive abide by those in authority. Credibility can also be achieved. Achieved credibility refers more directly to the skills and actions of the therapist in treatment. The therapist does something that is perceived by the client as being competent or helpful. Ascribed and achieved credibility undoubtedly are related, but they tend to have distinct and different implications for ethnic clients in terms of the psychotherapeutic process. The lack of ascribed credibility may be the primary reason for underutilization and avoidance of treatment, whereas decrements in achieved credibility may better explain premature termination and problems related to poor rapport.

Giving. In one way or another, clients often wonder how talking about problems to psychotherapists can result in the alleviation of emotional and behavioral distress. Almost immediately, clients need to feel a direct benefit from treatment. I have called this benefit a "gift" (Sue & Zane, 1987). The gift essentially constitutes this gesture of caring on the part of the therapist. The therapist cannot simply raise the client's expectations about outcomes. Direct benefits must be given, almost immediately. These are needed because of the need to demonstrate the achieved credibility of the therapist (and of therapy) and because of skepticism over Western forms of treatment on the part of many ethnic minority group clients. Providing a gift is difficult, particularly in the initial session, because the therapist may be interested in gathering information for assessment purposes.

What kinds of gifts can be given in therapy? Depending upon the client and situation, the therapist can strive to provide certain benefits. For example, clients who are depressed or anxious will perceive gains in therapy if there is an alleviation or reduction of these negative emotional states. For clients in a state of crisis and confusion, the therapist frequently helps clients to develop cognitive clarity or a means of understanding the chaotic experiences these clients encounter. Such a technique is often used in crisis intervention. Also, *normalization,* a process by which clients come to realize that their thoughts, feelings, or experiences are common with others, may be a gift to those who mistakenly believe that others do not have the same problems. Gift giving does not imply short-term treatment or even the necessity of finding quick solutions. However, it does imply the need for attaining some type of meaningful gain early in therapy. The process of giving, of course, can be conceptualized as a special case of building rapport or establishing a therapeutic relationship. The main point is that therapists need to focus on gift giving and attempt to offer benefits from treatment as soon as possible. Therapists should think of the gifts that can be offered, even in the first session.

Value Conflicts

In the search for ways to improve research, theory, and practice for ethnic minority groups, I have presented some major problems faced by psychologists and have offered some suggestions for addressing the problems. The problems have been discussed on a concrete level, as if the most important tasks are to gain knowledge of ethnic minority groups and use more appropriate research and intervention strategies. But there is a more fundamental task that involves a thorough understanding of the value conflicts that Americans face within themselves and with other Americans. I believe that these value conflicts are at the core of the problems that we face in responding to ethnic minorities. Without properly identifying the assumptions and effects of the conflicting views, it is very difficult to attempt to resolve ethnic minority issues. Let me indicate the nature of the conflicts, which have been the subject of several of my previous papers (Sue, 1983; Sue & Padilla, 1986; Zane & Sue, 1986).

We are all aware of several significant social issues facing Americans. For example, gun control versus the right to bear arms, and prochoice versus prolife are major conflicts. On some social conflicts, there are not only opposing sides, but also individuals endorsing both elements of the conflict. This is apparent in the issue of freedom of speech. Freedom of expression and speech is a strong principle advocated by many Americans. Yet, a large segment of the population also values protection from exposure to unwanted or allegedly harmful materials. Should one, for instance, have the right under the principle of freedom of speech to expose others to pornographic materials or to express racial slurs? Although it is possible to find individuals on the opposite extremes of the conflict, individuals can also be found who endorse both conflicting principles in the abstract. The contradiction is most apparent when these two equally valid or morally justifiable positions are applied in a concrete situation.

I believe that many ethnic minority issues in teaching, research, and practice reflect conflicts in which there are value clashes. Moreover, in trying to resolve issues, one side has been dominant, often to the detriment of ethnic minority groups. Perhaps I can best illustrate this point by noting some value conflicts and the concomitant problems that arise.

I will address five value conflicts that often occur in ethnic group relations. Examples of each side of the conflict and the nature of the conflict are based on the ideas expressed by a paper by Sue and Padilla (1986). Possible means to approach the paradox of values are also examined. It should be noted that the value conflicts are presented as dichotomies for heuristic purposes. In actuality, individuals may adhere to each value to differing degrees along a continuum.

Conflict 1: Etic Versus Emic

John is an 11-year-old Japanese student who was referred by his teacher to the school psychologist. John was excessively quiet and shy in school. Although his grades were slightly above average, the teacher noted that John was extremely anxious when asked to speak in front of the class. The psychologist administered some psychological tests to John and concluded that John was emotionally disturbed, excessively timid, and overanxious. When informed of the test results, John's parents were shocked. They perceived him as being quiet and well-behaved, but able to relate to them and his close friends in an appropriate manner. The parents then took John to a psychotherapist. After reviewing the psychological test results and seeing John for several sessions, the psychotherapist indicated that John was not emotionally disturbed. He felt that the test results were not valid indicators of John's emotional state because the tests had not been standardized on Japanese Americans. John was shy but not emotionally disturbed.

The case illustrates a major controversy in ethnic issues that involves the concepts of emics and etics. The emic approach is culture-specific. It examines the behaviors and values in one specific culture and interprets behaviors from within the cultural system. The etic approach applies criteria or standards that are absolute or universal (Brislin et al., 1973). It assumes that different cultures can be compared on these standards. In John's case, those who favor emics would argue that John's apparent shyness cannot be evaluated by tests that have not been developed or at least standardized on Japanese Americans. Etic proponents would adopt a more universal interpretation arguing that regardless of culture, if a person scores high on a psychological measure, they are disturbed.

Each perspective has some validity. Some characteristics are evident in all groups—for instance, the development of language and communication, ability to utilize abstract concepts, or motives to survive. On the other hand, other characteristics are specific to a cultural group such as particular patterns of social interaction, attitudes, and values. The problem occurs when one perspective dominates the other. An extreme emic perspective would not allow cross-cultural generalizations or cultural comparisons to be made. A strong etic orientation fails to appreciate the legitimacy of cultural relativity and diversity. As mentioned in the next conflict to be discussed, the problem is that society's standards (which are largely emic and Anglo-oriented) are presumed to be etics or universals. Ethnic minority groups are then inappropriately judged according to these assumed etics. Deviations from these norms are considered to be indicative of personal problems or maladjustment.

In ethnic minority issues, we need to recognize that some standards or criteria assumed to be universal (etics) are actually specific (emics) to mainstream American society. Furthermore, in the conflict between emic and etic positions, one must specify the exact standard, criterion, or issue being discussed. If we assume that each position has validity on some particular issues (e.g., human motivation, test performance) by specifying the issue, we may be able to achieve greater consensus. In other words, rather than saying, "Human beings are alike" or "You can't compare people from different cultures," one should indicate in what precise ways people are the same or are culturally different.

Conflict 2: Assimilation Versus Pluralism

During a faculty meeting at university, one faculty member mentioned that he was glad the department was interested in teaching students about ethnic and cultural issues. He felt that by becoming aware of the cultures and rituals of different groups, students could better understand their own heritage and those of other groups. Another faculty member, however, disagreed. While she felt that students should have knowledge of different cultures, she thought that the department's scarce resources should not be devoted to ethnic courses. She stated that: "Focusing too much on the culture and heritage of different students only causes friction and segregation between groups. We all live in this society and must learn the same skills in order to succeed."

Each faculty member in advocating a position illustrates a fundamental conflict of values: assimilation versus pluralism. Assimilation involves the absorption of ethnic minority groups into the dominant group and, quite often, the loss of the values and behavioral patterns of their ethnic cultures. Those who advocate for assimilation usually want ethnic groups to become "Americanized." On the other hand, pluralism refers to the coexistence of distinct cultural groups in society. Those who encourage pluralism believe that cultural differences should be maintained and appreciated and that different groups with various cultural orientations can coexist alongside each other. In the past, assimilation or Anglo-conformity of ethnic groups was expected because Anglo-Saxon culture was deemed superior or desirable (Gordon, 1978). Even though many persons no longer believe that Anglo-Saxon culture is intrinsically superior to other cultures, the assimilation push is resurfacing. Its advocates now use practical or functional arguments rather than references to intrinsic superiority. For instance, they may assert that educational programs for immigrant children should stress learning of English as rapidly as possible, rather than bilingual education, because any language other than English is not very functional and may, in fact, be a handicap in classroom learning. The controversy over achievement and intelligence testing is also one involving assimilation versus pluralism. Although many investigators no longer take the view that such tests are totally free from cultural biases, they may still advocate their use since these tests can moderately predict academic performance in school. Since school performance is highly valued, testing is considered useful and an essential part of education. Those who favor pluralism feel that under the notion of educational pragmatism, ethnic cultural patterns are being eliminated or being compared to a single standard. Again, there is a clash of fundamental values. How can one argue against the acquisition of functional skills, the development of good predictors, and some degree of Americanization? Similarly, how can one doubt that encouragement of pluralism, diversity, and respect for different cultures is also a valid principle? The dominance of the assimilation perspective, to the detriment of diversity, is the problem.

In the drive for assimilation, the fact is overlooked that consensus may be lacking on what constitutes functional skills or that time and circumstances may alter what skills are considered useful. For instance, with an increasing immigrant population, the abilities to speak Chinese and Spanish and to work with diverse groups are important assets. The point is that the learning of functional skills required for participation in society at large does not necessarily entail a diminution of ethnic cultural patterns. Thus, although the positions of assimilation and pluralism clash (because the strengthening of one weakens the other), the assumption underlying assimilation—that effective functioning can occur only if one assimilates—is not valid. Therefore, the challenge before us is to continually define what is meant by "functional" and to find ways to maintain pluralism.

Conflict 3: Equal Opportunity Versus Equality of Outcomes

In discussing his stance on ethnic issues, a Vice Chancellor from a large university recently said, "I believe in equality and do not discriminate against any group. In our hiring of teachers, we are color- and ethnic-blind. We depend upon applicants' qualifications." Another administrator at a small college said, "We are very active in affirmative action efforts to recruit students and faculty from different ethnic groups. We will not be satisfied until the ethnic composition of the college reflects that in our community."

The statements by the two administrators illustrate a conflict of values over the appropriate action to take in addressing ethnic minority group concerns. The first position focuses on establishing a process that ensures that all members of society have the same opportunity. Irrespective of ethnicity, individuals should be treated equally with respect to education, employment, housing, and so on. In contrast, the college administrator is attempting to achieve equality of outcomes (e.g., seeing that there is proportionate representation of ethnic minority groups). Through affirmative action procedures, he is attempting to directly influence outcomes. Such procedures may include efforts to increase the pool of ethnic applicants, selection procedures that take into account ethnicity, and different criteria for selecting different groups.

Proponents of equal opportunity want to eliminate discrimination. The goal is to abolish racial or ethnic bias, intentional patterns of ethnic group segregation, and discriminatory admissions or selection procedures so that an ethnic- or color-blind system is operating. However, even if the goal is accomplished, there is no reason to believe that educational outcomes will be equal for all groups. Although equal outcomes may not be attainable because of between-group differences in motivation, interests, and backgrounds, there are other reasons. Because of the long history of ethnic relations in the United States and the cultural interaction patterns that have emerged (as previously described), some ethnic groups will continue to be a step behind.

Realizing these problems, those favoring equality of outcomes have argued for affirmative action and special programs (e.g., compensatory education, bilingual education, educational reforms, multicultural education) in order to narrow the gap between ethnic minority groups and Whites. In their view, color-blind procedures that are applied to groups already showing disparate educational performances can only serve to maintain differential achievements. The dilemma between the two conflicting positions is quite apparent. Advocates of equal educational opportunities and nondiscrimination run the risk of perpetuating unequal outcomes; those who argue for equal outcomes (e.g., seeing that minority groups are as likely to graduate, enroll, or otherwise benefit from education) may have to discriminate by treating some groups differently because of social, cultural, and historical factors. By emphasizing one principle, the other principle may have to be sacrificed.

Unfortunately, the controversy has often been translated into one involving discrimination: "If it is unfair to discriminate against ethnic minority groups, should we now discriminate in reverse in order to favor ethnic minority groups (via affirmative action, ethnic quotas, and special programs)?" The controversy is unfortunate in the sense that in focusing on discrimination one cannot see the forest for the trees. The more important and broader question is, "What kind of society do we want?" If one values a society in which a primary goal is to maximize the potential of every individual irrespective of color, ethnic group, or sex, then extraordinary measures must be taken. This means that immediate and long-term attempts must be made to correct differential achievement patterns. Only after opportunities become truly equal can a color- or ethnic-blind system have any meaning.

Conflict 4: Modal Personality Versus Individual Differences

One of our colleagues (Mizokawa & Morishima, 1979) conveyed the following story to us:

> His daughter's fourth-grade teacher had just returned from a human relations workshop where she had been exposed to the necessity of incorporating "ethnicity" into her instructional planning. Since she had a Japanese American student in her class, she asked the child to be prepared to demonstrate to the class how the child danced at home. When the child danced in typical American fashion on the following Monday, the teacher interrupted and said, "No! No! I asked you to show the class the kinds of dances you danced at home." When the child indicated that she had done just that, the teacher said, "I wanted you to show the class how you people danced at the Bon Odori" (a Japanese festival celebrated in some Japanese American communities at which people perform Japanese folk dances). (p. 9)

In this example, the teacher had incorrectly assumed that the Japanese American child knew how to perform a Japanese folk dance, simply because the child was Japanese American. However, the student was quite assimilated and unfamiliar with Japanese dances.

The conflict involved in the modal personality versus individual differences refers to one's values regarding between- and within-group differences. The teacher in this case sought to appreciate ethnic differences (e.g., "Japanese dance differently from Americans"). Since the student was Japanese American, the teacher believed that the student must know how to perform the ethnic dance. The between-group approach largely ignores individual differences. It typically relies upon the concept of modal personality in describing cultural patterns (Inkeles & Levinson, 1969). As mentioned earlier, cultures may vary in the extent to which their members exhibit certain traits. By comparing various groups, one can calculate the average (or modal) characteristics in each group and then determine how different the groups are. Carried to an extreme, modal personality has an apparent stereotypic quality to it. For instance, the observation that the typical American is more individualistic than the typical Japanese is often translated into the belief that Americans are individualistic and Japanese are not.

The emphasis on individual differences is concerned with group variations. Members of an ethnic population are quite heterogeneous. Some are acculturated, speak no ethnic language, are individualistic in orientation, live in ethnically mixed neighborhoods, and are quite different from nonacculturated members of their group who maintain a more traditional orientation. Proponents of individual differences argue that the danger in formulating modal or average personalities for each ethnic group is that stereotypes emerge. In the case of the Japanese American student described previously, individual differences advocates state that one cannot assume that she is traditionally Japanese in behavior and values simply by virtue of her ethnicity. Although correct in asserting ethnic group heterogeneity, the individual differences notion tends to deny commonalities due to culture, if carried to the extreme. It is focused upon individuals and their uniqueness.

The strengthening of one principle (modal personality or individual differences) has the effect of weakening the other. What must be realized, however, is that each may be appropriate in a given context, for a given purpose. Discussions of cultures imply that generalizations and abstractions will be made. Knowledge of cultures provides a background for understanding different groups. However, given the context, it is then appropriate to examine the heterogeneity within groups. For example, American Indians come from many different tribes with distinct languages, values, and rituals of their own. Chinese and Mexican Americans are composed of immigrants as well as individuals who may be sixth- or seventh-generation Americans. We must be able to identify critical differences between *and* within ethnic minority groups.

Conflict 5: Presence Versus Absence of Prejudice and Discrimination

During a workshop on multicultural education, one instructor said, "When it comes down to it, ethnic minorities are still oppressed by direct and indirect forms of discrimination and stereotypes. I can see this in the attitudes of some teachers and administrators, especially when I advocate for changes on behalf of minority groups." Adopting a different point of view, another instructor said, "I disagree. The school I work for does not discriminate. I think a lot of minorities see discrimination when it doesn't exist. Americans have made great strides in ethnic and race relations—if you visit other countries, you'll see what discrimination is really like."

The final issue is that of the current existence of prejudice and discrimination—that is, racism. According to a recent Gallup Poll, Americans generally believe that the United States is ethnically tolerant and that overt racism is largely unacceptable ("Poll Finds," 1990). Yet, many ethnic minority groups continue to see prejudice and discrimination.

One perspective praises society for changes and for the absence of racism; the other claims that despite changes, society is still implicated in racial and ethnic problems. The disturbing fact is that despite the popular belief, the notion that prejudice and discrimination have all but disappeared has not received much support. Crosby, Bromley, and Saxe (1980) found that individuals often discriminate against Blacks in subtle ways that are difficult to observe in everyday life. Prejudice and discrimination are often maintained by depictions in the media, interpersonal interactions, daily conversations, children's books, and so on, about the crimes, strangeness, poverty, mistakes, and deterioration attributed to "foreigners" or people who are ethnic minority group members (van Dijk, 1987). Furthermore, others have argued that prejudice and racism are now expressed in a more indirect fashion (McConahay, Hardee, & Batts, 1981; Sears & Allen, 1984). The main point is that there are opposing views over ethnic relations and that many ethnic minority issues involve value clashes. On one side are those who value and praise the great strides made in recent years with respect to civil rights and who point to affirmative action programs as proof of these advances in civil rights. On the other side are individuals who are critical of American institutions such as education who feel that prejudice and discrimination persist in a variety of forms. The inability to resolve the differences in perspectives has led to debates over the necessity of having civil rights legislation and the form such legislation should take. Progress has been made in ethnic and race relations; however, prejudice and discrimination still exist and equality has not been achieved. We must confront the fact that positive changes have occurred and that there is still much that needs to be accomplished.

Toward Solutions for the Value Conflicts

From the discussion of value conflicts, it is clear that attempts must be made to find solutions to these value conflicts. The conflicts need resolution for several reasons. First, the values or principles involved have some degree of validity. Thus, individuals who argue for one side may feel quite self-righteous about their position. Another problem is that because of the kernels of truth associated with each value or principle, individuals may experience indecision or confusion over the resolution of the conflicts within themselves. The clash of values, therefore, can be seen between individuals who hold different values or within persons who cannot come to terms with the conflicts. Second, dominance of one side of the conflict weakens the other. The possibility exists that the dominant position may blind individuals to the validity of the other position. Third, it is my belief that the dominant position, more often than not, has reflected the majority group stance at the expense of ethnic minority groups.

In presenting the conflicts, I have alluded to ways of addressing the clashes of values. It should also be clear that solutions must maintain a dynamic balance between the conflicting positions because each has some validity. At this point, I want to suggest certain processes that may be helpful in moving toward the resolution of conflicts. The processes involve divergent thinking, mediation, alternation, coexistence, and level of abstraction.

Divergent thinking. Divergence refers to the act of departing from a set course or norm. In divergent thinking, conflicts are addressed by conceptualizing or redefining issues in innovative ways that may depart from norms or convention. For example, in the assimilation–pluralism conflict, one can diverge from the typical manner in which the conflict is approached. Rather than to deal with the assumption that assimilation is necessary in order to develop functional skills, one could focus on the ever-changing definition of what skills are considered functional or the possibility that development of functional skills does not preclude the existence of pluralism. For example, the classroom instructor can employ multicultural examples when giving lessons in social studies. This can be done at the same time that the instructor discusses emic and etic approaches to studying the United States as well as other cultures.

Mediation. At times, mediation or compromises may be necessary. In the case of modal personality versus individual differences approaches, one may want to discuss cultural characteristics of groups at an abstract and general level and then spend some time indicating the importance of variation within a culture. Conversely, one can primarily focus upon differences within a cultural group and acknowledge that different groups have distinct core features.

Alternation. One may alternate by emphasizing one element of the conflict at one particular time or in one context and then by emphasizing the other element at another time or in another context. As noted earlier, we may want to see to it that outcomes for various groups are equal before engaging in equal-opportunity or color-blind procedures. In this case, we apply one strategy and then change strategies over time. In some circumstances or contexts, one side of the conflict may be more appropriate than another. Discrimination may be present in some situations but absent in other situations.

It should be clear that these various solutions are not mutually exclusive of each other. Alternation requires a certain degree of flexibility and divergent thinking. The important thing to recognize in value alternation is that both values may be correct and that one can take a position that supports both values for different purposes in the same situation. For instance, equal opportunity without reverse discrimination, is important, but so is equality of outcome without lessening of standards.

Coexistence. If each side of a paradox has some validity, it is important to realize that both sides must exist. Attempts to abolish the other side, if successful, result in an unbalanced view of reality. For instance, the elimination of an emic approach would result in the dominant view that all human beings are alike and can be judged according to universal standards. Such an extreme view is absurd. The coexistence of conflicting but valid, positions is necessary in order to reflect reality and to create the tension necessary to find solutions to ethnic issues.

Level of abstraction. In addressing value conflicts, it may be helpful at times to move to a higher level of questioning about values. For example, proponents of equal opportunity value color-blind procedures, whereas those favoring equal outcomes value results (outcomes) rather than procedures. We noted earlier that the important question may be, "What kind of society do we want?" The answer to this question, which is asked at a higher level of abstraction, may enable both sides of the conflict to find unifying aspects or common goals.

I have tried to illustrate some of the tactics that might be used in approaching the value conflicts generated by ethnic minority issues. Obviously, the conflicts may be amenable to several different tactics. The main point is that we must continually find means of balancing elements in the conflicts and enhancing the performance of ethnic minority groups.

Issues of ethnic diversity must be addressed in the field of psychology. Central to these issues are the concepts of culture, ethnicity, and minority group status. By understanding these concepts, as well as the value conflicts that are experienced, we can begin to devise more adequate research and theoretical paradigms and intervention tactics that are consistent with the goal of psychology, namely, to promote human welfare.

References

Abe, J. S., & Zane, N. W. S. (1990). Psychological maladjustment among Asian and Caucasian American college students. Controlling for confounds. *Journal of Counseling Psychology, 37*, 437–444.

Acosta, F. X. (1984). Psychotherapy with Mexican Americans: Clinical and empirical gains. In J. L. Martinez & R. H. Mendoza (Eds.), *Chicano psychology* (2nd ed.; pp. 163–189). New York: Academic Press.

Albert, R. D. (1988). The place of culture in modern psychology. In P. Bronstein & K. Quina (Eds.), *Teaching a psychology of people* (pp. 12–20). Washington, DC: American Psychological Association.

Allport, G. W. (1954). *The nature of prejudice.* Reading, MA: Addison-Wesley.

American Psychological Association, Division 45. (1990, June). *Focus.* Washington, DC: Author.

Andersen, P. (1991). 7.3 million Asian and Pacific Islanders in U.S. *Asian Week, 12*, 1–17.

Atkinson, D. R., Morten, G., & Sue, D. W. (1979). *Counseling American minorities: A cross-cultural perspective.* Dubuque, IA: Brown.

Attneave, C. L. (1985). Practical counseling with American Indian and Alaska Native clients. In P. Pedersen (Ed.), *Handbook of cross-cultural counseling and therapy* (pp. 135–140). Westport, CT: Greenwood.

Baldwin, J. (1957). *Notes of a native son*. Boston: Beacon.

Banks, J. A. (1987). *Teaching strategies for ethnic studies*. Boston: Allyn and Bacon.

Banks, W. C. (1984). Toward a cultural–social learning analysis of self-concept in Blacks. In S. Sue & T. Moore (Eds.), *The pluralistic society: A community mental health perspective* (pp. 167–178). New York: Human Sciences Press.

Berry, J. W., Trimble, J. E., & Olmedo, E. L. (1986). Assessment of acculturation. In W. J. Lonner & J. W. Berry (Eds.), *Field methods in cross-cultural research* (pp. 291–324). Beverly Hills, CA: Sage.

Brislin, R. W., Lonner, W. J., & Thorndike, R. M. (1973). *Cross-cultural research methods*. New York: John Wiley & Sons.

Bronstein, P., & Quina, K. (Eds.) (1988). *Teaching a psychology of people*. Washington, DC: American Psychological Association.

Burnam, M. A., Hough, R. L., Escobar, J. I., Karno, M., Timbers, D. M., Telles, C. A., & Locke, B. Z. (1987). Six-month prevalence of specific psychiatric disorders among Mexican Americans and non-Hispanic Whites in Los Angeles. *Archives of General Psychiatry, 44*, 687–694.

California State Department of Education. (1986). *Beyond language: Social and cultural factors in schooling language minority students*. Los Angeles: Evaluation, Dissemination and Assessment Center.

Casas, J. M. (1985). The status of racial- and ethnic-minority counseling: A training perspective. In P. Pedersen (Ed.), *Handbook of cross-cultural counseling and therapy* (pp. 267–274). Westport, CT: Greenwood.

Clark, K. B. (1972). Foreword. In A. Thomas & S. Sillen (Eds.), *Racism and psychiatry*. New York: Brunner/Mazel.

Clark, K., & Clark, M. (1947). Racial identification and preference in Negro children. In T. M. Newcombe & E. C. Hartley (Eds.), *Readings in social psychology*. New York: Holt.

Comas-Diaz, L. (1988). Cross-cultural mental health treatment. In L. Comas-Diaz & E. E. Griffith (Eds.), *Clinical guidelines in cross-cultural mental health* (pp. 335–362). New York: John Wiley & Sons.

Comas-Diaz, L., & Griffith, E. E. (Eds.). (1988). *Clinical guidelines in cross-cultural mental health*. New York: John Wiley & Sons.

Crosby, G., Bromley, S., & Saxe, L. (1980). Recent unobtrusive studies of Black and White discrimination and prejudice: A literature review. *Psychological Bulletin, 87*, 546–563.

Cross, W. E. (1978). The Cross and Thomas models of psychological nigrescence. *Journal of Black Psychology, 5*, 13–19.

Dohrenwend, B. P., & Dohrenwend, B. S. (1969). *Social status and psychological disorder*. New York: John Wiley & Sons.

Dudley, G. R., & Rawlins, M. R. (1985). Psychotherapy with ethnic minorities. *Psychotherapy, 22*, 308–478.

Gibbs, J. T., & Huang, L. N. (1989). A conceptual framework for assessing and treating minority youth. In J. T. Gibbs & L. N. Huang (Eds.), *Children of color: Psychological interventions with minority youth* (pp. 1–30). San Francisco: Jossey-Bass.

Gordon, M. M. (1978). *Human nature, class, and ethnicity*. New York: Oxford University Press.

Gynther, M. D. (1972). White norms and black MMPIs: A prescription for discrimination? *Psychological Bulletin, 78*, 386–402.

Hodgkinson, H. L. (1983). Guess who's coming to college. *Academe, 69*, 13–20.

Hsu, F. L. K. (1985). The self in cross-cultural perspective. In A. J. Marsella, G. DeVos, & F. L. K. Hsu (Eds.), *Culture and self: Asian and western perspectives* (pp. 24–55). New York: Tavistock Publications.

Inkeles, A., & Levinson, S. J. (1969). National character: The study of modal personality and sociocultural systems. In G. Lindzey & E. Aronson (Eds.) *The handbook of social psychology*. Reading MA: Addison-Wesley.

Jackson, J. S., Neighbors, H. W., & Gurin, G. (1986). Findings from a national survey of Black mental health: Implications for practice and training. In M. R. Miranda & H. H. L. Kitano (Eds.), *Mental health research and practice in minority communities: Development of culturally sensitive training programs* (pp. 91–116). Washington, DC: U.S. Government Printing Office.

Jenkins, A. H. (1985). Attending to self-activity in the Afro-American client. *Psychotherapy, 22*, 335–341.

Jones, A., & Seagull, A. A. (1977). Dimensions of the relationship between the Black client and the White therapist: A theoretical overview. *American Psychologist, 32*, 850–855.

Jones, E. E., & Korchin, S. J. (1982). *Minority mental health*. New York: Praeger.

Jones, J. M. (1990). A call to advance psychology's role in minority issues. *APA Monitor, 21*, p. 23.

Keefe, S. E., & Padilla, A. M. (1987). *Chicano ethnicity*. Albuquerque, NM: University of New Mexico Press.

Kim, S. C. (1985). Family therapy for Asian Americans: A strategic–structural framework. *Psychotherapy, 22*, 342–348.

Kramer, M., Rosen, B. M., & Willis, E. M. (1973). Definitions and distributions of mental disorders in a racist society. In C. V. Willie, B. M. Kramer, & B. S. Brown (Eds.), *Racism and mental health* (pp. 363–462). Pittsburgh, PA: University of Pittsburgh Press.

Kroeber, A. L., & Kluckhohn, C. (1952). *Culture: A critical review of concepts and definitions*. Paper of the Peabody Museum of American Archeology and Ethnology, *47*, No. 1.

LaFromboise, T. D. (1988). American Indian mental health policy. *American Psychologist, 43*, 388–397.

LeVine, E. S., & Padilla, A. M. (1980). *Crossing cultures in therapy: Pluralistic counseling for the Hispanic*. Monterey, CA: Brooks/Cole.

Leong, F. T. (1986). Counseling and psychotherapy with Asian-Americans: Review of the literature. *Journal of Counseling Psychology, 33*, 196–206.

Li-Repac, D. (1980). Cultural influences on clinical perception: A comparison between Caucasian and Chinese-American therapists. *Journal of Cross-Cultural Psychology, 11*, 327–342.

Lopez, S. R. (1989). Patient variable biases in clinical judgment: Conceptual overview and methodological considerations. *Psychological Bulletin, 106*, 184–203.

Manson, S. M. (1986). Recent advances in American Indian mental health research: Implications for clinical research and training. In M. R. Miranda & H. H. L. Kitano (Eds.), *Mental health research and practice in minority communities: Development of culturally sensitive training programs* (pp. 51–90). Washington, DC: U.S. Government Printing Office.

Marcos, L. R. (1979). Effects of interpreters on the evaluation of psychopathology in non-English-speaking patients. *American Journal of Psychiatry, 136*, 171–174.

McConahay, J. B., Hardee, B. B., & Batts, V. (1981). Has racism declined in American? It depends on who is asking and what is asked. *Journal of Conflict Resolution, 25*, 563–579.

Mizokawa, D. T., and Morishima, J. K. (1979). The education for, by, and of Asian/Pacific Americans. *Research Review of Equal Education, 3*, 1–33.

Munoz, R. F. (1982). The Spanish-speaking consumer and the community mental health center. In E. E. Jones & S. J. Korchin (Eds.), *Minority mental health* (pp. 362–398). New York: Praeger.

Neighbors, H. W. (1984). The distribution of psychiatric morbidity in Black Americans: A review and suggestions for research. *Community Mental Health Journal, 20*, 169–181.

Neighbors, H. W., Jackson, J. S., Campbell, L., & Williams, D. (1989). The influence of racial factors on psychiatric diagnosis: A review and suggestion for research. *Community Mental Health Journal, 25*, 301–311.

The 1990 almanac. New York: Houghton-Mifflin.

O'Sullivan, M. J., Peterson, P. D., Cox, G. B., & Kirkeby, J. (1989). Ethnic populations: Community mental health services ten years later. *American Journal of Community Psychology, 17*, 17–30.

Padilla, A. M. (1987). Special issue: Acculturation research. *Hispanic Journal of Behavioral Sciences, 9*, 105–225.

Padilla, A. M., & Salgado De Snyder, N. (1985). Counseling Hispanics: Strategies for effective intervention. In P. Pedersen (Ed.), *Handbook of cross-cultural counseling and therapy* (pp. 157–164). Westport, CT: Greenwood Press.

Parham, T. A., & Helms, J. E. (1981). The influence of Black students' racial identity attitudes on preferences for counselor's race. *Journal of Counseling Psychology, 28*, 250–257.

Poll finds racial tension decreasing. (1990, June 29). *Asian Week*, p. 4.

President's Commission on Mental Health. (1978). *Report to the President*. Washington, DC: U.S. Government Printing Office.

Price-Williams, D. R. (1985). Cultural psychology. In G. Lindzey & E. Aronson (Eds.), *Handbook of social psychology: Volume II* (3rd ed.; pp. 993–1042). New York: Random House.

Ridley, C. R. (1984). Clinical treatment of the nondisclosing Black client: A therapeutic paradox. *American Psychologist, 39*, 1234–1244.

Rogoff, B., & Morelli, G. (1989). Perspectives on children's development from cultural psychology. *American Psychologist, 44*, 343–348.

Rogler, L. H., Malgady, R. G., & Rodriguez, O. (1989). *Hispanics and mental health: A framework for research*. Malabar, FL: Krieger Publishing Company.

Schofield, W. (1964). *Psychotherapy: The purchase of friendship*. Englewood Cliffs, NJ: Prentice-Hall.

Sears, D. O., & Allen, H. M. (1984). The trajectory of local desegregation controversies and Whites' opposition to busing. In N. Miller & M. B. Brewer (Eds.), *Groups in contact: The psychology of desegregation* (pp. 123–151). Orlando, FL: Academic Press.

Snowden, L. R. (Ed.). (1982). *Reaching the underserved: Mental health needs of neglected populations*. Beverly Hills, CA: Sage.

Snowden, L. R. (1984). Toward evaluation of Black psycho-social competence. In S. Sue & T. Moore (Eds.), *The pluralistic society: A community mental health perspective* (pp. 179–192). New York: Human Sciences Press.

Snowden, L. R., & Cheung, F. K. (1990). Use of inpatient mental health services by members of ethnic minority groups. *American Psychologist, 45*, 347–355.

Somervell, P. D., Leaf, P. J., Weissman, M. M., Blazer, D. G., & Bruce, M. L. (1989). The prevalence of major depression in Black and White adults in five United States communities. *American Journal of Epidemiology, 130*, 725–735.

Sue, D. W., & Sue, D. (1985). Asian-Americans and Pacific Islanders. In P. Pedersen (Ed.), *Handbook of cross-cultural counseling and therapy* (pp. 141–146). Westport, CT: Greenwood.

Sue, S. (1977). Community mental health services to minority groups: Some optimism, some pessimism. *American Psychologist, 32*, 616–624.

Sue, S. (1983). Ethnic minority issues in psychology: A reexamination. *American Psychologist, 38*, 583–592.

Sue, S., Fujino, D. C., Hu, L., Takeuchi, D. T., & Zane, N. W. S. (in press). Community mental health services for ethnic minority groups: A test of the cultural responsiveness hypothesis. *Journal of Consulting and Clinical Psychology.*

Sue, S., & Padilla, A. M. (1986). Ethnic minority issues in the United States: Challenges for the educational system. In California State Department of Education (Ed.), *Beyond language: Social and cultural factors in schooling language minority students* (pp. 35–72). Los Angeles, CA: Evaluation, Dissemination and Assessment Center.

Sue, S., & Zane, N. (1987). The role of culture and cultural techniques in psychotherapy: A critique and reformulation. *American Psychologist, 42*, 37–45.

Suinn, R. M., Richard-Fuguerod, K., Lew, S., & Vigil, P. (1985). Career decisions and an Asian acculturation scale. *Journal of the Asian American Psychological Association, 10*, 20–28.

Triandis, H. C., & Brislin, R. W. (1984). Cross-cultural psychology. *American Psychologist, 39*, 1006–1016.

Trimble, J. E., & LaFromboise, T. (1985). American Indian and the counseling process: Culture, adaptation, and style. In P. Pedersen (Ed.), *Handbook of cross-cultural counseling and therapy* (pp. 127–134). Westport, CT: Greenwood.

Tung, T. M. (1985). Psychiatric care for Southeast Asians: How different is different? In T. Owan (Ed.), *Southeast Asian mental health: Treatment, prevention, services, training, and research* (pp. 5–40). Washington, DC: U.S. Department of Health and Human Services.

Tyler, F. B., Sussewell, D. R., & Williams-McCoy, J. (1985). Ethnic validity in psychotherapy. *Psychotherapy, 22*, 311–320.

van Dijk, T. A. (1987). *Communicating racism.* Newbury Park, CA: Sage.

Westermeyer, J., Vang, T. F., & Neider, J. (1983). Migration and mental health: Association of pre- and post-migration factors with self-rating scales. *Journal of Nervous and Mental Disease, 171*, 92–96.

Wilson, M. N. (1989). Child development in the context of the black extended family. *American Psychologist, 44*, 380–385.

Wu, I. H., & Windle, C. (1980). Ethnic specificity in the relative minority use and staffing of community mental health centers. *Community Mental Health Journal, 16*, 156–168.

Yamamoto, J., James, Q. C., & Palley, N. (1968). Cultural problems in psychiatric therapy. *Archives of General Psychiatry, 19*, 45–49.

Zane, N., & Sue, S. (1986). Reappraisal of ethnic minority issues: Research alternatives. In E. Seidman & J. Rappaport (Eds.), *Redefining social problems* (pp. 289–304). New York: Plenum.

CAROL TAVRIS

THE MISMEASURE OF WOMAN: PARADOXES AND PERSPECTIVES IN THE STUDY OF GENDER

C arol Tavris earned her PhD in social psychology from the University of Michigan in 1971; she then began developing an idiosyncratic career as a writer, teacher, and lecturer, with the goal of communicating psychology to a variety of "publics." Tavris is author of *The Mismeasure of Woman* (Simon & Schuster), which expands upon material in this chapter and is projected to appear in early 1992, and *Anger: The Misunderstood Emotion* (Simon & Schuster/Touchstone, 1989). She is senior author with Carole Wade of *The Longest War: Sex Differences in Perspective* (Harcourt Brace Jovanovich, 1984). Wade and Tavris are authors also of *Psychology* (HarperCollins, 2d. ed., 1990), a textbook that represented the first major effort to "mainstream" human diversity—gender, ethnicity, and culture—into the introductory course. In addition to professional addresses and book chapters, Tavris has written numerous articles and book reviews on many aspects of psychology for a wide variety of general-interest magazines, and she regularly writes editorials for *The Los Angeles Times*.

Tavris taught at the Human Relations Center of the New School for Social Research and is currently a lecturer in the department of psychology at UCLA. She has served as Chair of the Division 35 Task Force on Public Information and as Consulting Editor for numerous magazines, including UNESCO's international science journal, *Impact of Science on Society*. She is a Fellow of APA Divisions 1, 9 and 35 and also is a member of Division 8; a charter member of the American Psychological Society; a Fellow of the Committee for the Scientific Investigation of Claims of the Paranormal; and a member of the International Society for Research on Emotion, PEN Center USA West, and the Authors Guild.

THE MISMEASURE OF WOMAN: PARADOXES AND PERSPECTIVES IN THE STUDY OF GENDER

W hen I entered graduate school in 1966, at the first rumblings of what would become an avalanche of scholarship about women, there were great pressures on women who wanted to follow in the traditional (male) career path. One was supposed to travel up the academic ladder without a break for distracting activities like marriage, children, travel, a job, or family obligations. Many graduate schools were reluctant to accept women in those days, and the reason, they said, was that women were so unpredictable and unprofessional. They were for-ever dropping out to support their husbands, have children, or take jobs that allowed them to eat.

In the ensuing 25 years, I have observed three waves of theory and research that would interpret this situation quite differently. The first was what Crawford and Marecek (1989b) call the "Woman as Problem" approach, in which researchers generally sought to prove no major differences between women and men. For example, research in the late 1960s was designed to provide reassuring evidence to administrators that women would finish their graduate programs and that they would eventually publish good research.

By the late 1970s and early 1980s, we entered what I call the "Woman as Solution" era. This approach holds that women do indeed follow different career paths and life patterns from those of men, but that the "woman's way," being less linear and goal-directed, is better. Why is it so desirable for an academic career to be uninterrupted by experience and outside work? Isn't it strange to assume that a person could build a career in psychology by studying only the creatures nearest at hand—college students and rats? In this view, administrators should be worrying about the deficient training of male students, so woefully unweathered by life.

Today we are in a third, even more interesting phase in the study of gender. Postmodern views assume that we will never know the essences of male and female, for these are endlessly changing, endlessly constructed from the eye of the observer and the conditions of our lives (K. J. Gergen, 1985; Hare-Mustin & Marecek, 1990; Morawski, 1990; Tiefer, 1987; Unger, 1990). These approaches transcend the literal and limited question of whether men and women differ and ask instead why everyone is so interested in differences and what function the *belief* in differences serves. Social constructionists might examine, for instance, the functions of the belief that women's experiences do not fit them for the academic life the way men's experiences do. (One result, of course, is that women were excluded from the academy.) They would ask how it came to be that only one correct academic path is acceptable, and who decides which one is "correct." They would observe that the very question of whether "women's ways" are worse or better than men's deflects us from the fact that men are setting the standard of normalcy.

All three approaches, which co-exist today, must confront what Faye Crosby (1989) calls the "paradox of gender"—the persistent belief that men and women differ in important qualities, in spite of countless studies that have failed to pin these qualities down and keep them pinned. As Kay Deaux and Brenda Major (1987) observed, "researchers attempting to document and replicate sex differences have often found them elusive, a case of 'now you see them, now you don't' " (p. 369). Meta-analyses of social behaviors, such as helpfulness, find that differences are due more to role than to gender (Eagly, 1987), and meta-analyses of intellectual skills, such as mathematical, verbal, and spatial abilities, find that differences have virtually vanished or are too trivial to matter (Caplan, MacPherson, & Tobin, 1985; Feingold, 1988; Hyde, Fennema, & Lamon, 1990; Hyde & Linn, 1986, 1988). And numerous gender differences have faded quickly with changing times (K. J. Gergen, 1973), as was the fate of "finger dexterity" (when men got hold of computers) and "fear of success" (when women got hold of law schools).

In this chapter I will argue that the paradox of gender is a result of the continuing use of the male as norm; the specific skills, behaviors, and qualities that are studied; and the popular zeitgeist that continues

I wish to express my gratitude and thanks to colleagues who read and commented on earlier versions of this chapter, especially Paula Caplan, Jacqueline Goodchilds, Letitia Anne Peplau, Leonore Tiefer, and Carole Wade.

to locate the primary source of gender differences in biology, personality, and intrapsychic dynamics (which appear to be permanent) rather than in life experiences, resources, and power (which change culturally and historically).

It is not the study of difference that is a problem; of course people differ, which is the theme of these Master Lectures on diversity. The problem occurs when one group is considered the norm with others differing from it, thereby failing to measure up to the ideal, superior, dominant standard, and when the dominant group uses the language of difference to justify its social position (Scott, 1988). In *The Mismeasure of Man*, Stephen Jay Gould (1981) used the study of "race differences" in intelligence to illustrate how science has been used and abused to serve a larger cultural agenda: namely, to confirm prejudices that "Blacks, women, and poor people occupy their subordinate roles by the harsh dictates of nature" (p. 74). The mismeasure of woman serves the same function, as I hope to show with two examples of research on female hormones and the brain. The antidote, as Gould reminds us, is always to ask: Who is doing the measuring, and for what purpose?

This chapter will address these questions, concluding with new perspectives that go beyond differences in examining the complexities of gender.

Traditional Biases in Approaches to Gender

In psychology and other fields, there have typically been three approaches to gender differences. They share an assumption that the male is the human norm, but they place the female in various locations in orbit around him: (a) Women are opposite and lesser; (b) women are opposite and superior (Hare-Mustin and Marecek, 1990, call these first two views "alpha bias," the exaggeration of differences and the belief that differences are fundamental); (c) women are the same as men. This last approach, which would seem to be the antidote to the fundamental-difference schools, commits an intrinsic error of its own by ignoring the differences that *do* exist between men and women in resources and life experiences. Hare-Mustin and Marecek (1990) call this error "beta bias."

"Women are Opposite and Deficient"

Women, as Simone de Beauvoir wrote in 1949, are the second sex, the other sex, the sex to be explained. Her observation still holds. In popular political thought, there are "important issues" (drugs, economics, war) and "women's issues" (daycare, housework, peace). We worry about "the feminization of poverty," but do not see its connection to the masculinization of wealth. Society ponders the problem of unwed teenage mothers, not the problem of unwed teenage fathers. Indeed, reproductive freedom in general is a "women's issue," as if men were merely disinterested bystanders on the matter of sexuality.

In the last 20 years, feminist psychologists have uncovered the hidden biases in the study of gender differences that resulted from using men as the human standard (Denmark, Russo, Frieze, & Sechzer, 1988; Gilligan, 1982; Sherif, 1987). But the bias persists in subtle ways. Consider this good study of the reasons that women and men offer, in a mock job interview, for their success or failure on creativity tests (Olson, 1988). The researcher reports that women attributed their successes less often to their own abilities than to luck, and they reported less overall confidence in their present and future performance. Why, she asks, do women make less self-serving attributions than men do? "The feminine social goal of appearing modest inhibits women in making self-promoting attributions in an achievement situation which involves face-to-face interaction" (p. 2). The premise of this study—to explain why the women didn't behave like men—is apparent if we rephrase the question and its answer thus: "Why do men make more self-serving attributions than women do? The masculine social goal of appearing self-confident inhibits them from making modest explanations of their abilities or acknowledging the help of others and the role of chance."

Of course, the bias of seeing women's behavior as something to be explained in relation to the male norm makes sense in a world that takes the male norm for granted. In this case, the researcher showed that the female habit of modesty does women a disservice in job interviews, because they appear to be unconcerned with achievement and unwilling to promote themselves. (This information would be useful to *both* sexes in cultures that value modesty, if they want to do business in the United States.) However, the research masks the fact that the male norm frames the very questions and solutions that investigators explore, and then creates the impression that women have "problems" and "deficiencies" if they differ from the norm. For example, consider these findings:

- Women have lower self-esteem than men do (Sanford & Donovan, 1984).
- Women do not value their efforts as much as men do, even when they are doing the same work (Major, 1987).
- Women are more likely than men to say they are "hurt" than to admit they are "angry" (Biaggio, 1988).
- Women have more difficulty than men in developing a "separate sense of self" (Aries & Olver, 1985).

Surely, these are things to worry about. Surely it is desirable for women to have high self-esteem, value their work, be self-confident, express anger, and develop autonomy, and such studies usually conclude with discussions of "the problem" of why women are so insecure and what can be done about it. But had these studies used women as the basis of comparison, the same findings might then lead to a different notion of what the "problems" are:

- Men are more conceited than women.
- Men overvalue the work they do.
- Men are not as realistic and modest as women in assessing their abilities.
- Men are more likely than women to accuse and attack others when they are unhappy, instead of stating that they feel hurt and inviting sympathy.
- Men have more difficulty than women in forming and maintaining attachments.

When the "problems" are stated this way, the biased tone is apparent. But the reverse, seeing female behavior as problematic, is so ingrained that it feels normal—until the assumption is questioned. Major, McFarlin, and Gagnon (1984) found that when men and women were given the same amount of money and told to work until they felt they had earned it, women worked significantly longer and did more accurate and efficient work than the men did. Perhaps women do not undervalue their labor, Major et al. concluded; perhaps men overvalue theirs.

The point, however, is not that one way of doing things is right and the other is wrong or biased. The point is that whichever side is considered the norm, the other will be perceived as deviating from it, and deviation is quickly enshrined as "opposition." For example, some studies of physical aggression report that females, in not behaving as aggressively as males, are *opposite* from them, that is, "unaggressive" or "submissive." But these studies do not find that women are submissive; only that women are less likely than men to behave aggressively. By describing the women's behavior as the opposite of the men's, researchers not only are mistaken; they also lose critical information about *female* aggressiveness (this example is from Denmark et al., 1988).

There have been two major responses to the view of women as opposite and deficient: (a) to agree with the notion of "opposition," but to reinterpret women's deficiencies as strengths; and (b) to deny differences and to assume a fundamental sameness of women and men. Both approaches have contributed to our understanding of gender, but both have basic flaws, as I will argue next.

"Women Are Opposite and Superior"

Proponents of this view accept the idea that there are profound differences between women and men, but they believe that women's ways are better. They emphasize aspects of female experience or female "nature"—such as menstruation, childbirth, compassion, spirituality, attachment, cooperation, "care-based" moral reasoning, pacifism—and celebrate them as being morally superior to men's experiences and qualities. This view is gaining ground in many areas, including psychoanalysis, religion, history, psychology, politics, and feminist theory. Cultural feminists hope to overcome sexism in law and social life by celebrating women's "special qualities," culture, and experiences (Echols, 1984; see also West, 1988); ecofeminists hope to transform the globe into an environmental Eden by celebrating women's alleged proximity to nature and peacefulness.

I am sympathetic to the impulse to retrieve the best "female" qualities and experiences from the dustbin of slander in which they have reposed. Nevertheless, although the judgments of women are kinder, the male is still the norm against which women are judged. Further, framing the issue in polarities—regardless of which pole is the valued one—immediately sets up false choices for women and men. It ignores the fact that the opposing qualities associated with masculinity and femininity are caricatures to begin with (Hare-Mustin & Marecek, 1986). As Bernice Lott (1990) and Martha Mednick (1989) have observed, it perpetuates the ago-old belief that there is something special and mystical about woman's nature, an attitude that historically has served to keep women in their place (Tavris & Wade, 1984). And it represents an attitude that has the potential to be as oppressive to women as the denigrating attitude it replaces. By oversentimentalizing women's "natural" birthing capacities, for example, such views make women who have a difficult time with childbirth feel guilty that they have pain (Standing, 1980).

Rachel Hare-Mustin and Jeanne Marecek (1986), using the example of autonomy, have dissected the consequences of false polarizations. In this society, autonomy—generally meaning independence, self-sufficiency, and the ability to pursue one's own goals—has been considered the sign of maturity and health. At first, therefore, feminists argued that women should become more independent, more "like men." Now many are arguing that the pursuit of autonomy is a snare and delusion, a male value that serves no one but the Marlboro Man, and that women should celebrate their "natural relatedness" and nurturance as a healthier sign of maturity.

Yet the endorsement of female relatedness, while important, is not a sufficient alternative to the model of autonomy. Hare-Mustin and Marecek (1986) argue that both extremes overlook the complexities of people's lives. Men are not wholly autonomous; they depend on others to keep their households and businesses running, to make sure they get to the doctor, to raise their children, to provide love and moral support. Nor are women wholly selfless in their devotion to others; many derive satisfaction, power, and sense of achievement from managing their families and homes, having close friendships, caring for those they love, and raising children.

Second, Hare-Mustin and Marecek observe, women's new emphasis on relatedness tastes of sour grapes. Under current conditions, "pure" autonomy is not feasible for many women because of their economic insecurity, responsibility for children, and lack of power. The proper response to these conditions, they say, is not to give up the goal of self-determination because women cannot easily achieve it, but to understand what it will take for women to have it. Likewise, it is better to specify what it will take for men to become more "related" or "connected" (or, in actuality, to admit that they already are!) than to dismiss them as hopelessly lacking this "female" skill.

Ultimately, the problem with all theories that divide men and women into different psychological camps is that in their needs, capabilities, and values, men and women aren't as different as the Moral Majority or cultural feminists believe. In a study of 130 college students, of an age where we might expect the most exaggerated sex differences, Cochran and Peplau (1985) found no differences in attachment values; and the women, if anything, valued autonomy more than the men did. Men and women may express their feelings differently, but in their *behavior*—their need and desire for attachment and love—they do not differ in significant ways, Gilligan's ideas of male "fear of attachment" notwithstanding (Cancian, 1987; Riessman, 1987; Shaver, Hazan, & Bradshaw, 1988).

Similarly, there is little evidence to support the prevalent belief that men and women differ in moral reasoning, as Carol Gilligan (1982) has maintained. Gilligan did not say that women's "care-based" moral reasoning is better than men's "justice-based" reasoning, only that it is different, and that both styles have strengths and weaknesses. This point was lost on many of her adherents, who replaced the former male bias in moral-development studies with a female bias. Yet most researchers report no average differences in the kind of reasoning that men and women use in evaluating moral dilemmas (Cohn, 1991; Colby & Damon, 1987; Friedman, Robinson, & Friedman, 1987; Greeno & Maccoby, 1986; Thoma, 1986). Thoma (1986) concluded that "there is little support for the notion that males are better able to reason about hypothetical dilemmas, or that moral reasoning is in some way a male domain" (p. 176).

Yet the conviction that women speak in a "different voice" has tremendous appeal (Chodorow, 1978; Goldberger, Clinchy, Belenky, & Tarule, 1986). As Mednick (1989) observes, "the simplicity of such ideas is appealing; such gender dichotomy confirms stereotypes and provides strong intuitive resonance" (p. 1122). She cites Greeno and Maccoby's (1986) warning: "Women have been trapped for generations by people's willingness to accept their own intuitions about the truth of gender stereotypes" (p. 315).

Let's examine one such intuition more closely. One of the constructive impulses behind cultural feminism is the dream of a world that will be egalitarian, peaceful, and ecologically balanced. This dream, and visions of how to achieve it, rest on a belief in the most basic male–female dichotomy: that men are the warlike, dominating, planet-destroying sex, and women are the peacemaking, nonaggressive, planet-saving sex. Some members of the woman-is-better school, represented by the growing movement of ecofeminism, have concluded that the saving of the world depends on the ascendancy of women, who will stop pillaging the environment and allow all to live in harmony (except for men, who presumably will have to be enclosed on restricted preserves).

I admit that I've entertained this fantasy too. The trouble is that the only sex that might replace men is women, and there is no evidence that women are naturally more pacifistic, empathic, or earth-loving than men: They are just as likely to depersonalize enemies into vermin and beasts, to be carried away with patriotic fervor, and to justify brutality (Anderson & Zinsser, 1988; Kohn, 1990; Lott, 1990; Zur, 1989).

Moreover, throughout history women have been just as militant in wartime as men, participating as their societies permitted: as combatants, as defenders, as laborers in the work force to produce war materials, as supporters of their warrior husbands and sons, as resistance fighters themselves (Elshtain, 1987). Women have joined in the glorification of nation above family, finding honor in playing the "Spartan Mother" (a reference to the nameless woman who lost five sons in battle and thanked the gods that Sparta won). We think of war as a male activity and value, but war also gives women a route out of domestic confinement—a public identity and a chance to play a heroic role, usually denied them in their private lives. Conversely, not all men in wartime fought bloodthirstily to kill. Many throughout history have refused, and many sacrificed their lives for their comrades, families, and nations. The archetypes of Man as Just Warrior and Woman as Beautiful Soul, Elshtain (1987) shows, are flattering to both sexes, but they are untrue. Archetypes are not blueprints for human beings.

In a similar vein, other writers have sought evidence of a past age when, allegedly, women were worshiped, when women ruled, when everyone lived in peace. The search for such a feminist Eden has recurred in history. In the 19th century, Bachofen's theory of "mother right"—the view that human society progressed from a matriarchal structure to a patriarchal one—attracted many followers, including Elizabeth Cady Stanton, who felt it was an inspiring theory that would motivate women and give them self-respect (Pomeroy, 1986). Perhaps for the same reasons, we are seeing a resurgence of this belief today. For example, Riane Eisler (1987) and Gerda Lerner (1986) maintain that in earliest history, religions were peace-loving and woman-worshipping, women were deities and priestesses, and neither sex, as it were, wore the pants. In Eisler's view, all was well until barbarians swept through Europe, creating societies based on male dominance and aggression.

This argument likewise has much intuitive appeal and is currently the source of lively debate, focused on the archeological evidence of figurines of women—the voluptuous "Venuses" found in archeological sites from Spain to Siberia. The belief that religions originally were woman-centered rests on the hypothesis that these figurines represent mother goddesses and their priestesses. It is not certain, however, that such artifacts were objects of worship. Even powerful goddesses such as Ishtar, Athena, and Isis—or the Hindu Kali, and Mary and female saints in the Christian tradition—are found where men have been in political and religious control and where misogyny is rampant. Such goddesses most likely reflect men's images of women, not women's actual power (Anderson & Zinsser, 1988; Pomeroy, 1975). These romantic accounts of the past reduce the complexities of history into a morality play of good versus evil, female versus male. But we cannot assume that all barbarians were male; what about the female barbarians who joined their conquests and cheered them on? What about all the nonbarbarian males, past and present, who do not share the view of Western nations that nature is to be conquered and plundered?

For all these reasons, many feminist scholars argue that it is time to stop thinking in opposites (Gilbert, 1988; Hare-Mustin & Marecek, 1986; Minnich, 1990). Thinking in opposites leads to what philosophers call "the law of the excluded middle," which is where most men and women fall in terms of their qualities, beliefs, values, and abilities (Hyde & Linn, 1986; Jacklin, 1981). By dividing the world into two gender categories, we lose sight of the fact that human beings of both genders are diverse. All women are not alike; all men are not alike; many women and men are alike. The very term "opposite sex" implies that women and men act in opposition to one another (Gilbert, 1988; Lott, 1990). It implies an underlying antagonism or conflict, the pitting of one side against the other, one way (which is right and healthy) versus the other's way (which is wrong and unhealthy). Yet, as Hare-Mustin (1987) asks, what is the "opposite" of man: woman? mouse? beast? machine? Superman? Nothing in the nature of gender requires us to emphasize difference and opposition. We can emphasize similarity and reciprocity, human variation rather than gender rigidities. But it has not suited our society to do so.

As long as we think in opposites, we will be prevented from envisioning a future that would combine, for example, "male" access to power and resources with "female" values and skills. We will continue to define problems narrowly instead of expanding visions of possibility. We will continue to provoke animosities across the gender line, instead of alliances. That is why the woman-is-better school is ultimately as self-defeating as the woman-is-deficient school it hopes to replace.

"Women Are Just Like Men"

To question the belief that men and women differ in profound and basic ways is not to deny that men and women differ at all. Of course they do. They differ in power and resources, life experiences, and reproductive processes. Ironically, the belief in the normalcy of men has generated a third common error: Generalizing from the experiences of men to all humanity on the grounds that everyone is like men, usually a narrow band of educated, white middle-class men at that (Minnich, 1990).

The law, for example, regards the male body as the legal standard of a human being (Eisenstein, 1989; Littleton, 1987; MacKinnon, 1990; Rothman, 1989; West, 1988). The male body doesn't menstruate, lactate, or become pregnant, but the "abnormal" female body does. Therefore, women may be treated like men, in which case they are "equal" to them, or not like men, in which case they are "deficient." But they are never treated specifically *as women*. There is no concept in the law of what is normal for women.

Christine Littleton (1987) argues for a model of "equality as acceptance"—acceptance of existing differences—rather than equality as assimilation, which attempts to squeeze women into male careers, life paths, and models of behavior. Women's inequality, she suggests, results from devaluing women's real biological and cultural differences from men. Efforts to achieve equality through precisely equal treatment, therefore, are doomed to fail: "As a concept, equality suffers from a 'mathematical fallacy'—that is, the view that only things that are the same can ever be equal" (p. 1282).

This fallacy is revealed in studies finding that by treating women the same as men, the law often produces unequal results. The most well-known example is what happened after changes in the divorce and custody laws, which falsely assumed that women and men have equal social and economic standing, equal wages and benefits. A New York State Task Force found that on virtually all issues of specific concern to women—notably domestic violence, rape, child support, day care, and pregnancy—being treated "equally," i.e. like men, under the law leads to unequal results in life (Eisenstein, 1989). So did a major review of gender bias in the courts conducted by the Judicial Council of California (1990).

As Catherine MacKinnon (1990) has observed, "Clearly there are many differences between women and men. One could not systematically elevate one half of a population and denigrate the other half and produce a population in which everyone is the same" (pp. 220–221). Many feminist legal scholars, therefore, are arguing that we cannot ignore these differences but must instead find ways to include women's experiences (and bodies) under the law, and to assure equal *outcomes*, so that women do not pay—in income, loss of pensions and benefits, in status, in health— for differences imposed or chosen (Littleton, 1987).

Medicine, like law, takes the male as its norm. In anatomy textbooks, the illustrations that show a full body typically show a male body, except for the illustrations of the female reproductive system, (Giacomini, Rozée-Koker, & Pepitone-Arreola-Rockwell, 1986). In medical school, students learn from a paradigm patient called "the 70-kilogram man" (Klass & Wallis, 1989). Students learn what the "average man's" heart weighs and what his minimum urine output should be; they treat him for allergies, appendicitis, and prostate problems; but the 70-kilogram man never gets endometriosis, fibroids, or any other female disorder. In professional journals, research based on samples only of males is titled as if it applied to everyone (e.g., "Work Activity and Coronary Heart Mortality"; no one assumes that a study done only on women would apply to men. Eichler, Reisman, and Borins (1990) examined all 1988 issues of four medical journals. Two thirds of the articles revealed gender bias in titles, methods, data collection and interpretation, or treatment recommendations, either by ignoring the reality of gender differences or by overgeneralizing inappropriately from samples of men to women.

Women and men are different biological entities, with different hormones, different patterns of health and disease, different responses to stress (Jensvold & Hamilton, 1989). But the assumption that findings about the 70-kilogram man will apply equally to women has proven wrong, over and over again. Consider this small sampling of topics:

● *Alcohol.* In general, alcohol behaves more unpredictably in women than in men, possibly because of its interactions with women's hormonal and metabolic changes. Many women who are taking birth control pills, for instance, are more susceptible to adverse reactions to liquor than are women not on the pill (Jeavons [Wilkinson] & Zeiner, 1984).

● *Drugs.* Women receive about 70% of all prescriptions for antidepressant medications, but most of the studies of these drugs have been conducted only on men, and few studies have investigated the ways in which women and men might differ. The index of a leading text in psychopharmacology lists only two citations under *gender*, and it minimizes the effects of gender in those two instances (Hamilton & Parry, 1983; Jensvold & Hamilton, 1989; McGrath, Keita, Strickland, & Russo, 1990).

● *Cholesterol.* Before menopause, estrogen seems to counteract the risk effects of cholesterol for women, but no one has specifically studied cholesterol in postmenopausal women to see if high cholesterol is a risk for them. Even that ideal cutoff point of 200 is specific to men; it is not known what level, if any, increases the risk of heart disease in women (Palumbo, 1989).

● *Hypertension and responses to stress.* Women with high blood pressure are at less risk than men with the same level of hypertension; complications from hypertension appear an average of 10 years later than they do for men. And a large body of research finds gender differences in neuroendocrine reactions to stressors; for example, males excrete higher levels of epinephrine than females do (Polefrone & Manuck, 1987).

The acceptance of the 70-kilogram man has two dangerous medical consequences for women. First, many physicians regard conditions that are normal or medically safe for women as if they were abnormal (such as menopause) and treat them inappropriately. Second, many physicians ignore conditions that *are* problems for women. In a group of patients who had taken tests that showed evidence of heart disease, for example, 40% of the men but only 4% of the women were referred by their physicians for the next test to see if bypass surgery was warranted. The women had the same symptoms and abnormal test results, but apparently the doctors did not take these warning signs seriously (Tobin et al., 1987). One result is that by the time women are referred for coronary artery surgery, they are older and sicker than men would be with identical symptoms. Thus women are nearly twice as likely as men to die from this surgical procedure (Khan et al., 1990).

But of all the dilemmas for women that occur because of inappropriate comparisons to a male norm, one of the most psychologically destructive has to do with body image and weight. The normal female body has been biologically designed to store fat reserves for menstruation, pregnancy, nursing, and the production and storage of estrogen after menopause. This seems to be one reason that weight gain in older women is not as risky to health as it can be for men, and why such weight gain offsets the risk of osteoporosis (Bennett & Gurin, 1982). Most white teenage girls no longer regard necessary weight gain as normal signs of maturation, but as signs of (unpleasant) fatness. A representative survey of more than 2,000 girls in Michigan, ages 11–18, found that nearly 40% considered themselves overweight; dieting and dissatisfaction with body image were the typical responses to the onset of puberty (Drewnowski & Yee, 1988). Many other studies of nationally representative samples find that dieting, unrealistic body image, and dissatisfaction with weight are chronic stressors and sources of low self-esteem for White women (Attie & Brooks-Gunn, 1987).

Ideal body image, in turn, is related to larger social and economic factors. Curvy, full-breasted women are in fashion during pronatalist eras, such as the early 1900s, the 1950s, and, increasingly, today; thin, muscular, boyish bodies are in fashion whenever women have entered the work force, specifically the traditionally male occupations, as they did in the 1920s and late 1960s (Silverstein, Perdue, Peterson, Vogel, & Fantini, 1986). One reason seems to be that the voluptuous body is associated with femininity, and femininity is associated with nurturance, domesticity, and incompetence (Silverstein, Peterson, & Perdue, 1986). Therefore, women who want to be thought professional and competent must look more "male-ish." In such eras, the number of articles and books on dieting increases dramatically, and eating disorders and "fat panic" among women and girls become epidemic.

The belief that a woman's body is never right as it is and always needs to be fixed will continue as long as women seek to be opposite from the male body, or to be like the male body, but never satisfied with the woman's body they have (Striegel-Moore, Silberstein, & Rodin, 1986).

The Social Uses of Theory: Two Cases

In 1980, Benbow and Stanley published their famous article in *Science*, arguing that males have an "endogenous" superiority in math. The media were on this news like a duck on a June bug ("A New Study Says Males May Be Naturally Abler Than Females"; "Boys Have Superior Math Ability, Study Says"; cited in Eccles & Jacobs, 1986, p. 377).

As it happened, at the time of this excitement, Jacquelynne Eccles and Janis Jacobs (1986) were conducting a longitudinal study of 7th- and 9th-grade children's math achievement. At the start of the study, the children were equal in math ability (as tests and teacher evaluations showed). Eccles and Jacobs assessed the impact of this media blitz, comparing parents who heard the Benbow and Stanley news with those who did not. The reports of a "natural" male superiority had a strong negative impact on parents' confidence in their daughters' math abilities: for example, they would praise their sons' good performance as reflecting natural ability, but commend their daughters' equally good performance as evidence of how hard the daughters had worked. This attitude (of which the parents were unaware) decreased the likelihood of the girl taking further math courses and valuing math in general. Why should she, if math is going to be so hard and unnatural an enterprise?

We are today in the midst of many similar media reports that emphasize biological explanations of gender differences; these are part of a larger trend, a tidal wave of biomedical research and explanations of human behavior in general (Bleier, 1988; Hubbard, 1990; Jacklin, 1989). Biological research itself is not the problem; much of it has benefited women. It is important to know that morning sickness during pregnancy is a hormonal matter, and not, as a male physician once said to a friend of mine, "a woman's way of saying she doesn't want to be pregnant." It is important for physicians and psychotherapists not to dismiss women's medical concerns as being "all in their minds." It is important for women to know that the hormonal changes of menopause do not indicate a "psychological resistance to the loss of femininity." Indeed, ignorance of the normal changes of aging causes an overpsychologizing of older women's physical health problems (Rodeheaver & Datan, 1988).

The problems occur when normal hormonal changes become viewed as abnormalities and disorders, and when the biological explanation for the goose is not the explanation for the gander. It was front-page news in The New York Times (November 18, 1989) that "Female Sex Hormone Is Tied To Ability to Perform Tasks"—the tasks being tongue twisters and "precise hand movements"—but not front-page news that "Male Sex Hormone Is Tied to Lapses in Hand Steadiness" (Houser, 1979) or that "Male Sex Hormone Is Tied to Pathological Behaviors" (Dabbs & Morris, 1990). Biological theories of gender, which travel as far back as Plato's theory of the wandering uterus as the cause of hysteria, are never socially neutral and do not have the same consequences for both sexes (Hubbard, 1990; Tiefer, 1988). The problems that are more characteristic of men than women—such as drug abuse, violence, and antisocial behavior—are rarely related to male hormones, brain structure, or anatomy. When men have problems, it is because of their upbringing, personality, or environment (Canetto, in press); when women have problems, it is because of something in the nature of being female.

Here I wish to discuss some research behind the headlines: two stories that highlight the social repercussions of the biological measure and mismeasure of woman.

The Creation of Female "Syndromes"

The invention of "Premenstrual Syndrome" (PMS) as an individual and social problem illustrates how impoverished women are in having a language of their own bodies, which are not like the bodies of men. It shows the complex interaction of mind, body, and culture. And it reveals the double-edged sword of diagnosis: the social stigma it confers and the validation of personal experience.

The idea that menstruation is a debilitating condition that affects women emotionally and behaviorally has it own cycle. It comes and goes in phase with women's participation in the labor market. Worry about the effects on women workers of their "premenstrual tension" emerged during the Depression, when the gains that women had made in the labor force because of World War I were eroding (Laqueur, 1987; Martin, 1987). At the start of World War II, however, studies suddenly found that menstruation and "premenstrual tension" were not problems for working women. One researcher, who had argued in 1934 that menstruation was debilitating, changed her mind 10 years later: "Any activity that may be performed with impunity at other times," she wrote during the War, "may be performed with equal impunity during menstruation" (cited in Martin, 1987, p. 120). But after World War II, with women returning home from the labor force, the news changed again. In the early 1950s, Katharina Dalton and a colleague coined the term "premenstrual syndrome," and in 1964 she published *The Premenstrual Syndrome*. In the ensuing decades, "PMS" became an increasingly popular research topic, as Table 1 indicates.

Along the way, "PMS" was coopted by biomedical researchers. As Mary Brown Parlee describes (1989), psychologists had been studying the psychology and physiology of menstruation, but they were focusing on normal menstrual cycles. The money, the grants, increasingly went to biomedical researchers on the assumption that "PMS" was a disease or a physiological abnormality that was best studied by radioimmunoassays of gondal hormones and by other new weapons in the medical arsenal.

When Parlee was first writing about "PMS," she put it in quotation marks, in order to denote it as an odd or unusual concept that was

Table 1
Growing Popularity of Articles in Medical and Psychological Journals on "PMS," Premenstrual Syndrome, and Premenstrual Tension, 1964–1989

	Number of citations in:	
Year(s)	Medical journals [Medline]	Psychological journals [PsycInfo]
1964	1	—[a]
1965	16	—[a]
1966–1967	67	8
1968–1969	84	9
1970–1971	74	5
1972–1973	87	9
1974–1975	114	16
1976–1977	146	20
1978–1979	128	16
1980–1981	148	25
1982–1983	187	36
1984–1985	218	77
1986–1987	260	107
1988–1989	305	120

Note. This list *omits* other menstrual-cycle research that did not use these terms or categories.
[a]Figures not available in PsycInfo database for these years.

supposedly scientific but not supported by data. In a recent speech (Parlee, 1989), she described what happened:

> A copy editor took out all the quotation marks, and with them the meaning I wanted to establish. I lost—was silenced—then in my effort to shape in a small way the scientific discourse about PMS. The processes through which "PMS" has come to mean what it does today are too powerful, too internally and mutually self-sustaining, for that meaning to be affected by the results of good science. . . . People—women, researchers, the media, drug company representatives—now use the term PMS as if it had a clearly understood and shared meaning; the only question is how to help women who "have" it. Thus PMS has become real. The quotation marks have been removed. (p. 12)

Indeed, the biomedical model has won. Today most laypeople regard PMS as a clearly defined disorder that most, if not all, women "suffer." A news item in *Psychology Today* (June 1989, p. 13) began:

"Premenstrual Syndrome (PMS) remains as baffling to researchers as it is troublesome to women." *Troublesome*? To all women, as implied? The article is about a study of 188 nursing students and tea factory workers in China. In the tea factory, "almost 80% suffered from PMS." *Suffered*? "Overall, nearly 74% rated their symptoms as mild, 24% as moderate and 3% said they were severe." In short, 97% of these women were far from "suffering."

The confusion between that 3% who report severe symptoms and the 97% who do not is exacerbated by popular "checklists" of up to 150 symptoms, which do not leave much out. One "complete checklist" includes weight gain, eye diseases, asthma, nausea, skin disorders and lesions, joint pains, headaches, backaches, general pains, epilepsy, cold sweats and hot flashes, sleeplessness, forgetfulness, confusion, impaired judgment, accidents, difficulty concentrating, lowered school or work performance, lethargy, decreased efficiency, drinking or eating too much, mood swings, crying and depression, anxiety, restlessness, irritability, tension, and loss (or increase!) of sex drive (cited in Martin, 1987). With so many symptoms, accounting for most of the possible range of negative human experience, who *wouldn't* have PMS?

Once PMS was defined as a troubling syndrome that millions of women "suffer," and as soon as its symptoms included "forgetfulness," "confusion," and "trouble concentrating at work," employers were bound to worry about the productivity of their female workers. The *Wall Street Journal* (January 22, 1986) has already reported on the possible "billions" to the economy that is lost to PMS in an article headlined "Premenstrual Distress Gains Notice as a Chronic Issue in the Workplace" (cited in Golub, 1988).

Physicians and clinicians themselves do not agree on whether they are talking about a phenomenon that a few women experience or that all women experience sometimes. In a conference that was held to discuss "PMS—an important and widespread problem," the participating physicians tried to estimate the scope of the "widespread problem." One thought it affected "between 20% and 40% of women at some stage in their lives." Another said that "probably fewer than 5% of them are sufficiently moved by these symptoms to seek medical help." A third said that "Probably all women at some time in their lives have disturbing premenstrual symptoms . . . but only 5–10% of women have clearcut PMS" (quoted in Fisher, 1987, pp. 1–2).

Researchers are now reduced to speaking of "clearcut" or "true" PMS to distinguish the small group of women who have severe premenstrual physical and emotional symptoms from those who have normal menstrual changes and from those who have other disorders (Parlee, 1989). In some studies of women who present for treatment for PMS and who are tested with daily rating diaries (instead of with fallible retrospective measures), three groups emerge: (a) women who have severe premenstrual symptoms but no history of affective disorders; (b) women whose depressive symptoms are aggravated by menstruation; and (c) women who prove not to have premenstrual problems although they believe they do. Women with a history of affective disorders are over-represented in the latter two categories (DeJong et al., 1985; Hammarback & Backstrom, 1989).

In spite of this confusion over prevalence, diversity, and nature of premenstrual changes, and in spite of the confounding of premenstrual symptoms with a history or presence of affective and other psychiatric disorders, by 1987 the DSM-III-R included, in an appendix, "Late Luteal Phase Dysphoric Disorder" (LLPDD) as a category "needing further study." There is considerable confusion among researchers and clinicians as to whether PMS and LLPDD are the same or even related phenomena. LLPDD is a psychiatric diagnostic category that attempts to describe symptoms that are severe enough to "seriously interfere with work or with usual social activities or relationships with others" (DSM-III-R, p. 369)—but that is precisely how some clinicians define PMS or "true" PMS. Some researchers consider LLPDD to be a subset of PMS; others think that PMS simply refers to normal menstrual changes, whereas LLPDD is a distinct disorder; still others think the two labels refer to the same phenomenon (Caplan, McCurdy-Myers, & Gans, 1990). In practice, however, most of the studies attempting to confirm LLPDD as a diagnostic category have failed to conform to the DSM-III-R criteria (e.g., the specific comparison of symptoms during the late luteal phase with those in the early follicular phase, after onset of menstruation); they use the same problematic measures as studies of PMS do; and they lack criteria for degree of symptom severity, let alone criteria of "interference with work or relationships" (Caplan et al., 1990).

Research on the physiology and psychology of the menstrual cycle paints a different picture from the public impression that PMS is a proven biomedical syndrome. Some physical changes normally occur (such as breast tenderness and water retention), varying with a woman's age, parity, nutritional conditions, and general health. But women around the world interpret, experience, and label these symptoms differently (Ericksen, 1987; Golub, 1988)—*just as men and women vary in how they interpret, experience, and label all symptoms of pain or physical discomfort* (Pennebaker, 1982). Further, in spite of the effort to document the existence of a disorder that so may women are "suffering" from, no biological marker has been found that distinguishes women who have severe premenstrual changes from those who do not, and no biological treatment has proved superior to a placebo (Hamilton & Gallant, 1988), including the popular prescription of progesterone (Freeman, Rickels, Sondheimer, & Polansky, 1990).

Moreover, recent evidence finds that most of the emotional and behavioral symptoms reportedly associated with normal menstrual cycles may not have much to do with menstruation, and in any case are not limited to women. Some findings follow:

Failure to observe positive changes. In prospective studies, women's responses vary widely over a 35-day span. Some women do become irritable premenstrually; but many report feeling better and having a burst of creativity and energy. In one such study, Parlee (1982) concluded wryly that she had found evidence for a "premenstrual elation syndrome." Yet when she interviewed the women later, many believed that they had been more irritable and depressed premenstrually, although their own diaries failed to bear them out.

The power of expectations and circumstances. As Parlee showed, studies of PMS that are based on women's retrospective accounts are now known to be distorted by unreliable recall (Gallant & Hamilton, 1988; for a different view, see Richardson, 1990). But prospective studies also have a problem because distortion of daily symptom ratings increases when women know that menstruation is the focus of the research.

In a study by AuBuchon and Calhoun (1985), women with normal cycles and a comparison group of men completed daily mood and symptom diaries. Half of the women knew that menstrual cycle changes were the foucs of the study; the rest did not. The "aware" women reported a significantly higher level of negative moods and physical complaints during the premenstrual phase than did the "unaware" women or the men. The latter two groups did not differ from one another. Thus the belief in PMS itself influences a woman's likelihood of noticing some symptoms and ignoring others at different times, resulting in an increase of negative symptom ratings "by as much as 70%" (Gallant & Hamilton, 1988, p. 274). But when women are unaware that menstrual-cycle changes are the focus of the study, their moods generally have less to do with their "time of the month" than with their "time of the week": positive moods, for both sexes, peak on weekends (McFarlane, Martin, & Williams, 1988).

Failure to use a male comparison. When men fill out checklists of symptoms (with female-specific items, such as breast tenderness, omitted), they report having as many "premenstrual symptoms" as women do. If the list is titled "Menstrual Distress Questionnaire," however, men miraculously lose their headaches, food cravings, and insomnia (Gallant & Hamilton, 1988). As McFarlane et al. (1988) summarized:

> The women were not "moodier" than the men; their moods were not less stable within a day or from day-to-day. Evidence of weekday mood cycles in both sexes suggests that *treating emotional fluctuations as unhealthy symptoms, and assuming that only women usually manifest them, is misleading.* (pp. 216–217; italics added)

Hormones and behavior. Golub (1988) reviewed studies that have tried to find effects of menstruation on the ability to work, from the ability to perform simple motor tasks to complex problem solving. The results, she reports, "confirmed the findings of almost 50 years of research in this area. The menstrual cycle has no consistent demonstrable effect on cognitive tasks, work, or academic performance despite beliefs to the contrary that persist" (p. 17).

In contrast, Dabbs and Morris (1990), in a recent study of 4,462 male veterans, found that unusually high testosterone was associated with delinquency, drug use, having many sex partners, conduct disorders, abusiveness, and violence. Men of higher socioeconomic status had lower testosterone levels and were less likely to commit antisocial acts. Of course, these are correlational data, and it is also true that some behaviors raise testosterone levels. But Dabbs and Morris noted that high testosterone is directly associated only with negative behaviors: "While high testosterone theoretically might lead to prosocial behavior, the present data provide no indication of such redeeming social value" (p. 210).

I do not wish to replace the biological reductionism of female behavior with a biological reductionism of male behavior, but rather to highlight the different diagnoses that society favors and to raise some questions. Of course women are influenced by their bodies—by aches, pains, puffiness, water retention, and headaches; but so are men. Why, then, are women's mood changes a "syndrome," but men's mood changes just "normal ups and downs"? Why are women, but not men, considered "moody," and why are mood changes, which are normal, considered undesirable (Shields, 1987)? Why is the *Wall Street Journal* unruffled about the cost to the economy of men's hormones? Why does the DSM lack a label, such as "Excessive Testosterone Syndrome" or "Amenorrheic Lability Disorder," that reduces male moodiness and antisocial behavior to their hormones?

To ask these questions is to ask who benefits, and who loses, by the creation and application of labels and diagnosis. As Parlee (1989) has shown, the move toward the medicalization of "PMS" has been actively supported by drug companies, which stand to profit greatly if every menstruating woman would take a pill or two every month. Many other groups benefit from this concept: biomedical researchers, medical schools, insurance companies, gynecologists (who have a new problem to treat), and psychiatrists. Obstetricians and psychiatrists are already quarreling over who is best suited to diagnose and treat it. (Similar observations have been made about the medicalization of male erectile dysfunction [Tiefer, 1987].)

But Parlee (1989) reminds us that we must also ask why so many women have warmly embraced the label and resist any argument that menstrual symptoms involve expectation, experience, and situation *as well as* physical changes. She suggests that "the language of 'PMS' is a means by which many women can have their experiences of psychological distress or actions they do not understand validated as 'real' and taken seriously" (p. 16). The label of PMS is empowering for women, she observes, because it gives a medical reality to their experiences that were previously ignored, trivialized, or misunderstood. And it gives women permission to express anger, resentment, and unhappiness that otherwise might be threatening or taboo (Koeske, 1987; Martin, 1987).

I have told this story in some detail because we will hear it over and over, with different words but always the same tune. As the baby-boom generation ages, the saga of PMS will be replayed with another normal stage of women's lives, menopause; as soon as women recover from the "disease" of PMS, they suffer the "disease" of Menopausal Estrogen Deficiency. The *Los Angeles Times* has already featured a report on "Menopause, Baby Boomers' Next Step" (December 5, 1989), subtitled: "Thirty million women are on the verge of the change of life. Although some will suffer little, others are facing challenges . . ." *Some* will suffer little? Then most women will suffer (and need treatment).

As usual, the evidence contradicts these predictions. A study of 2,500 randomly chosen menopausal women in Massachusetts found that, apart from reporting some "temporarily bothersome symptoms," such as hot flashes, sweating, and menstrual irregularity, most of these women said that menopause was "no big deal." The vast majority either regarded menopause as a relief and a pleasure or had no particular feelings about it; only 3% felt regretful (McKinlay, McKinlay, & Brambilla, 1987). The women in this study who reported an increase in depression were primarily those who had had surgical menopause (hysterectomy), and many of them also had a history of affective disorders, physical ailments unrelated to menopause, and a higher than average number of surgeries.

The transformation of women's normal physiology into diseases and syndromes is part of a general pervasive negativity, in science and in the culture, toward normal female reproductive processes. As Martin (1987) showed, textbooks universally describe the process of menstruation in terms of deprivation, deficiency, loss, shedding and sloughing: ". . . disintegration starts, the entire lining begins to slough, and the menstrual flow begins." Before one says, "Well, how else would you describe it?" one should consider the way textbooks describe other bodily processes that are analogous to menstruation. The lining of the stomach is shed and replaced regularly, but textbooks do not describe this process as one of degenerating or sloughing of the stomach lining. They emphasize the "secretion" and "production" of mucous, Martin found, and "—in a phrase that gives the story away—the periodic *renewal* of the lining of the stomach" (p. 50, her emphasis). And although a large proportion of the male ejaculate is composed of waste material, "the texts make no mention of a shedding process let alone processes of deterioration and repair in the male reproductive tract" (p. 51).

If menstruation is a monthly deterioration and failure, menopause represents a permanent deterioration and failure; in 1981, the World Health Organization actually defined menopause as an estrogen-deficiency disease. But why should a process that is normal for all women be construed as a disease? Why aren't the advantages to women of ceasing reproduction emphasized? Of course menopause does involve a reduced production of estrogen and the inability to conceive, and the risks of osteoporosis and heart disease do rise after menopause. Nevertheless, most women do not die from these conditions; most live another active 25 or 30 years. Martin (1987) found only one medical textbook that acknowledges that perhaps menopause is not a disease requiring medical cures. It describes the changes of menopause as a "physiologic phenomenon which is protective in nature—protective from undesirable reproduction and the associated growth stimuli" (cited in Martin, 1987, p. 52).

Like the evidence for "premenstrual elation syndrome," research supports what Jacqueline Goodchilds (personal communication) calls PMF—("Post-Menstrual Freedom")—and what Margaret Mead called "post-menopausal zest." But I predict that we won't be hearing much about PMF or the protective nature of menopause as baby-boom women go through this phase. It is too big a market.[1]

The Pursuit of the Female Brain

The belief that men's and women's brains differ in fundamental ways has a long and inglorious history. Typically, when scientists did not find the anatomical differences they were seeking, they did not abandon the goal or their belief that such differences exist; they just moved to another part of the brain (Shields, 1975). We look back with amusement at the obvious biases of research a century ago, research designed to "prove" the inferiority of women and minorities, but biases and values are just as embedded in research today—old prejudices in new technologies (Bleier, 1988; Epstein, 1988; Harding, 1987; Hubbard, 1990; Keller, 1985).

For example, two widely accepted hypotheses are that the left and right hemispheres develop differently in boys and girls and that the corpus callosum, the bundle of fibers connecting the hemispheres, also differs. As a result, males process visual–spatial information predominantly with the right hemisphere, whereas females use both hemispheres more symmetrically. According to Geschwind and Behan (1982), this sex difference originates during fetal development, when testosterone in

---

[1]Some gynecologists are prepared to prescribe hormone replacements for all menopausal women indefinitely. One physician told a reporter: "The consensus of doctors, the *worldwide* consensus, is that unless there is a contraindication, every menopausal woman should be given estrogen indefinitely to prevent osteoporosis and because of its other beneficial effects." Quoted in Andrea Boroff Eagan, "The Estrogen Fix," *Ms.*, April 1989, p. 43.

male fetuses selectively attacks the left hemisphere, briefly slowing its development and resulting in right-hemisphere dominance in men, which in turn explains why men excel in art, music, and mathematics. Geschwind and Behan's theory has had tremendous scientific and popular appeal. *Science* (December 23, 1983, p. 1312) hailed it with the headline, "Math Genius May Have Hormonal Basis."

The late neuroscientist Ruth Bleier (1988) reviewed Geschwind and Behan's data and original references. One study they had cited, of 507 fetal brains, reported finding no significant sex differences in these brains. If testosterone had an effect on the developing brain, it would surely have been apparent in this large sample. Yet Geschwind and Behan cited this study for other purposes and utterly ignored its findings of no sex differences, reporting as evidence for their hypothesis a study of *rats'* brains. Bleier argued that it is an "unsupported conceptual leap" (p. 157) to generalize from male rat cortices to greater spatial orientation in rats, let alone from rats to humans, especially since there is at present no evidence that spatial orientation is related to asymmetry of the cortex in the first place. *Science* did not publish Bleier's critical paper or even her letter to the Editor.

Another well-publicized study by de Lacoste-Utamsing and Holloway (1982) reported evidence of gender differences in the corpus callosum. The researchers speculated that "the female brain is less well lateralized—that is, manifests less hemispheric specialization—than the male brain for visuospatial functions" (p. 1432). (Notice the language: the female brain is *less well lateralized* than, and by implication inferior to, the male brain, not *more integrated*.)

This article, which also achieved professional acclaim, had a number of major flaws (Bleier, 1988). It was based on a small sample of only 14 brains. Its methodology of sample selection was unstated, so it is possible that pathology was present in some of the brains. It contained numerous unsupported assumptions (for example, there is at present no evidence that the size of the corpus callosum is related to hemispheric specialization). Most damning, the reported sex differences in size of the corpus callosum were not statistically significant ($p = .08$). Bleier wrote to *Science*, delineating these criticisms and also citing four subsequent studies, by her and by others, that independently failed to find gender differences in the corpus callosum. *Science* failed to publish this criticism, as it has failed to publish all studies that find no gender differences in the brain.

The point is not that there are no sex differences in the corpus callosum. Some studies have found differences. The point is that the studies are small and inconclusive, and weak data have been used to support unwarranted speculations, like using pebbles as the foundation for a castle (Caplan et al., 1985). Because these speculations, like those about PMS, fit the dominant beliefs about gender, they receive far more attention and credibility than they warrant.

The irony is that the very things that brain lateralization theories are attempting to account for—gender differences in verbal, spatial, and math abilities—are fast disappearing. In the last 30 years, gender differences in SAT scores have declined sharply (Feingold, 1988). Hyde and Linn (1988) reviewed 165 studies of verbal ability (i.e., skills in vocabulary, writing, anagrams, reading comprehension, and speaking fluency), which represented tests of 1,418,899 people. The concluded that there are no gender differences in verbal ability at this time in America, adding: "Thus our research pulls out one of the two wobbly legs on which the brain lateralization theories have rested" (p. 63).

The other leg—the assumption of differences in mathematics and spatial ability—is being eroded too. Caplan et al. (1985), in their critique of research on spatial abilities, found the construct itself to be problematic, as well as a pattern either of no sex differences or differences of marginal statistical significance. And Hyde et al. (1990), in a meta-analysis of 100 studies of mathematics performance representing the testing of 3,985,682 students, found that gender differences were smallest and favored *females* in samples of the general population, and grew larger, favoring males, only in selected samples of highly precocious individuals. Is everybody's brain changing?

I consider it good news that cognitive gender differences are diminishing rapidly, but that is not the major lesson to be drawn here. Although meta-analyses are a powerful and important tool, they describe only the studies that go into them (Unger, 1990). If, in 10 years, cognitive gender differences return, will we conclude that it was all a matter of brain lateralization differences after all? I hope not. For gender differences or similarities in cognitive abilities to change so rapidly, they must be a result of education, motivation, and opportunity, not innate differences between male and female brains (Epstein, 1988).

Biological theories of gender differences cannot account for changes over time (Unger, 1990). Two decades ago, theories postulated numerous internal psychological barriers and biological limitations that were thought to keep women out of "men's work" like medicine, law, and bartending. When the external barriers to these professions fell, the speed with which women entered them was dizzying (Nieva & Gutek, 1981; Tavris & Wade, 1984). Today we would be amused to think that women have a fear-of-success problem or a brain-lateralization deficiency that is keeping them out of law school. But we hear often about internal psychological barriers and biological limitations that are keeping women out of science, math, and politics (Epstein, 1988).

Moreover, the focus on small, measurable definitions of cognitive abilities deflects us from more important questions. Does it really matter, asked Hyde and Linn (1988), that men and women no longer differ on tests of reading comprehension or vocabulary, when, in terms of total talking time in the workplace, frequency of interruptions, and control of conversational topics, men far exceed women? Ultimately, the significance and appeal of biological reductionism (as opposed to biological interactionism) is precisely that it avoids such real-world questions. As Ruth Bleier (1987) concluded:

> Such efforts directed at the callosum (or any other particular structure in the brain, for that matter) are today's equivalent of 19th century craniology: if you can find a bigger bump here or a smaller one there on a person's skull, if you can find a more bulbous splenium here or a more slender one there . . . you will know something significant about their intelligence, their personality, their aspirations, their astrological sign, their gender and race, and their status in society. We are still mired in the naive hope that we can find something that we can *see* and *measure* and it will explain everything. It is silly science and it serves us badly. (pp. 11–12; Bleier's italics)

Deconstructing and Reconstructing Gender

If women are not deficient men, or better men, or different from men, or the same as men, what are they? Where are all the differences that everyone knows exists?

In a critical appraisal of approaches to the study of gender, Crawford and Marecek (1989b) described the recent emergence of the "transformation framework"—so labeled because it questions the assumptions that psychologists bring to the study of gender itself, and requires us to break out of the usual frameworks and conceptions in research, psychotherapy, and social problems (Morawski, 1990; for a bibliography on these new directions, see Crawford & Marecek, 1989a).

The transformation framework includes a daunting variety of names: social constructionism, literary deconstructionism, postrealism, feminist poststructuralism, postmodernism. However, I believe this movement, by any name, may be as significant an intellectual revolution as those wrought by Copernicus, Darwin, and Freud in their fields. The earth is not the centerpiece of the solar system, human beings are not the centerpiece of creation, the ego is not the centerpiece of the mind, and man is not the centerpiece of experience and knowledge—neither the generic man nor the individual man (M. Gergen, 1988; Keller, 1985; Minnich, 1990).

What all of these approaches have in common "is an emphasis on the person's active role, guided by his or her culture, in structuring reality" (Tiefer, 1987, p. 71); they therefore contrast with empiricism and positivism, which emphasize objective facts and possibility of finding single truths, single essences (K. Gergen, 1985; Morawski, 1990). Although this movement is considered new to the American academy and is causing impassioned debate about threats to the curriculum and basic notions of science, it has long been intrinsic to Eastern philosophy. Zen teaches that the universe is in a constant state of flux, that art and science exist in an always-shifting context rather than as autonomous entities, that events and objects depend on the perception of the beholder as much as on their own qualities.

The transformationist goal is to reveal how the concepts and categories we use, which seem timeless and universal, vary in their meanings and connotations throughout history and across cultures. Concepts such as "romantic love," "childhood," "mother's love," "the self," and "emotion" have meant different things at different times (K. Gergen, 1985); there is no single essence to being, let alone defining, a "homosexual," a "nymphomaniac" (a label for its era, as "inhibited sexual desire" is the label in ours), a "man" or a "woman."

This movement is sweeping social science, literature, history, sociology, law, and other fields. In linguistics, George Lakoff (1989) attacked the premise of 2,000 years of Western philosophy that linguistic categories accurately mirror patterns of nature; on the contrary, Lakoff argues, we impose our categories, schemas, and stereotypes on nature. In anthropology, Renato Rosaldo (1989) shows that the belief in universal, timeless truths is no longer the monopoly view. It now competes with the many truths of case studies that are embedded in specific contexts. And in sexology, Tiefer (1987, 1988) argues that current writing about sexuality has been dominated by a narrow medical perspective, the view that if we can only identify the universal physiological responses, the simple steps of a "response cycle," and the magic button or spot, sexual satisfaction would be assured. Social constructionists have countered that there are no essences or universalities to sexual experience—gay or straight, male or female (see Kitzinger, 1987).

These new approaches are a source of heated controversy among feminists as well as between liberals and conservatives. I do not have space here to consider the debate in detail, and I refer the interested reader to Marecek (1989) and previous citations. But I disagree with those who fear that this movement means that we must throw up our hands in despair on the grounds that no one can know anything, or that because perceptions vary there can be no common discourse or agreement, or that the traditional methods and findings of social science are useless. (I've relied on many of them in this chapter.) In my view, postmodern approaches do not require us to abandon former methods, but to examine them, to add new ones, to expand our views of the problems we investigate (Peplau & Conrad, 1989). As Marecek (1989) noted: "The turn to metatheory and epistemology allows us to see how the discipline of psychology disciplines us: how it structures the categories we think in, regulates the knowledge we produce, and restrains our imagination" (p. 375).

This last section will address two areas of research that help resolve the paradox of gender and reinvigorate our imaginations. They provide alternatives to the familiar goal of counting vanishing gender differences in personality traits, skills, and cognitions, while illuminating the profound differences that still divide men and women in their daily lives. The first seeks a renewed emphasis on the external factors and contexts that perpetuate or reduce gendered behavior. The second focuses on the ways that women and men perceive, interpret, and respond to events that befall them—the stories they tell about their lives.

The Power of Context and the Context of Power

In 1988 Ann Hopkins sued Price Waterhouse for discrimination in not granting her partnership status. Hopkins' supporters described her behavior as outspoken, independent, self-confident, and courageous. Her detractors interpreted the same behavior as overbearing, arrogant, self-centered and abrasive. They thought she should be more "feminine."

At the same time that Hopkins case was wending its way to the Supreme Court (where she eventually won), an attorney named Brenda Taylor lost her job because she appeared *too* feminine: she favored short skirts, designer blouses, ornate jewelry, and spike heels. Her boss told her that she looked like a "bimbo," and she was fired after she complained about his remarks to the Equal Employment Opportunity Commission.

Ann Hopkins and Brenda Taylor illustrate the pressures on modern women to be both feminine and masculine, to be different from men but also the same. How is a woman supposed to behave? Like an ideal male, in which case her male colleagues will accuse her of not being feminine enough, or like an ideal female, in which case her male colleagues will accuse her of not being masculine enough?

In the transformationist perspective, we will never know the truth about Ann Hopkins' personality, because both sets of perceptions are true, from the beholder's standpoint. But by framing the problem as one of her personality, her colleagues deflected attention from the systematic practices of their company and from their own behavior. Suppose, instead, we ask this question: "Under what conditions are negative evaluations of women like Hopkins more likely to occur?" The answer is, when the woman (or member of a minority) is a token member of the organization; when the criteria used to evaluate the woman are ambiguous; and when observers lack necessary information to evaluate the woman's work (American Psychological Association, 1988). All three conditions were met in Hopkins's situation. She could have gone to work dressed in a muumuu or Saran Wrap, and she still would have lost that promotion. Her personality had nothing to do with it.

As this example suggests, gender does not consist fo a set of fixed "masculine" or "feminine" traits; the qaulities and behaviors expected of women and men vary across settings and interactions (Morawski,

1990; Unger, 1990). The result is what West and Zimmerman (1987) call "doing gender": gender is defined, redefined, and shaped by ongoing social processes. Deaux and Major (1987) have identified some of these processes, finding that gender-related behaviors are influenced by the expectations of perceivers, self-perceptions of the target, and the situation that both participants are in. That is, the behavior that we link to gender depends more on what an individual is doing and needs to do than on his or her biological sex or even sex role.

For example, Barbara Risman (1987) compared the parenting skills and personality traits of single fathers, single mothers, and married parents. If biological predispositions or sex-role socialization create stable personality differences between men and women, then fathers should differ from mothers in their baby-care skills, regardless of marital status. In fact, Risman found that having responsibility for child care was as strongly related to "feminine" traits, such as nurturance and sympathy, as being female was. The single men who were caring for children were more like mothers than like married fathers. (Neither were these men an atypical group of "nurturant" men; they had custody of their children through circumstances beyond their control—widowhood, the wife's desertion, or the wife's lack of interest in shared custody.)

If we look closely at what men and women do as a result of their roles, statuses, and obligations, we find a wealth of gender differences, of which Table 2 presents a small sampling. For instance, research has found that women have more than the two basic roles of home and work. Women have many jobs. They do the "interaction work" in conversations—making sure feelings aren't hurt and keeping the ball rolling (Fishman, 1983; McConnell-Ginet, 1983). They do the invisible but time-consuming "kin work" of managing extended family relationships, such as organizing celebrations, sending holiday and birthday cards, making phone calls to keep in touch (Di Leonardo, 1987). They do the "emotion work" in close relations, monitoring the course of the relationship and participants' feelings, and are more likely than men to be in occupations that require the display of cheerful emotion (Hochschild, 1983; Shields, 1987). And they work fully an extra month of 24-hour-days per year in comparison to husbands, doing a "second shift" of child care and housekeeping (Hochschild, 1989).

Rhoda Unger (1990) recently noted that "Research on sex differences does not cocnern itself with behaviors in which the rate is virtually zero for one sex" (p. 104)—such as rape. Studies of sex differences, she noted, have focused on those that are the least significant and the most variable. But sexual coercion, rape, and other forms of violence against women—in dating relationships (Gavey, 1989), in marriage (Gelles & Straus, 1989; Russell, 1982), by strangers (Koss, 1990; Walker, 1989)—permeate the lives of women as they do not permeate the lives of men.

The traditional focus on gender differences in personality traits has overshadowed the importance of experiences and activities, and also of

Table 2
Gender Comparisons: A Summary of Selected Topics

Where the comparisons are not	Where the comparisons are
Attachment, affiliation	Caretaking
Cognitive abilities	Communication, influence styles,
Verbal[a], mathematical[b],	"interaction work"
reasoning, rote memory,	Context analysis (e.g., roles)
vocabulary, reading, etc.	Discourse: Constructing the world
Dependency	Emotional context and display
Empathy	Contexts that produce emotions
Moods and "moodiness"	Emotion work
Moral reasoning	"Feminization of distress"
Need for achievement	"Feminization of love"
Need for affiliation	Forms of expression
Need for power	Employment, income, work roles
Nurturance[c]	Health
Pacifism, belligerence	Medication and treatment
(e.g., depersonalizing enemies)	Longevity differences
Verbal aggression	Income
	Life narratives, life dreams
	Life-span development
	Effects of children
	Family and career "clocks"
	Power and status at work, in
	relationships, in society
	Reproductive experiences
	Reproductive technology and its
	social/legal consequences
	"Second shift": housework, child
	care, kinship obligations
	Sexual experiences and concerns
	Violence, public and intimate
	Weight and body image

[a]Males more susceptible to some verbal problems; however, the sex difference in dyslexia, long assumed to be more prevalent among boys than girls, turns out to be an artifact of referral bias: more boys are reported for help than girls, but there are no sex differences in the prevalence of reading disabilities (Shaywitz, Shaywitz, Fletcher, & Escobar, 1990).
[b]Males excel at highest levels of math performance; in general population, females have slight advantage.
[c]As a capacity; in practice, women do more of the actual care and feeding of children, parents, relatives, friends.

the immediate *context* in which men and women live (Deaux, 1984; Frieze, 1990). For example, studies of aging find few significant gender differences per se in adjustment, satisfaction, cognitive abilities, and the like, but older women experience the "double jeopardy" of being old and female (Rodeheaver & Datan, 1988). They are more vulnerable than aging men because of their greater likelihood of poverty, widowhood (and ensuing economic insecurities), caregiving responsiblities, and biases in the mental health system that lead to overmedicating their problems and underestimating their capabilities.

Eleanor Maccoby (1990) has recently described the importance of contexts in understanding child development. Starting in earliest childhood, boys and girls develop different styles of play and influence. But they do not differ in "passivity" or "activity" in some consistent, trait-like way; *their behavior depends on the gender of the child with whom they are playing.* Among children as young as three, for example, girls are seldom passive with each other; however, when paired with boys, girls typically stand on the sidelines and let the boys monopolize the toys. This gender segregation, Maccoby (1988) found, is "essentially unrelated to the individual attributes of the children who make up all-girl or all-boy groups" (p. 755). Instead, it is related to the fact that between the ages of 3½ and 5½, boys stop responding to the influence strategies of girls. When a boy and girl compete for a shared toy, the boy dominates—unless there is an adult in the room. Girls in mixed classrooms stay nearer to the teacher, this research suggests, not because they are more "dependent" as a personality trait, but because they want a chance at the toys! Girls play just as independently as boys when they are in all-girl groups, when they will actually sit *farther* from the teacher than boys in all-male groups do.

By elementary school, the interaction and influence styles of boys and girls have diverged significantly. Girls tend to form intimate "chumships" with one or two other girls; boys form group friendships organized around games and other activities. Boys in all-boy groups are more likely than girls to interrupt one another; use commands, threats, or boasts; refuse to comply with another child's wishes; heckle a speaker; call another child names; top someone else's story; and tell jokes. Girls in all-girl groups are more likely than boys to agree with another speaker verbally; pause to give another girl a chance to speak; and acknowledge what a previous speaker said (Maltz & Borker, 1982). Among boys, Maccoby (1990) concluded, "speech serves largely egoistic functions and is used to establish and protect an individual's turf. Among girls, conversation is a more socially binding process" (p. 516).

Yet just as Maccoby observed with children, Linda Carli (1990) has found that people's ways of speaking often depend more on the gender of the person with whom they are speaking than on their own "conversational style." Women speak more tentatively than men do, she found, primarily when they are speaking to men. With men, they offer more disclaimers, use more hedges and moderating terms (like the use of *like*), and use more tag questions that solicit agreement. Many young women use such hesitations and tags when they speak with men, Carli also found, because young men are more *influenced* by a woman who speaks hesitatingly than one who speaks assertively. When a woman uses tentative language with a man, Carli concludes, she may be communicating that she has no wish to enhance her own status or challenge his.

This line of research is evidence for the view that gender, like culture, organizes for its members different influence strategies, ways of communicating, nonverbal languages, and ways of perceiving the world (Maltz & Borker, 1982). Just as when in Rome most people do as Romans do, the behavior of women and men depends more on the gender of the person with whom they are interacting than on anything intrinsic about the gender they themselves are.

But there is an important qualification to the "two cultures" approach to gender differences, because the two cultures of gender are not equal in power, resources, or status. This is why women are more likely to become "bilingual" than men are—better able to "read" men and "speak" male-speak than men are at "reading" and "speaking" female-speak. Men are often charmed and amused by what they regard as the "mysterious" behavior of women, but they typically feel no need to decipher it; women learn that for their own safety they had better try to understand and predict the behavior of men (Lakoff, 1990). Some researchers (e.g., Hall, 1984) believe that women are superior to men in nonverbal skills, regardless of contexts. But other research suggests that many behaviors thought to be typical of women are artifacts of a power imbalance. Consider the following:

• Snodgrass (1985) found that "women's intuition"—the ability to read nonverbal cues—was a function of powerlessness rather than gender; when men interact with a more powerful woman, they show as much "female intuition" as women do when interacting with a more powerful man.

• Dovidio, Ellyson, Keating, Heltman, and Brown (1988) found that both men and women who were high in expertise or reward power displayed high visual dominance (the ratio of looking while speaking to looking while listening). High visual dominance ratios are associated with high power, and both sexes behave the same way when they have power. When they do not, their visual behavior confirms the gender stereotype.

• O'Barr & Atkins (1980), in a study of male and female witnesses in a courtroom setting, found that the hesitations and uncertainties of so-called women's speech (pauses, hedges, "sort ofs," and the like) are a function of powerlessness, social position, and the courtroom context. See also McConnell-Genet, 1983, 1984.

In psychology, as in society at large, interest in power and roles as explanatory variables has faded in favor of individual, internal processes such as biology and psychodynamics (Kahn & Yoder, 1989; Mednick, 1989). One practical result has been the continual reinvention of the wheel, in theory and psychotherapy. Thus every few years another best-selling book sweeps over the land, purporting to explain to women the origins of their unhappiness. The symptoms these books attempt to treat are always the same: low self-esteem, passivity, depression, an "exaggerated" sense of responsibility to others, and an inability to break out of bad relationships. The problem has been diagnosed as a fear of success, a Superwoman Syndrome, a Cinderella Complex, a Wendy Dilemma, or "loving too much." Today the problem is defined as the "disease" of "codependence"—women are addicted to abusers, bad relationships, and people with addictions (Gomberg, 1989; Tavris, in press).

The codependency language does reflect an important aspect of family dynamics, namely that every member of a group affects every other member (H. Lerner, 1988). But codependency's emphasis on inner feelings and the language of chronic sickness obscures the external limitations, power inequities, and *normal female role obligations* that keep many women trapped in bad relationships. In a review of research investigating why women leave abusive relationships and why they stay, Strube (1988) found "a picture of women who lack the economic means to leave an abusive relationship, are willing to tolerate abuse so long as it does not become too severe or involve the children, and who appear to be very committed to making their relationships last" (p. 240). Many are also opposed to divorce for religious reasons and are trapped in a network of friends and family who pressure them to stay in the marriage and who look disapprovingly on their efforts to leave.

Likewise, popular explanations of why more women have not reached the highest pinnacles of power have tended to blame women, in one way or an other, for a failure of motivation or a personal inability to combine family and career. In a review of the literature on gender and power in organizations, Ragins and Sundstrom (1989) examined the longitudinal development of gender differences in power. Women, more than men, typified, a "psychological cycle of powerlessness," blaming themselves, losing self-confidence, and limiting their ambitions. But these psychological symptoms proved to be results of powerlessness, not causes. The levels of power outside and inside organizations interact differently for men and women such that men tend to develop more power as they progress through their careers, whereas most women do not. Ragins and Sundstrom (1989) concluded, "Research reveals a consistent difference favoring men in accessibility to, and utility of, resources for power. It suggests that the processes involved in the development of power differ for men and women and that the path to power for women resembles an obstacle course" (p. 51). Powerlessness perpetuates powerlessness.

Gender as Narrative

George Gerbner once defined the human being as "the only species that tells stories—and lives by the stories we tell" (personal communication, November 3, 1984). Contemporary magazines reveal one possible gender difference in the stories that men and women tell about their lives, as shown in Table 3. That is, most magazines directed to women include a horoscope, a mystic, or a numerologist; not one men's magazine does.

Table 3
Presence or Absence of Horoscopes in Leading Magazines Directed Primarily to Women or Men

Women's magazines		Men's magazines	
Cosmopolitan	yes	*Esquire*	no
Elle	yes[a]	*Fame*	no
Glamour	yes	*Field & Stream*	no
Harper's Bazaar	yes	*Forbes*	no
In Fashion	yes	*Fortune*	no
Lear's	yes	*Gentleman's Quarterly*	no
Mademoiselle	yes	*Golf*	no
Marie Claire	yes	*M (The Civilized Man)*	no
Mirabella	yes[b]	*MGF (Men's Guide to Fashion)*	no
Moxie	yes[c]	*Manhattan, Inc.*	no
New Woman	yes	*Men's Fitness*	no
Sassy	yes	*Money*	no
Self	yes	*Penthouse*	no
Seventeen	yes	*Playboy*	no
Taxi	yes	*Popular Mechanics*	no
Vogue	yes	*Soldier of Fortune*	no
Woman	yes	*Sports Afield*	no
Family Circle	no	*Sports Illustrated*	no
Good Housekeeping	no	*Success*	no
Ladies Home Journal	no	*Tennis*	no
McCall's	no		
New York Woman	no		
Redbook	no		
Working Woman	no		

Note. General-interest magazines directed at both sexes (*Atlantic, Harper's, People, Time,* etc.) have been omitted. Most of these do not have horoscopes, with the notable exception of *TV Guide.*
[a]Has a horoscope *and* a numerology column.
[b]Has a "Mystic of the Month" column.
[c]Had a column by a self-proclaimed psychic answering readers' queries.

Even new magazines for older women, such as *Lear's* and *Mirabella*, have them. Why? Horoscopes are cheap to produce, advertisers compete to position their ads next to them, and readers demand them.

I do not suggest that women are more gullible or superstitious than men—or, in the positive construction of this difference, more open-minded and spiritual! Actually, studies of the general population find that women are only slightly more likely than men to believe in astrology, and that this difference is largely a function of differences in age and education (Gallup & Newport, 1991). But if we examine one meaning of horoscopes, we find an unobtrusive measure of a difference in female and male locus of control, in the perception of opportunities and "destinies." It is no coincidence that the magazines (which both sexes read) called *Fame, Success, Money,* and *Fortune* do not have horoscopes, because astrology contradicts the capitalist message that anyone can become anything with enough hard work. Likewise it is significant that magazines about careers, families, and motherhood—*Working Woman, New York Woman, Family Circle, Good Housekeeping*—do not have horoscopes. Mothers and employed women, apparently, know that their fate has little to do with the stars and everything to do with time management. But in the magazines for women about relationships, beauty, youth, and the pursuit of perfection—goals which women feel increasingly to be out of their control, increasingly a source of anxiety—the implicit narrative tells women they can have it all, at least if their stars and their cosmetics are in place.

Theodore Sarbin (1986) has proposed that the life story is the key metaphor in understanding human behavior: Plans, memories, love affairs, and hatreds "are guided by narrative plots" (p. 11). Sarbin argues that using narratives as a metaphor for understanding human behavior is a more fruitful direction for psychology than the dated positivistic model of natural science on which psychology was built.

Men and women have a repertoire of life stories relevant to their own gender, observes Mary Gergen (in press): "Understanding one's past, interpreting one's actions, evaluating future possibilities—each is filtered through these stories. Events 'make sense' as they are placed in the correct story form" (p. 10). In the classic myth of the hero, the man ventures forth from everyday life to conquer supernatural forces in the name of his quest; he returns, victorious, and is richly rewarded. "Where is the woman in this story?" asks Gergen. "She is only to be found as a snare, an obstacle, a magic power, or a prize" (p. 7). Women are not even heroes of their own stories. What effect does this have on their identities and dreams? Here, in the stories that men and women tell about their lives, we find the greatest divergence between them (Heilbrun, 1989).

For example, Catherine Riessman (1990) contrasted the stories that wives and husbands tell about their divorces in order to make sense of what happened to them: the protagonists, the inciting provocations, the culminating events. Women and men tell different stories, designed to persuade both teller and listener that the divorce was inevitable, justified, and for the best. The accounts reveal a paradox: "Women and men construct heavily gendered definitions of what marriage ought to be, but at the same time they mourn these gender tensions and blame their divorces on them," Riessman found (p. 23). Women and men define the meaning of emotional intimacy differently. Women want deep talk about feelings and problems, and small talk about mundane events; in men's definitions of emotional closeness, talk is not critical.

Reissman (1990) suggests that this difference stems from the "feminization of psychological distress": the fact that traditional ways of measuring distress are constructed on typically female responses such as crying, sadness, and eating disorders. The result is that many men are excluded from the very languages of love and distress, leading to incorrect inferences that men suffer less than women when relationships are in trouble, or that men are "incapable" of love. Riessman (1990) found that after divorce, most men do not report the usual symptoms of depression, because these are not the "culturally approved idioms for men" (p. 157). Men turn to responses that are stereotypically masculine, that they have a vocabulary for, that they can reveal without conflict or shame. By not understanding men's discourse of grief, Riessman argues, many psychologists and laypeople infer that there is something wrong with men because they seem not to feel anything after divorce or loss.

By usurping the language of emotion—a component of the female role that specifies greater emotional responsiveness in general (Eagly, 1987)—women seem to differ from men not only in that famous negative emotion, depression (Nolen-Hoeksema, 1990; Strickland, 1988) but also in positive emotions. Wood, Rhodes, and Whelan (1989), in a meta-analysis of 93 studies of well-being, found that women are slightly but significantly more likely than men to report greater happiness and satisfaction *and* that they are more likely to report greater negative affect. But these results are role-related; they obtain primarily among married people.

Other evidence likewise suggests that the genders differ primarily in the contexts that produce emotion, not in emotions themselves (Shields, 1987; Tavris, 1989). Stapley and Haviland (1989) found that for adolescent boys, "emotional salience"—the frequency, intensity, and duration of emotion—was highest in response to activities and achievement, whereas girls found affiliation to be of greatest emotional salience. Boys were more likely to report having had feelings of sadness when they were alone; girls, when they were with others. Like Riessman, Stapley and Haviland (1989) suggested that depression scales are biased by measuring deviation from female emotional experience and do not contain many items reflecting male emotional experience.

Wood et al. (1989) concluded that because men and women differ in positive and negative emotions, neither gender has an advantage "in the adaptiveness and desirability of their different styles of emotional life" (p. 260). I wish to underscore this point. Women gain much from their greater "emotional expertise"—social support, being understood by psychotherapists, validation of experience—but they pay a price in rehearsing and brooding over problems rather than learning to distract themselves or take action against them (Nolen-Hoeksema, 1990).

If women have articulated a language of emotion and distress, they are inarticulate, I would argue, in a language of sexuality, of the body. Harriet Lerner (1988) has observed that women do not even accurately name their genitals; at best, little girls are taught that they have a vagina, which becomes the word for everything "down there"; girls rarely learn that they also have a vulva and clitoris. As I noted earlier, the scientific "stories" of menstruation and menopause are almost uniformly told in a language of loss and deterioration (Martin, 1987). Should we then be surprised that women are vulnerable to the diagnoses, labels, and theories—that is, the language, the story—provided by "experts" (Tavris, in press)?

The social–constructionist approach to the stories that men and women tell has two important implications for researchers and psychotherapists. The first is that it alerts us to the hazard of imposing our theories prematurely, especially when the subjects of study are of a different gender, class, or culture (Peplau & Campbell, 1989). Riessman (1987), who contrasted interviews with Anglo American and Puerto Rican women talking about their marital separations, found that culture overrode gender. The Anglo American middle-class woman told a linear story of events through time; the Puerto Rican working-class woman described episodes. Each story symbolized to the speaker what her marital problems were, but whereas the Anglo American interviewer could "hear" and understand the first woman, she remained "out of sync" with the second. Many psychologists may be "out of sync" with what different cultures are saying to them. New trends in discourse analysis (e.g., Gavey, 1989) sharpen the ability to observe and hear what interviewees say.

The second implication of studying gender as narrative is that rather than trying to find the "right" story or the "official" story, we can direct our attention to the origins, contexts, and consequences of stories. What are the supports for stories that use a vocabulary of "disease," "deficiency," and astrological destiny rather than a vocabulary of power, context, and roles? If a woman wishes to believe that her problem is PMS or codependency rather than an abusive or simply unresponsive husband, how does she benefit? How does she lose? One consequence might be survival of the marriage (Hochschild, 1989); another might be depression, which is tied closely to women's greater likelihood of having had experiences with abuse and violence (Koss, 1990; McGrath et al.,

1990; Russo, 1990) and blaming themselves for these events (Nolen-Hoeksema, 1990).

But social constructionists would emphasize that there is nothing essential to men's and women's *natures* that causes the difference in their stories. Francesca Cancian (1987) traced the "feminization of love" in this century, the economic and social events that caused women to become the "love experts" as part of their roles and expertise, in contrast to male roles. And women's "emotion work" in occupations developed with the rise of a service industry (Hochschild, 1983). Stories have consequences, but stories change, and how and why they do is the heart of the psychological enterprise.

Conclusions

The mismeasure of woman has done serious harm to women's feelings about themselves, to their relationships, and to their position in society. It is responsible for the analyses that leave women feeling that once again they lack the right stuff and aren't doing the right thing. It has made sicknesses and syndromes of women's normal bodily processes, and diseases of women's role obligations. It has turned societal attention inward, to biology and psyche. And it has polarized the discourse between men and women, relegating to women's "special nature" the human qualities of feeling, attachment, connection, and care.

Future research and applications can, however, begin to build bridges between the concepts of "normal" men and "different" women in the following ways:

1. Recognizing that female physiology is not "abnormal," but normal for women, and that there are many ways to be "normal." Women experience menstruation, pregnancy, childbirth, and menopause in many diverse ways, a result in class, culture, physiology, temperament, and experience. Yet menopause and menstruation need not be perceived as sicknesses, losses, and legal disabilities but as healthy states, renewals, and transitions.

2. Reclaiming the psychological qualities historically associated with female deficiency, but within a framework of synthesis rather than opposition (Goodrich, Rampage, Ellman, & Halstead, 1988). For example, dependence, typically viewed as feminine and bad, is a basic human need—and can be good. Women do not need to stop being conciliatory in order to be leaders, or to stop caring for others in order to be autonomous. Connection and autonomy are both necessary in human life. The goal for both sexes should be to add qualities and skills, not lose old ones.

3. Realizing that qualities, skills, and behaviors change over the life span, and identifying the factors and contexts that produce or retard change. The exaggerated sex games of adolescence are not, thank God, a blueprint for life. People develop, learn, have adventures and new experiences; and as they do, their notions of masculinity and femininity change, too (Gutmann, 1987; Josselson, 1987). Gender rules and behavior are not frozen at one moment in time, whether the psychologically fashionable time is thought to be infancy, childhood, or adolescence (Maccoby, 1990; Stacey & Thorne, 1985; Unger, 1990).

4. Turning our attention to the way that questions are posed, influencing the answers that are produced. Typically, when people wonder why some battered wives stay with their husbands, they ask "Are these women masochistic? Do they believe they deserve abuse?" The problem is constructed as the battered wives. Yet when people wonder why husbands batter wives, they rarely use comparable language: "Are men sadistic? Do they believe they deserve to abuse others?" Instead, their explanations focus on the pressures men are under, their own abuse as children, or the wife's provocations (Caplan, 1989; Walker, 1989). Similarly, Paula Caplan (1989) showed that the widespread assumption that mothers are to blame for all of their children's problems has deflected attention from fathers, peers, the children themselves, and environmental factors.

5. Examining the biases and values we bring to the processes of research and psychotherapy and to their findings. Social constructionism simply makes explicit the processes that are going on all the time. We can easily discern the political purpose of the diagnosis of "drapetomania," a pre–Civil War "disease" that afflicted slaves with an uncontrollable urge to run away from slavery (Landrine, 1988); it is equally important to identify the social and political uses of diagnoses such as PMS and Self-Defeating Personality Disorder today. We can discern political motives behind Freud's refusal to listen to the stories of abuse his patients told him (Lerman, 1986); we must be just as aware of political motives behind modern observers' categories of "abuse" and "sexual coercion" when participants do not construct their experiences this way (Gavey, 1989). We recognize the bias in labeling as "sick" those women, years ago, who did not play the traditional role; we must also recognize the bias in labeling as "sick" (e.g., "addicted") those women today who play the same role too well.

6. Opening our perceptions to the stories people tell as well as to the stories we expect them to tell. By setting aside predetermined categories, we have learned that the male model of adult development does not apply to all women (Gilligan, Ward, & Taylor, 1989; Josselson, 1987); that the Masters and Johnson medical model of sexuality does not apply to all women or men (Tiefer, 1987); that the female model of emotional expressivity does not apply to all men (Riessman, 1990). We have learned that there is no one right way to have (or combine) a marriage, a baby, a career (Crosby, 1987), no one right way to be straight or gay (Kitzinger, 1987), no one right way to be a parent (Caplan, 1989).

This does not mean, in my view, that we must abandon the scientific enterprise. As Ellen Kimmel (1989) observed, "I am convinced . . . that the personal is not only political or professional, but also scientific" (p. 144). We can, she said, recognize the pitfalls and limitations of self-report, but also acknowledge "that a young science needs to look and describe before it constructs and explains" (p. 144).

Ultimately, I believe that the study of gender will lead us to an appreciation of diversity and commonality if we can transform and transcend the oldest vision of difference. As long as the question is framed as "What do we do about *them*, the other, the opposite?"—it can never be answered. The question, rather, is this: "What shall we do about *us*, so that our relationships, our work, our children, and our planet will flourish?"

References

American Psychological Association. (1988). Brief for amicus curiae in support of respondent Ann B. Hopkins. Washington, DC: American Psychological Association.

Anderson, B. S., & Zinsser, J. P. (Eds.). (1988). *A history of their own: Women in Europe from prehistory to the present: Vols. I and II*. New York: Harper & Row.

Aries, E. J., & Olver, R. R. (1985). Sex differences in the development of a separate sense of self during infancy: Directions for future research. *Psychology of Women Quarterly, 9*, 515–532.

Attie, I., & Brooks-Gunn, J. (1987). Weight concerns as chronic stressors in women. In R. Barnett, L. Biener, & G. Baruch (Eds.), *Gender and stress* (pp. 218–254). New York: The Free Press.

AuBuchon, P. G., & Calhoun, K. S. (1985). Menstrual cycle symptomatology: The role of social expectancy and experimental demand characteristics. *Psychosomatic Medicine, 47*, 35–45.

Benbow, C., & Stanley, J. (1980). Sex differences in mathematical ability: Fact or artifact? *Science, 210*, 1262–1264.

Bennett, W., & Gurin, J. (1982). *The dieter's dilemma: Eating less and weighing more*. New York: Basic Books.

Biaggio, M. K. (1988, August). *Sex differences in anger: Are they real?* Paper presented at the 96th annual convention of the American Psychological Association, Atlanta, Georgia.

Bleier, R. (1987, February). *Sex differences research in the neurosciences.* Paper presented at the annual meeting of the American Association for the Advancement of Science, Chicago.

Bleier, R. (1988). Sex differences research: Science or belief? In R. Bleier (Ed.), *Feminist approaches to science* (pp. 147–164). New York: Pergamon.

Cancian, F. M. (1987). *Love in America: Gender and self-development*. Cambridge, England: Cambridge University Press.

Canetto, S. S. (in press). Suicide attempts and substance abuse: Similarities and differences. *Journal of Psychology*.

Caplan, P. J. (1989). *Don't blame mother: Mending the mother–daughter relationship.* New York: Harper & Row.

Caplan, P. J., MacPherson, G. M., & Tobin, P. (1985). Do sex-related differences in spatial abilities exist? *American Psychologist, 40,* 786–799.

Caplan, P. J., McCurdy-Myers, J., & Gans, M. (1990). *Should PMS be called a psychiatric abnormality?* Unpublished manuscript (under review), Ontario Institute for Studies in Education, Toronto.

Carli, L. L. (1990). Gender, language, and influence. *Journal of Personality and Social Psychology, 59,* 941–951.

Chodorow, N. (1978). *The reproduction of mothering.* Berkeley, CA: University of California Press.

Cochran, S. D., & Peplau, L. A. (1985). Value orientations in heterosexual relationships. *Psychology of Women Quarterly, 9,* 477–488.

Cohn, L. D. (1991). Sex differences in the course of personality development: A meta-analysis. *Psychological Bulletin, 109,* 252–266.

Colby, A., & Damon, W. (1987). Listening to a different voice: A review of Gilligan's *In a different voice.* In M. R. Walsh (Ed.), *The psychology of women: Ongoing debates* (pp. 321–329). New Haven, CT: Yale University Press.

Crawford, M., & Marecek, J. (1989a). Feminist theory, feminist psychology: A bibliography of epistemology, critical analysis, and applications. *Psychology of Women Quarterly, 13,* 477–491.

Crawford, M., & Marecek, J. (1989b). Psychology reconstructs the female: 1968–1988. *Psychology of Women Quarterly, 13,* 147–165.

Crosby, F. J. (Ed.). (1987). *Spouse, parent, work: On gender and multiple roles.* New Haven, CT: Yale University Press.

Crosby, F. J. (1989). *Gender and personality: Illusions and reality.* Paper presented at Rutgers University, New Brunswick, NJ.

Dabbs, J. M., Jr., & Morris, R. (1990). Testosterone, social class, and antisocial behavior in a sample of 4,462 men. *Psychological Science, 1,* 209–211.

Deaux, K. (1984). From individual differences to social categories: Analysis of a decade's research on gender. *American Psychologist, 39,* 105–116.

Deaux, K., & Major, B. (1987). Putting gender into context: An interactive model of gender-related behavior. *Psychological Review, 94,* 369–389.

DeJong, R., Rubinow, D. R., Roy-Byrne, P., Hoban, M. C., Grover, G. N., & Post, R. M. (1985). Premenstrual mood disorder and psychiatric illness. *American Journal of Psychiatry, 142,* 1359–1361.

de Beauvoir, S. (1949/1952). *The second sex.* New York: Bantam.

de Lacoste-Utamsing, C., & Holloway, R. L. (1982). Sexual dimorphism in the human corpus callosum. *Science, 216,* 1431–1432.

Denmark, F., Russo, N. F., Frieze, I. H., & Sechzer, J. A. (1988). Guidelines for avoiding sexism in psychological research. *American Psychologist, 43,* 582–585.

Di Leonardo, M. (1987). The female world of cards and holidays: Women, families, and the work of kinship. *Signs, 12,* 1–20.

Dovidio, J. F., Ellyson, S. L., Keating, C. F., Heltman, K., & Brown, C. E. (1988). The relationship of social power to visual displays of dominance between men and women. *Journal of Personality and Social Psychology, 54,* 233–242.

Drewnowski, A., & Yee, D. K. (1988, August). *Adolescent dieting: Fear of fatness and the role of puberty.* Paper presented at the 96th annual convention of the American Psychological Association, Atlanta, GA.

Eagly, A. H. (1987). *Sex differences in social behavior: A social-role interpretation*. Hillsdale, NJ: Erlbaum.

Eccles, J. S., & Jacobs, J. E. (1986). Social forces shape math attitudes and performance. *Signs, 11*, 367–380.

Echols, A. (1984). The taming of the id: Feminist sexual politics: 1968–1983. In C. S. Vance (Ed.), *Pleasure and danger: Exploring female sexuality*. Boston: Routlege and Kegan Paul.

Eichler, M., Reisman, A., & Borins, E. (1990). *Gender bias in medical research*. Unpublished manuscript, Ontario Institute for Studies in Education, Toronto, Ontario, Canada.

Eisenstein, Z. R. (1989). *The female body and the law*. Berkeley, CA: University of California Press.

Eisler, R. (1987). *The chalice and the blade*. San Francisco: Harper & Row.

Elshtain, J. B. (1987). *Women and war*. New York: Basic Books.

Epstein, C. F. (1988). *Deceptive distinctions: Sex, gender, and the social order*. New Haven, CT: Yale University Press.

Ericksen, K. P. (1987). Menstrual symptoms and menstrual beliefs: National and cross-national patterns. In B. E. Ginsburg & B. F. Carter (Eds.), *Premenstrual syndrome: Ethical and legal implications in a biomedical perspective*. New York: Plenum.

Feingold, A. (1988). Cognitive gender differences are disappearing. *American Psychologist, 43*, 95–103.

Fisher, H. W. (Ed.). (1987). *The premenstrual syndrome*. London, England: Royal Society of Medicine Services.

Fishman, P. M. (1983). Interaction: The work women do. In B. Thorne, C. Kramarae, & N. Henley (Eds.), *Language, gender and society*. Rowley, MA: Newbury House.

Freeman, E., Rickels, K., Sondheimer, S. J., & Polansky, M. (1990, July 18). Ineffectiveness of progesterone suppository treatment for premenstrual syndrome. *Journal of the American Medical Association, 264*, 349–353.

Friedman, W. J., Robinson, A. B., & Friedman, B. L. (1987). Sex differences in moral judgments? *Psychology of Women Quarterly, 11*, 37–46.

Frieze, I. H. (1990, August). *Adding context to the study of gender: Considering the self-context of the college student*. Carolyn Wood Sherif Award Lecture, presented at the 98th annual convention of the American Psychological Association, Boston.

Gallant, S. J., & Hamilton, J. (1988). On a premenstrual psychiatric diagnosis: What's in a name? *Professional Psychology: Research and Practice, 19*, 271–278.

Gallup, G. H., Jr., & Newport, F. (1991, Winter). Belief in paranormal phenomena among adult Americans. (Special Report/Gallup Poll). *Skeptical Inquirer, 15*, 137–146.

Gavey, N. (1989). Feminist poststructuralism and discourse analysis. *Psychology of Women Quarterly, 13*, 459–475.

Gelles, R. J., & Straus, M. A. (1989). *Intimate violence: The causes and consequences of abuse in the American family*. New York: Touchstone.

Gergen, K. J. (1973). Social psychology as history. *Journal of Personality and Social Psychology, 26*, 309–320.

Gergen, K. J. (1985). The social constructionist movement in modern psychology. *American Psychologist, 40*, 266–275.

Gergen, M. M. (Ed.). (1988). *Feminist thought and the structure of knowledge*. New York: New York University Press.

Gergen, M. M. (in press). Life stories: Pieces of a dream. In G. Rosenwald & R. Ochberg (Eds.), *Storied lives*. New Haven CT: Yale University Press.

Geschwind, N., & Behan, P. (1982). Left-handedness: Association with immune disease, migraine, and developmental learning disorder. *Proceedings of the National Academy of Sciences, 79*, 5097–5100.

Giacomini, M., Rozée-Koker, P., Pepitone-Arreola-Rockwell, F. (1986). Gender bias in human anatomy textbook illustrations. *Psychology of Women Quarterly, 10*, 413–420.

Gilbert, L. (1988). *Sharing it all*. New York: Plenum.

Gilligan, C. (1982). *In a different voice*. Cambridge, MA: Harvard University Press.

Gilligan, C., Ward, J. V., & Taylor, J. M. (Eds.). (1989). *Mapping the moral domain: A contribution of women's thinking to psychological theory and education*. Cambridge, MA: Harvard University Press.

Goldberger, N. R., Clinchy, B. M., Belenky, M. F., & Tarule, J. M. (1986). *Women's ways of knowing: The development of self, voice, and mind*. New York: Basic Books.

Golub, S. (1988). A developmental perspective. In L. H. Gise, N. G. Kase, & R. L. Berkowitz (Eds.), *The premenstrual syndromes* (pp. 7–20). New York: Churchill Livingstone.

Gomberg, E. S. L. (1989). On terms used and abused: The concept of "codependency." *Drugs and Society: Current issues in alcohol/drug studies, 3*, 113–132.

Goodrich, T. J., Rampage, C., Ellman, B., & Halstead, K. (1988). *Feminist family therapy: A casebook*. New York: W. W. Norton.

Gould, S. J. (1981). *The mismeasure of man*. New York: Norton.

Greeno, C. G., & Maccoby, E. E. (1986). How different is the "different voice"? *Signs, 11*, 310–316.

Gutmann, D. (1987). *Reclaimed powers: Toward a new psychology of men and women in later life*. New York: Basic Books.

Hall, J. A. (1984). *Nonverbal sex differences: Communication accuracy and expressive style*. Baltimore, MD: The Johns Hopkins University Press.

Hamilton, J. A., & Gallant, S. (1988). Premenstrual symptom changes and plasma beta-endorphin/beta-lipotropin throughout the menstrual cycle. *Psychoneuroendocrinology, 13*, 505–514.

Hamilton, J. A., & Parry, B. (1983). Sex-related differences in clinical drug response: Implications for women's health. *Journal of the American Medical Women's Association, 38*, 126–132.

Hammarback, S., & Backstrom, T. (1989). A demographic study in subgroups of women seeking help for premenstrual syndrome. *Acta Obstetrics & Gynecology Scandinavia, 68*, 247–253.

Harding, S. (Ed.). (1987). *Feminism and methodology*. Bloomington, IN: Indiana University Press.

Hare-Mustin, R. T. (1987). The problem of gender in family therapy theory. *Family Process, 26*, 15–27.

Hare-Mustin, R. T., & Marecek, J. (1986). Autonomy and gender: Some questions for therapists. *Psychotherapy, 23*, 205–212.

Hare-Mustin, R. T., & Marecek, J. (1990). Gender and the meaning of difference: Postmodernism and psychology. In R. T. Hare-Mustin & J. Marecek (Eds.), *Making a difference: Psychology and the construction of gender*. New Haven,

CT: Yale University Press. An earlier version of this chapter appeared in *The American Psychologist, 43*, 455–464.

Heilbrun, C. G. (1989). *Writing a woman's life.* New York: Ballantine.

Hochschild, A. R. (1983). *The managed heart.* Berkeley: University of California Press.

Hochschild, A. R. (1989). *The second shift: Working parents and the revolution at home.* New York: Viking.

Houser, B. B. (1979). An investigation of the correlation between hormonal levels in males and mood, behavior, and physical discomfort. *Hormones and Behavior, 12*, 185–197.

Hubbard, R. (1990). *The politics of women's biology.* New Brunswick, NJ: Rutgers University Press.

Hyde, J. S., Fennema, E., & Lamon, S. J. (1990). Gender differences in mathematics performance: A meta-analysis. *Psychological Bulletin, 107*, 139–155.

Hyde, J. S., & Linn, M. C. (Eds.). (1986). *The psychology of gender: Advances through meta-analysis.* Baltimore, MD: The Johns Hopkins University Press.

Hyde, J. S., & Linn, M. C. (1988). Gender differences in verbal ability: A meta-analysis. *Psychological Bulletin, 104*, 53–69.

Jacklin, C. N. (1981). Methodological issues in the study of sex-related differences. *Developmental Review, 1*, 266–273.

Jacklin, C. N. (1989). Female and male: Issues of gender. *American Psychologist, 44*, 127–133.

Jeavons [Wilkinson], C. M., & Zeiner, A. R. (1984). Effects of elevated female sex steroids on ethanol and acetaldehyde metabolism in humans. *Alcoholism: Clinical and Experimental Research, 8*, 352–358.

Jensvold, M. F., & Hamilton, J. (1989, August). *Pharmacologic treatment of depression in women.* Paper presented at the 97th annual convention of the American Psychological Association, New Orleans.

Josselson, R. (1987). *Finding herself: Pathways to identity development in women.* New York: Jossey-Bass.

Judicial Council of California (1990). *Achieving equal justice for women and men in the courts: The draft report of the Judicial Council Advisory Committee on gender bias in the courts.* Unpublished manuscript, San Francisco.

Kahn, A. S., & Yoder, J. D. (1989). The psychology of women and conservatism: Rediscovering social change. *Psychology of Women Quarterly, 13*, 417–432.

Keller, E. F. (1985). *Reflections on gender and science.* New Haven, CT: Yale University Press.

Khan, S. S., Nessim, S., Gray, R., Czer, L. S., Chaux, A., & Matloff, J. (1990). Increased mortality of women in coronary artery bypass surgery: Evidence for referral bias. *Annals of Internal Medicine, 112*, 561–567.

Kimmel, E. B. (1989). The experience of feminism. *Psychology of Women Quarterly, 13*, 133–146.

Kitzinger, C. (1987). *The social construction of lesbianism.* London: Sage.

Klass, P., & Wallis, L. (1989, October). Macho medicine. *Lear's*, pp. 65, 67.

Koeske, R. D. (1987). Premenstrual emotionality: Is biology destiny? In M. R. Walsh (Ed.), *The psychology of women: Ongoing debates.* New Haven, CT: Yale University Press.

Kohn, A. (1990). *The brighter side of human nature: Altruism and empathy in everyday life.* New York: Basic Books.

Koss, M. P. (1990). The women's mental health research agenda: Violence against women. *American Psychologist, 45*, 374–380.

Lakoff, G. (1989). *Women, fire, and dangerous things*. Chicago: University of Chicago Press.

Lakoff, R. T. (1990). *Talking power: The politics of language*. New York: Basic Books.

Landrine, H. (1988). Revising the framework of abnormal psychology. In P. Bronstein & K. Quina (Eds.), *Teaching a psychology of people*. Washington, DC: American Psychological Association.

Laqueur, T. (1987). Orgasm, generation, and the politics of reproductive biology. In C. Gallagher & T. Laqueur (Eds.), *The making of the modern body*. Berkeley, CA: University of California Press.

Lerman, H. (1986). *A mote in Freud's eye*. New York: Springer.

Lerner, G. (1986). *The creation of patriarchy*. New York: Oxford University Press.

Lerner, H. G. (1988). Parental mislabeling of female genitals. In H. G. Lerner, *Women in therapy* (pp. 25–41). Northvale, NJ: Jason Aronson Inc.

Littleton, C. A. (1987). Reconstructing sexual equality. *California Law Review, 75*, 1279–1337.

Lott, B. (1990). Dual natures or learned behavior: The challenge to feminist psychology. In R. T. Hare-Mustin & J. Marecek (Eds.), *Making a difference: Psychology and the construction of gender* (pp. 65–101). New Haven, CT: Yale University Press.

Maccoby, E. E. (1988). Gender as a social category. *Developmental Psychology, 24*, 755–765.

Maccoby, E. E. (1990). Gender and relationships: A developmental account. *American Psychologist, 45*, 513–520.

MacKinnon, C. A. (1990). Legal perspectives on sexual difference. In D. L. Rhode (Ed.), *Theoretical perspectives on sexual difference* (pp. 213–225). New Haven, CT: Yale University Press.

Major, B. (1987). Gender, justice, and the psychology of entitlement. In P. Shaver & C. Hendrick (Eds.), *Sex and Gender: 7* (pp. 124–148). Newbury Park, CA: Sage.

Major, B., McFarlin, D., & Gagnon, D. (1984). Overworked and underpaid: On the nature of gender differences in personal entitlement. *Journal of Personality and Social Psychology, 47*, 1399–1412.

Maltz, D. N., & Borker, R. A. (1982). A cultural approach to male–female miscommunication. In J. J. Gumperz (Ed.), *Language and social identity* (pp. 196–216). Cambridge, England: Cambridge University Press.

Marecek, J. (Ed.). (1989). Theory and method in feminist psychology [Special issue]. *Psychology of Women Quarterly, 13*(4).

Martin, E. (1987). *The woman in the body: A cultural analysis of reproduction*. Boston: Beacon.

McConnell-Ginet, S. (1983). Intonation in a man's world. In B. Thorne, C. Kramarae, & N. Henley (Eds.), *Language, Gender and Society* (pp. 69–88). Rowley, MA: Newbury House.

McConnell-Ginet, S. (1984). The origins of sexist language in discourse. In S. J. White & V. Teller (Eds.), *Discourses in reading and linguistics (Annals of the New York Academy of Sciences, col. 433)* (pp. 123–135). New York: New York Academy of Sciences.

McFarlane, J., Martin, C. L., & Williams, T. M. (1988). Mood fluctuations: Women versus men and menstrual versus other cycles. *Psychology of Women Quarterly, 12*, 201–223.

McGrath, E., Keita, G. P., Strickland, B., & Russo, N. F. (Eds.). (1990). *Women and depression: Risk Factors and treatment issues.* Washington, DC: American Psychological Association.

McKinlay, J. B., McKinlay, S. M., & Brambilla, D. (1987). The relative contributions of endocrine changes and social circumstances to depression in mid-aged women. *Journal of Health and Social Behavior, 28*, 345–363.

Mednick, M. T. (1989). On the politics of psychological constructs: Stop the bandwagon, I want to get off. *American Psychologist, 44*, 1118–1123.

Minnich, E. K. (1990). *Transforming knowledge.* Philadelphia, PA: Temple University Press.

Morawski, J. G. (1990). Toward the unimagined: Feminism and epistemology in psychology. In R. T. Hare-Mustin & J. Marecek (Eds.), *Making a difference: Psychology and the construction of gender* (pp. 150–183). New Haven, CT: Yale University Press.

Nieva, V. F., & Gutek, B. A. (1981). *Women and work: A psychological perspective.* New York: Praeger.

Nolen-Hoeksema, S. (1990). *Sex differences in depression.* Stanford, CA: Stanford University Press.

O'Barr, W. M., & Atkins, B. K. (1980). "Women's language" or "powerless language"? In S. McConnell-Ginet, R. Borker, & N. Furman (Eds.), *Women and language in literature and society* (pp. 93–110). New York: Praeger.

Olson, C. B. (1988, April). *The influence of context on gender differences in performance attributions: Further evidence of a "feminine modesty" effect.* Paper presented at the meeting of the Western Psychological Association, San Francisco.

Palumbo, P. J. (1989, July 7). Cholesterol lowering for all: a closer look. *Journal of the American Medical Association, 262*, 91–92.

Parlee, M. B. (1982). Changes in moods and activation levels during the menstrual cycle in experimentally naive subjects. *Psychology of Women Quarterly, 7*, 119–131.

Parlee, M. B. (1989, March). *The science and politics of PMS research.* Invited address presented at the annual meeting of the Association for Women in Psychology, Newport, R.I.

Pennebaker, J. W. (1982). *The psychology of physical symptoms.* New York: Springer-Verlag.

Peplau, L. A., & Campbell, S. M. (1989). The balance of power in dating and marriage. In J. Freeman (Ed.), *Women: A feminist perspective* (4th ed.; pp. 121–137). Mountain View, CA: Mayfield.

Peplau, L. A., & Conrad, E. (1989). Beyond nonsexist research: The perils of feminist methods in psychology. *Psychology of Women Quarterly, 13*, 379–400.

Polefrone, J. M., & Manuck, S. B. (1987). Gender differences in cardiovascular and neuroendocrine response to stressors. In R. C. Barnett, L. Biener, & G. K. Baruch (Eds.), *Gender and stress* (pp. 13–38). New York: The Free Press.

Pomeroy, S. B. (1975). *Goddesses, whores, wives, and slaves: Women in classical antiquity.* New York: Schocken.

Pomeroy, S. B. (1986, April 20). When no one wore the pants [Review of *The creation of patriarchy* by Gerda Lerner]. *The New York Times Book Review*, p. 12.

Ragins, B. R., & Sundstrom, E. (1989). Gender and power in organizations: A longitudinal perspective. *Psychological Bulletin, 105*, 51–88.

Richardson, J. T. E. (1990). Questionnaire studies of paramenstrual symptoms. *Psychology of Women Quarterly, 14*, 15–42.

Riessman, C. K. (1987). When gender is not enough: Women interviewing women. *Gender and Society, 1*, 172–207.

Riessman, C. K. (1990). *Divorce talk: Women and men make sense of personal relationships*. New Brunswick, NJ: Rutgers University Press.

Risman, B. J. (1987). Intimate relationships from a microstructural perspective: Men who mother. *Gender and Society, 1*, 6–32.

Rodeheaver, D., & Datan, N. (1988). The challenge of double jeopardy: Toward a mental health agenda for aging women. *American Psychologist, 43*, 648–654.

Rosaldo, R. (1989). *Culture and truth: The remaking of social analysis*. Boston: Beacon.

Rothman, B. K. (1989). *Recreating motherhood: Ideology and technology in a patriarchal society*. New York: W. W. Norton.

Russell, D. E. H. (1982). *Rape in marriage*. New York: Macmillan.

Russo, N. F. (1990). Overview: Forging research priorities for women's mental health. *American Psychologist, 45*, 368–373.

Sanford, L. T., & Donovan, M. (1984). *Women and self-esteem*. New York: Doubleday.

Sarbin, T. R. (1986). The narrative as a root metaphor for psychology. In T. R. Sarbin (Ed.), *Narrative psychology: The storied nature of human conduct* (pp. 129–151). New York: Praeger.

Scott, J. W. (1988, Spring). Deconstructing equality-versus-difference: Or, the uses of poststructuralist theory for feminism. *Feminist Studies, 14*, 33–50.

Shaver, P., Hazan, C., & Bradshaw, D. (1988). Love as attachment: The integration of three behavioral systems. In R. J. Sternberg & M. L. Barnes (Eds.), *The psychology of love*. New Haven: Yale University Press.

Shaywitz, S. E., Shaywitz, B. A., Fletcher, J. M., & Escobar, M. D. (1990, August 22–29). Prevalence of reading disability in boys and girls. Results of the Connecticut Longitudinal Study. *Journal of the American Medical Association, 264*, 998–1002.

Sherif, C. W. (1987). Bias in psychology. In S. Harding (Ed.), *Feminism and methodology* (pp. 37–56). Bloomington: Indiana University Press.

Shields, S. A. (1975). Functionalism, Darwinism, and the psychology of women: A study in social myth. *American Psychologist, 30*, 739–754.

Shields, S. A. (1987). Women, men, and the dilemma of emotion. In P. Shaver & C. Hendrick (Eds.), *Sex and gender: 7* (pp. 229–250). Newbury Park, CA: Sage.

Silverstein, B., Perdue, L., Peterson, B., Vogel, L., & Fantini, D. A. (1986). Possible causes of the thin standard of bodily attractiveness for women. *International Journal of Eating Disorders, 5*, 135–144.

Silverstein, B., Peterson, B., & Perdue, L. (1986). Some correlates of the thin standard of bodily attractiveness in women. *International Journal of Eating Disorders, 5*, 145–155.

Snodgrass, S. E. (1985). Women's intuition: The effect of subordinate role on interpersonal sensitivity. *Journal of Personality and Social Psychology, 49,* 146–155.

Stacey, J., & Thorne, B. (1985). The missing feminist revolution in sociology. *Social Problems, 32,* 301–316.

Standing, H. (1980). "Sickness is a woman's business?": Reflections on the attribution of illness. In Brighton Women and Science Group (Ed.), *Alice Through the Microscope: The Power of Science over Women's Lives* (pp. 124–138). London, England: Virago.

Stapley, J. C., & Haviland, J. M. (1989). Beyond depression: Gender differences in normal adolescents' emotional experiences. *Sex Roles, 20,* 295–308.

Strickland, B. (1988). Sex-related differences in health and illness. *Psychology of Women Quarterly, 12,* 381–399.

Striegel-Moore, R. H., Silberstein, L. R., & Rodin, J. (1986). Toward an understanding of risk factors for bulimia. *American Psychologist, 41,* 246–263.

Strube, M. J (1988). The decision to leave an abusive relationship: Empirical evidence and theoretical issues. *Psychological Bulletin, 104,* 236–250.

Tavris, C. (1989). *Anger: The misunderstood emotion* (2nd ed.). New York: Simon & Schuster/Touchstone.

Tavris, C. (in press). *The mismeasure of woman.* New York: Simon & Schuster.

Tavris, C., & Wade, C. (1984). *The longest war: Sex differences in perspective* (2nd ed.). San Diego: Harcourt Brace Jovanovich.

Thoma, S. (1986). Estimating gender differences in the comprehension and preferences of moral issues. *Developmental Review, 6,* 165–180.

Tiefer, L. (1987). Social constructionism and the study of human sexuality. In P. Shaver & C. Hendrick (Eds.), *Sex and Gender: 7* (pp. 70–94). Newbury Park, CA: Sage.

Tiefer, L. (1988). A feminist perspective on sexology and sexuality. In M. M. Gergen (Ed.), *Feminist thought and the structure of knowledge* (pp. 16–26). New York: New York University Press.

Tobin, J. N., Wassertheil-Smoller, S., Wexler, J. P., Steingart, R. M., Budner, N., Lense, L., & Wachspress, J. (1987). Sex bias in considering coronary bypass surgery. *Annals of Internal Medicine, 107,* 19–25.

Unger, R. K. (1990). Imperfect reflections of reality: Psychology constructs gender. In R. T. Hare-Mustin & J. Marecek (Eds.), *Making a difference: Psychology and the construction of gender* (pp. 102–149). New Haven, CT: Yale University Press.

Walker, L. E. (1989). Psychology and violence against women. *American Psychologist, 44,* 695–702.

West, C., & Zimmerman, D. H. (1987). Doing gender. *Gender & Society, 1,* 125–151.

West, R. (1988). Jurisprudence and gender. *The University of Chicago Law Review, 55,* 1–72.

Wood, W., Rhodes, N., & Whelan, M. (1989). Sex differences in positive well-being: A consideration of emotional style and marital status. *Psychological bulletin, 106,* 249–264.

Zur, O. (1989). War myths: Exploration of the dominant collective beliefs about warfare. *Journal of Humanistic Psychology, 29,* 297–327.

LESBIAN AND GAY MALE DIMENSIONS IN THE PSYCHOLOGICAL STUDY OF HUMAN DIVERSITY

Linda Garnets received her PhD in clinical/community psychology from the University of Michigan in 1978. She is a psychotherapist and organizational consultant in Los Angeles. She provides organizational consultation to city and county government agencies and commissions, human service and social purpose organizations, research projects, and universities. Garnets specializes in work with gay and lesbian individuals and with local and national gay and lesbian organizations. For the past 4 years, she has taught a course on the "Psychology of the Lesbian Experience" at UCLA. She was formerly a member of the core faculty of Wright Institute, Los Angeles, and has taught courses on community psychology and the psychology of gender at several universities in southern California. From 1979–1982, she was the Research Director of a NIMH-funded sexual assault research project.

Garnets has written and presented numerous papers on the state of the art in research and practice in gay and lesbian psychology. She is past Chair of the APA Committee for Lesbian and Gay Concerns (CLGC), Co-Chair of CLGC's Task Force on Bias in Psychotherapy with Lesbians and Gay Men, a member of the Executive committees of APA Divisions 9 (Society for the Psychological Study of Social Issues) and 44 (Society for the Psychological Study of Lesbian and Gay Issues), a member of the Editorial Board of the *Journal of Gay and Lesbian Psychotherapy*, and she was formerly a member of the Executive Committee of

Division 35 (Psychology of Women). She is a recipient of the Distinguished Professional Contribution Award from Division 44.

D ouglas C. Kimmel received a BA in 1965 from the University of Colorado. Supported by NIMH fellowships, he earned a PhD in Human Development in 1970, specializing in clinical psychology at the University of Chicago.

A professor of psychology at City College of the City University of New York, Kimmel has been a member of the faculty for 20 years; he is a licensed psychologist in New York and Maine, Fellow of the Gerontological Society of America, Fellow of APA Divisions 9, 20, and 44, former President of APA Division 44 (Society for the Psychological Study of Lesbian and Gay Issues), and recipient of a 1989 Outstanding Achievement Award from the APA Committee on Lesbian and Gay Concerns.

In 1974 he wrote the college text, *Adulthood and Aging*, now in its third edition (John Wiley & Sons, 1990). He is co-author with Irving B. Weiner of *Adolescence: A Development Transition* (Erlbaum, 1985) and co-author with Harry R. Moody of a chapter titled "Ethical Issues in Gerontological Research and Services" in the third edition of the *Handbook of the Psychology of Aging* (Academic Press, 1990). His research on gay male patterns of aging was first published in 1977 and he is co-investigator with Clarence L. Adams of an ongoing study of patterns of aging among African-American gay men. He has published several other book chapters and journal articles, presented a variety of scientific papers, and reviewed manuscripts for a range of journals. He is currently Chair of an NIMH Small Grants review panel.

In 1977 he was a cofounder of Senior Action in a Gay Environment (SAGE), a New York City nonprofit organization providing social services to older lesbians and gay men. He was Chair of the steering committee of the Association of Gay Psychologists in 1977, Chair of the APA Committee on Gay Concerns in 1983, member of the APA Board of Social and Ethical Responsibility from 1984–1986, and Chair of the APA task force on avoiding ageism in psychological research in 1986. He was a visiting professor at the University of Maine in 1982–1983 and 1985 and at Tokyo Metropolitan University in 1987.

LESBIAN AND GAY MALE DIMENSIONS IN THE PSYCHOLOGICAL STUDY OF HUMAN DIVERSITY

S exual orientation has become an aspect of the psychological study of human diversity during the last few years. We survey this emerging field from the perspective of four main themes: (a) the meaning of sexual orientation and why it is relevant to the psychological understanding of people; (b) the development of gay and lesbian identity within a multicultural society; (c) differences between lesbians and gay men; and (d) the impact of sexual orientation on two central themes of human development (relationships and parenting). Our basic assumption is that an understanding of sexual orientation will enhance psychological research and practice by reducing heterosexist bias, will increase the perception of similarity and appreciation of difference among those who differ in sexual orientation, and will support efforts to remove the stigma and discrimination against lesbians and gay men.

> Imagine, for example, a hypothetical society that attached a great deal of importance to the question of whether its citizens were dog lovers or cat lovers. Imagine that scientists constructed complicated psychological questionnaires to determine whether someone was a "feliphile" or a "caniphile," scored people on scales of "petual orientation," and received or were denied tenure on the basis of whether they could prove the existence of "bipetuality." (Weinrich & Williams, 1991, p. 47)

Introduction

Until the 1970s most psychological research on homosexuality focused on its presumed pathological aspects. Morin (1977) documented the bias that dominated the field up to that time as "heterosexist bias," which he defined as "a belief system that values heterosexuality as superior to and/or more 'natural' than homosexuality" (p. 631). Only a few pioneers, such as Kinsey, Pomeroy, and Martin (1948), Kinsey, Pomeroy, Martin, and Gebhard (1953), Ford and Beach (1951), and Hooker (1957), stood out as questioning the dominant model of homosexuality as a sign of mental illness. A significant change occurred as a result of a concerted effort by gay-affirmative mental health professionals who called attention to the empirical data that led the American Psychiatric Association in 1973 to remove homosexuality per se from its list of mental disorders (Bayer, 1981). The American Psychological Association (APA) supported this change and further urged mental health professionals to take the lead in removing the stigma that previously had been associated with homosexuality (Conger, 1975; Kooden et al., 1979). Subsequent psychological research on homosexuality has shifted from a preoccupation with the causes and pathology of homosexuality to a much greater focus on the characteristics and psychosocial concerns of lesbians and gay men, including social attitudes about homosexuals (Watters, 1986).

In recent years there has been much positive change, but the effects have been limited. On one hand, a gay-affirmative perspective has emerged within American psychology. Within this perspective homosexuality is viewed as a natural variant in the expression of erotic attractions and relationships, the adoption of a gay male or lesbian identity is considered to be a viable and healthy option, and many of the problems of living associated with being lesbian or gay are thought to result from negative social attitudes about homosexuality. On the other hand, a recent survey of a large and diverse sample of psychologists by an APA Committee on Lesbian and Gay Concerns Task Force (1990) showed that a wide range of negative biases and misinformation about homosexuality persisted that could affect therapy practice with lesbians and gay men.

Likewise, in recent years, social attitudes have been affected by the increased visibility and political power of lesbians and gay men. However, few aspects of human behavior evoke the intensity of opposition that homosexuality arouses in some circles. For example, in 1990, the United States Congress passed a bill to collect statistics on hate crimes,

We are grateful to several colleagues who read and commented on earlier drafts of this chapter: Connie Chan, Jacqueline Goodchilds, Greg Herek, Barrie Levy, Steve Morin, and Anne Peplau. We also thank Ron Schwizer for his technical assistance in preparing the manuscript and the slides for the lecture, and Elizabeth Sheldon for library research. The APA Continuing Education Committee was also very helpful in providing support for two lecturers to cover this topic.

significantly including those based on sexual orientation, and the president signed it at a ceremony that included openly lesbian and gay male community leaders. Moreover, empirical research has documented the persistence of institutional and personal hostility toward gay men and lesbians and the mental health consequences of hate crimes, victimization, and verbal abuse (Garnets, Herek, & Levy, 1990; Herek, 1991).

The emergence of acquired immune deficiency syndrome (AIDS) has focused considerable attention on gay male life-styles and has brought renewed stigma to and discrimination against lesbians and gay men (Herek, 1990b). Psychology, to its credit, has played a leading role in the fight against the epidemic and the related discrimination against those people affected by the disease (cf. Backer, Batchelor, Jones, & Mays, 1988). It has been a tragic episode and the end is not yet in sight. Certainly it has affected sexual behavior, intimate relationships, and the development experiences of bereaved survivors, but it is too soon to know the extent of the impact or the long-term consequences of this historical event.

Within this contradictory social–historical context, we seek to describe the complex phenomenon of sexual orientation from a psychological perspective in 1990. Time does not allow us to discuss AIDS or other important issues such as the extraordinary process of building a community that has taken place over the last two decades. We focus, instead, on the nature of sexual orientation, gay male and lesbian identity, gender differences, and some relevant life span development issues.

Definitions

At the outset, it is useful to define the terminology that we use (see Appendix A). We have selected these definitions for the purposes of this lecture; they are not engraved in stone. They are based on, but modified from, those developed by Money (1988, pp. 191–216). We have adopted some of his terms such as *homophilia* and *heterophilia* because they emphasize love (*philia*) instead of only sexual behavior and because they focus on affectional and erotic desire instead of viewing homosexuals as "certain kinds of people" (Risman & Schwartz, 1988).

These definitions make subtle distinctions that are important. First, an individual may be *homophilic* without being *lesbian* or *gay* because the latter terms involve a life-style that implies some degree of self-awareness and identification with the larger lesbian and gay male community. Second, *homosexuality* may involve sexual acts without a gay life-style or self-identification. Third, homophilia, similar to heterophilia, does not imply that an individual acts on the erotic feelings; for example, one may be celibate or may use heterophilic fantasy to facilitate a homosexual encounter or vice versa. Fourth, *sexual orientation* generally reflects the affectional–erotic attraction to same gender, other gender, or to both women and men. We consider it to be the relative balance between an individual's homophilia and heterophilia—not a bipolar dichotomy but instead two parallel dimensions (cf. Shively & DeCecco, 1977). That is, homosexuality and heterosexuality reflect correspondingly high and low degrees of homophilia and heterophilia. A bisexual status reflects relatively high homophilia and heterophilia (androgynophilia). An asexual status reflects relatively low levels of both homophilia and heterophilia.

Clearly, sexual orientation is more complex than either *homosexual* or *heterosexual*. It is similar to the continuum of colors in a rainbow. For example, Coleman (1987) pointed out the multiple dimensions involved in sexual orientation: self-identification, behavior, fantasies, emotional attachments, and current relationship status. F. Klein, Sepekoff, and Wolf (1986) proposed a similar model but also included a temporal dimension (past, present) and one's self-defined "ideal." In addition, Masters and Johnson's (1979) study of ambisexuals provided a fascinating example of the interaction of gender with sexual orientation and behavior: The same ambisexual men moved more quickly toward orgasm with female partners than with male partners; the same ambisexual women engaged in mutual "my turn, your turn" sexual interaction with their female partners but let their male partners "set the pace throughout the entire sexual interaction" (p. 169). Moreover, it should be noted that there is not a necessary relationship between biological gender, gender identity or role, and sexual orientation; they represent separate components of sexual identity (Larsen, 1981; Ross, 1987; Shively & DeCecco, 1977).

Limitations and Caveats Regarding Research

Because representative sampling of the population is problematic because many people will not disclose their sexual orientation, differing levels of confidence in research with regard to sexual orientation must be noted.

First, research that focuses on refuting universal stereotypes about lesbians and gay men does not require representative samples to be compelling because it focuses on disproving these generalizations. For example, Hooker's (1957) study showed that homosexual men cannot be distinguished from heterosexual controls on the basis of psychological tests, and Masters and Johnson's (1979) laboratory study showed that homosexual men and homosexual women showed the same physiological sexual response as did heterosexual men and heterosexual women, respectively. In neither study was a representative sample used, yet both were convincing. Likewise, studies of patterns of aging among gay men (Kimmel, 1978) can lead one to conclude that, contrary to stereotypes, there is considerable diversity—probably even more than was found among the limited sample—without claiming the findings are representative of all gay men.

Second, limited generalizations can be made from nonrepresentative samples if proper caution is taken. Because most research has focused on White gay male samples, we can be relatively comfortable describing this population, noting that the volunteer samples tend to be better educated and more affluent than their age group as a whole. Obvious biases such as samples of men from gay bars or from gay community organizations are typically noted. It is clear, however, that such samples cannot be generalized to gay men of color or to women; urban samples also cannot be generalized to rural gay men, youthful samples to older adults, and so on.

Third, we cannot claim certainty regarding the proportion of respondents manifesting various characteristics. For example, we do not know how many gay men have children or how many lesbians are living in committed relationships with another woman. We do not know how many parents accept their child's homosexuality or whether gay male or lesbian life expectancy is different from that of heterosexual men and women. Recently, however, survey researchers have developed techniques for sampling this population, (e.g., using telephone surveys that inquire about sexual orientation and related themes). Although problems exist, if limitations are specified, it may now become possible to describe some characteristics of the lesbian and gay male population (cf. Herek, 1990a, 1991).

Moreover, it is important that research be replicated before it is accepted with confidence. A study by Kolodny, Masters, Hendryx, and Toro (1971) showed that testosterone levels were lower in gay men than in heterosexual controls; this was not found in a careful replication study (Sanders, Bain, & Langevin, 1985). Similarly, research by Gladue, Green, and Hellman (1984) that showed different gonadotropic hormone response in homosexual and heterosexual men was not replicated in a later study (Hendricks, Graber, & Rodriguez-Sierra, 1989).

An additional problem is that research studies often include people with some heterosexual experience in the "homosexual" sample and rarely distinguish bisexuals as a distinct group. In that sense, as MacDonald (1983) and others have noted, "a little bit of lavender"—that is, a little same-gender sexual experience—can make an individual homosexual for research purposes. Thus, depending on how much other-gender interest is required, and the particular dimension measured, some people might more accurately be classified as bisexual instead of homosexual.

We must be cautious, therefore, about placing either too little or too much confidence in the research on which we rely. In this chapter, except where specifically noted, it may be assumed that the sample was predominately White with a higher than average level of education than the general population. Many findings have been replicated to a large extent in other studies and appear to be robust. However, many topics would benefit from additional research with different samples.

Sexual Orientation Is an Important Psychological Variable

Sexual orientation, similar to gender, age, race, and ethnicity, is an important psychological variable. The determinants of sexual orientation reflect a complex interaction of biology, culture, history, and psychosocial influences. The mix is unlikely to be identical for different individuals (Richardson, 1987). The result is a mosaic of diversity in life-style, behavior, and adaptation. Gender, economic and class differences, chronological age, ethnic and racial variation, and whether one is a parent are among other relevant dimensions of diversity in gay and lesbian lives.

There are several characteristics that stand out for lesbian and gay people within the context of Western society. These include the following:

1. Gay men and lesbians discover their sexual orientation at a relatively late point in the process of identity development, often at the time sexual desire begins to be recognized. It is not recognized or acknowledged from birth but is an *achieved* instead of an *ascribed* status (cf. M. S. Weinberg & Williams, 1974, p. 288). Often there is a time lag between the discovery and owning of one's identity.

2. Lesbians and gay men learn negative attitudes about homosexuality, gay men, and lesbians from others (both significant others and conventional society); do not imagine that such negative attitudes could apply to them; and then learn that they do indeed apply.

3. Because families of lesbians and gay men typically are heterosexual, they do not provide useful role models for normal transitions and developmental periods of gay and lesbian lives.

4. Family disruption often results when a gay or lesbian sexual orientation is revealed. Moreover, it may be revealed in different ways: by conscious decision, by positive transition (new relationship, birth of grandchild), or by some negative circumstance (e.g., arrest, divorce, illness).

5. Because lesbians and gay men are diverse and the majority are not easily identifiable, most move in and out of gay and straight identities, and many hide their sexual orientation from public view. In addition, they may be assumed to be gay or not gay as roles shift during the day or week, and often they are treated as if they were heterosexual.

6. Even when gay men and lesbians are open about their sexual orientation, they do not automatically invalidate stereotypes about them because each individual can be discounted as an exception to the general pattern.

7. The lesbian and gay male community encompasses diversity in terms of gender, race, ethnicity, age, socioeconomic status, relationship status, parenthood, health, disabilities, politics, and sexual behavior. For many lesbians and gay men, this community may introduce them to greater social diversity than they had experienced before coming out as gay or lesbian.

8. Gay and lesbian people have had little awareness of any community history until relatively recently. Although the gay and lesbian community has a history, it is not passed on through family traditions. There are few road maps; each person tends to be an individual creation. This may lead to greater potential for "normative creativity" (Brown, 1989).

9. Gay men and lesbians are often encouraged or permitted by their deviance from accepted norms to explore androgynous gender role behavior, independence, self-reliance, and educational and occupational options.

10. Lesbians and gay men raise issues that some members of the public may find potentially threatening, such as (a) anyone can be gay (stereotypes are inaccurate predictors); (b) same-sex sexual fantasies can be explored (everyone is not 100% heterosexual all of the time); and (c) relationships and sexual relations need not be based on gender role constraints. Moreover, gay men and lesbians without children may benefit economically from not having a family; two gay men in a relationship without children or alimony payments may be particularly advantaged because male income typically exceeds female income levels. Also, lesbians may be perceived as having greater power than heterosexual women because they live independently of men and do not depend on men for sexual, emotional, or financial support.

We might even think that gay men and lesbians are perceived as a threat to the traditional power structure because sexual orientation is nearly always excluded from the list of protected minorities in civil rights legislation except in a few cities and one or two states; conversely, same-gender sexual relations are illegal in nearly half of the states in the United States.

It should also be noted that people who are neither exclusively homosexual nor heterosexual tend to be viewed with suspicion by both groups. On one hand, they may be seen as trying to avoid the stigma of being homosexual; on the other hand, they may be viewed as being less normal than a heterosexual. Although research data are limited, there is some evidence of a different process of development for bisexuals. Many report no same-gender sexual experience until adulthood. Moreover, many bisexuals reported moving from a same-gender sexual relationship to an other-gender sexual relationship and then back again or vice versa (Blumstein & Schwartz, 1977; cf. Bell, Weinberg, & Hammersmith, 1981).

In summary, gay male and lesbian sexual orientations are important characteristics within the context of American culture at the present time. They represent complex psychosocial factors that affect heterosexuals as well as lesbians and gay men. We have pointed out the multidimensional nature of sexual orientation, suggested the extent of recent social change regarding the psychological understanding of sexual orientation, and outlined some of the issues related to contemporary research on sexual orientation. In the next section, we discuss the determinants of sexual orientation as an aspect of an individual's unique pattern of sexuality.

Sexual Orientation and an Individual's Lovemap

> My mother made me a homosexual.
> If I give her the yarn will she make me one too? (graffiti on a wall circa 1970)

Present research suggests that the origins of sexual orientation are not well understood. One perplexing issue concerns the stability of sexual orientation over the life span. On one hand, retrospective reports indicate that gay male and lesbian sexual orientation appears to be established by the time one reaches adolescence, often before sexual activity begins, and is frequently preceded by an awareness of same-gender sexual attraction (Bell et al., 1981). Also, cases of change from an exclusively homosexual sexual orientation as a result of psychotherapy have not been convincingly documented (Money, 1988, p. 87; Zuger, 1988). These data suggest that for some people, sexual orientation develops relatively early in life and does not undergo major changes in adulthood. On the other hand, some individuals appear to have flexibility in their sexual orientation or adopt one orientation after considerable experience with the other orientation in adulthood (J. K. Dixon, 1984, 1985; Golden, 1987; Kimmel, 1978; LaTorre & Wedenberg, 1983; Lowenstein, 1985). Money (1988) termed this phenomenon "sequential bisexuality." These data suggest that there may be different origins of sexual orientation for different individuals.

A second controversial issue concerns the possible biological–physiological origins of sexual orientation. One site of presumed difference has been located in the sexual dimorphic nucleus of the hypothalamus, but no difference in number of cells in this nucleus was found in an autopsy study between homosexual and heterosexual men despite a marked difference between men and women (Swaab & Hofman, 1988). Moreover, the data regarding endocrine factors and sexual orientation are inconsistent and contradictory (Gladue, 1987; Sanders et al., 1985).

Money (1987, 1988) proposed a process by which sexual orientation develops in stages beginning in prenatal development and results from an interaction among prenatal cultural, experiential, and socialization influences, with the mix depending on the individual situation. We find this model useful because sexual orientation (e.g., heterophilia and homophilia) can be conceptualized as aspects of an individual's unique "lovemap." The lovemap reflects the wide range of sexual interests and attractive characteristics in one's idealized lover (Money, 1988, chap. 4). This concept implies the developmental interaction of mind and brain, hormones and experience, and prenatal and postnatal influences that lead to a personalized template of erotic and sexual feelings, fantasy, and activity that is as unique as one's fingerprint or voiceprint.

Moreover, the concept of a unique lovemap sheds light on the debate between the social constructionist and essentialist perspectives on homosexuality (Hart & Richardson, 1981; Kitzinger, 1987; Plummer, 1981; Weeks, 1981). The former view is that sexual orientation is a creation of Western culture that can be traced back to the 19th century, when the terminology and supportive ideology of homosexuality as a pathology emerged. The latter view is that sexual orientation reflects an *essential* characteristic of people that is based in deep-seated biological or psychological influences.

> The debate currently raging between "essentialist" scholars, who propound a biological base for gender and sexuality, versus "social constructionists," who emphasize cultural origins, is perhaps more accurately viewed from the perspective that human lives are shaped by the interaction of both of these factors. (Williams, 1987, p. 137)

These differing perspectives may be integrated if the unique varieties of lovemaps are seen as reflections of some essential characteristics of persons that have been constructed by social convention into concepts such as a bipolar sexual orientation. In this sense, the lovemap may resemble a "script" defined by social convention as well as by an idiosyncratic "fingerprint" (cf. Tiefer, 1987). It should also be noted that the lovemap can evolve over time; it may be constructed and reconstructed by the individual and need not be the same at age 45 or 70 as it was at age 15 or 25.

In summary, homophilia and heterophilia are aspects of an individual's unique pattern of sexual responsiveness. To reduce this complex lovemap to a bipolar dichotomy of homosexuality versus heterosexuality is not only a gross oversimplification, but also a reflection of Western religious beliefs and "either–or" logic. This simplistic perspective has led to a denial of similarity between and diversity within these supposedly dichotomous sexual orientations. It may also be observed that whereas our culture has emphasized the importance of this dimension of human sexuality, other cultures and historical eras have structured the meaning of homosexual behaviors and heterosexual behaviors differently (cf. Blackwood, 1985; Greenberg, 1988; Weinrich & Williams, 1991).

Lesbian and Gay Male Identity

Since the 19th century, the meaning of homosexuality has evolved from a purely sexual act to a personal identity (Foucault, 1979; Hart & Richardson, 1981; Weeks, 1977, Weinberg, 1983). Thus, in American culture, as Herek has stated, "What a person *does* sexually defines who the person *is*" (Herek, 1986, p. 568). The social forces that have transformed the awareness and conditions of gay and lesbian life, in part through the homophile rights movement, to produce a greater recognition of group identity have been documented by social historians (Adam, 1987; Altman, 1981; D'Emilio, 1983). In addition, the feminist movement changed women's ideas about sexuality in general, raised questions about traditional gender roles, and reduced stigma surrounding lesbianism; this led to visible communities based on lesbian–feminist ideology (Faderman, 1984; Krieger, 1982; Lockard, 1985). To a surprising extent, lesbian and gay male identity has been transformed in recent history from abnormal to *normatively different* (Brown, 1989).

> Back in 1948 to 1950 . . . there wasn't as yet in the minds of my fellow Queers, let alone the American society at large, even the beginnings of such a concept as that of a GAY IDENTITY. Everywhere we were constantly being told . . . that we were heteros who occasionally performed nasty acts. . . . The tremendous leap forward in consciousness that was the Stonewall Rebellion changed the pronoun in Gay identity from "I" to "WE." (Hay, 1990, p. 5)

As a result of these social changes, in Western societies today individuals have the opportunity to construct gay male and lesbian identities in ways that did not exist earlier (Herdt, 1989; Herek, 1985): For example, as a member of an oppressed minority (D'Emilio, 1983; Herdt, 1989; Herek, 1991), as a publicly acknowledged member of a community (Herek, 1991; Paul, 1982), as "women-identified-women" (Radicalesbians, 1973), or as part of a "lesbian continuum" (Rich, 1980). Like racial and ethnic minority identity, the contemporary view is that gay male and lesbian identity formation represents an emergent, continuous life process that does not have any necessary static endpoint (Boxer & Cohler, 1989; Golden, 1987; Lowenstein, 1985; Peplau, 1991; Troiden, 1988).

Gay and Lesbian Identity as a Minority Status

Lesbians and gay men share some elements in common with other minority groups (Bierly, 1985; Bradford & Ryan, 1987). For example, society defines gay men and lesbians largely in terms of characteristics that relegate them to unequal status and set them apart from the dominant group (Adam, 1978; de Monteflores, 1986; Herek, 1991). Similarly, on the basis of group stereotypes, gay men and lesbians are still denied full social participation and civil rights (cf. Herek, 1990a). Gay men and lesbians, therefore, represent a minority as a consequence of conditions imposed by majority reaction and treatment (Paul, 1982; Yearwood & Weinberg, 1979). As a result, lesbians and gay men have developed strategies to manage their differences from the mainstream and to respond to overt and covert oppression (Barrett, 1990; de Monteflores, 1986). Lesbians and gay men show great resilience in the face of social oppression. As individuals, they typically manage to form a positive sense of self and do not suffer from low self-esteem. As members of groups, gay men and lesbians have worked together to form support networks and communities to facilitate a positive individual and group identity (Harry & Duvall, 1978; Kurdek, 1988; M. S. Weinberg & Williams, 1974).

> The political minority status of gay people was recognized by the California Supreme Court in 1979 (*Gay Law Students Association v. Pacific Telephone and Telegraph*). Noting that the civil rights struggle of the gay community "must be recognized as political activity" (p. 32) and that publicly acknowledging one's own homosexual orientation is an important aspect of this struggle, the Court ruled that discrimination against openly gay individuals constitutes illegal discrimination on the basis of political activity. (Herek, 1991)

The Process of Lesbian and Gay Identity Development

Gay male and lesbian identity development, or "coming out," includes realization of one's own homosexuality as well as disclosure of this realization to others. Coming out has been conceptualized as a rite of passage during which one constructs one's own sense of self as gay or lesbian within the context of contemporary society (Herdt, 1989; Kleinberg, 1986). Self-labeling as gay, accepting this label, self-disclosing, and feeling accepted by others have been found to be strongly related to psychological adjustment (Bell & Weinberg, 1978; McDonald, 1982; Miranda & Storms, 1989). Similarly, a more positive gay male or lesbian identity has been found to be correlated with significantly fewer symptoms of neurotic or social anxiety, higher ego strength, less depression, and higher self-esteem (Hammersmith & Weinberg, 1973; Savin-Williams, 1989; Schmitt & Kurdek, 1987).

Zimmerman (1984) discussed the power of shared storytelling of lesbians through telling their coming out experiences: "The personal narrative, particularly the coming out story, forms our 'tribal lore,' our myth of origins" (p. 674). Whenever gay men and lesbians meet, sooner or later they get around to practicing this ritual of telling their coming out stories.

Today, one can also speak about *coming in*: the realization of having entered into a community and the process of identifying with a larger group of gay and lesbian people (Petrow, 1990). The presence of a gay male and lesbian support system has been found to be associated with adaptive coping strategies and lower levels of stress (Gillow & Davis, 1987), positive well-being (M. S. Weinberg & Williams, 1974), psychological adjustment (Kurdek, 1988), and more emotional intimacy in relationships (Harry, 1984). For lesbians, feminist values and involvement in feminist activities may also provide sources of validation, self-esteem, self-acceptance, and social support that facilitates development of lesbian identity (Leavy & Adams, 1986; Peplau & Cochran, 1981; Sophie, 1985/1986). For gay men, the gay community can function as a kind of club that provides social support, professional contacts, and entrée into social networks when traveling or relocating.

Considerable research has been devoted to the topic of lesbian and gay identity development. We can summarize three major themes here: developmental tasks in the acquisition of a positive identity, cultural diversity in identity development, and the time lag in achieving a positive lesbian or gay identity.

Developmental tasks in acquisition of identity. Empirical studies of gay male and lesbian identity development have focused on how individuals identify, label, and construct their sense of identity as lesbians and gay men and on understanding the developmental tasks necessary to form and to maintain a positive gay male or lesbian identity. Numerous stage-sequential models have been developed to organize and interpret the data on lesbian and gay identity development; some have been empirically tested (Cass, 1984; Chapman & Brannock, 1987; Coleman, 1981/1982; Hanely-Hackenbruck, 1988; Hencken & O'Dowd, 1977; Lee, 1977; Lewis, 1984; Minton & McDonald, 1983/1984; Weinberg, 1983; Sophie 1985/1986). Five central points may be drawn from these studies:

1. Initial awareness of same-gender sexual desires initiates a developmental transition in which individuals report feeling different and being off course (Boxer & Cohler, 1989; Schaefer, 1977; Troiden, 1979). During the period from first awareness to self-labeling, many gay men and lesbians experience a period of identity confusion characterized by feeling in limbo between questioning a heterosexual identity and recognizing a potential gay male or lesbian one (Cass, 1979; Troiden, 1988). Cass (1984) described the in-limbo phase of identity confusion in the following way:

> You feel that you *probably* are a homosexual, although you're not definitely sure. . . . You feel distant or cut off from *other people*. . . . You are beginning to think that it might help to meet other homosexuals but you're not sure whether you really want to or not. . . . You prefer to put on a front of being completely heterosexual. (Cass, 1984, p. 156)

2. Gay male and lesbian identity development requires individuals to reconcile their own uniqueness with society's template, with only partial success. In order to form a positive lesbian or gay male identity one must assess, confront, and reject the negative identity provided by society and transform that identity into a positive and viable self-concept (Espin, 1987; Fein & Nuehring, 1981; Malyon, 1982; Ponse, 1984). This process is accomplished by transforming the cognitive category *gay* or *lesbian* from negative stereotypes to positive labels (Dank, 1971). This is followed by increased acceptance and commitment of the label as applied to oneself. Cass (1979) described the growth of self-acceptance in the following terms: "I might be gay, I'm different"; then "I probably am gay"; then "I'm proud I'm gay"; then "I am gay and being gay is one aspect of who I am."

3. Throughout the identity-formation process, gay men and lesbians use a variety of strategies to evade the stigma associated with homosexuality, to manage the boundary between the heterosexual and the gay worlds, and to manage discrepancies between their same-gender sexual feelings or behaviors and their self-definition as gay or lesbian (de Monteflores, 1986; Hencken, 1984).

4. An important aspect of identity development involves exploration of the lesbian and gay subcultures and socialization into their norms (Plummer, 1975). Contact with these subcultures is available today in most cities, by newspaper subscriptions, and by toll-free information services. This contact helps to foster group identity, provides role models, reveals the diversity among homosexuals, diminishes feelings of isolation or alienation, and facilitates learning the folkways, behavior, language, and structure of the lesbian and gay male community (Harry, 1984; Kurdek, 1988).

5. Over time, gay men and lesbians experience an increased desire to disclose their identity to an expanding group of others that may include other lesbians and gay men, heterosexual friends, family, coworkers, acquaintances, and the public at large (Troiden, 1988).

Although generally a stage-sequential linear progression is assumed in lesbian and gay male identity development, the data indicate that the process might be better conceptualized as a repeating spiral pattern (Ponse, 1978; Troiden, 1988). In common with other aspects of adult development, one may traverse the same psychological territory again and again, albeit at different "elevations" (cf. Shneidman, 1989). Moreover, some events do not happen to everyone and, if they do occur, they happen in different ways (McDonald, 1982; Sophie, 1985/1986; Troiden & Goode, 1980).

> A great variety exists in the order and timing of events. . . . self definition may precede contact with other lesbians . . . or it may

follow such contact; disclosure to others, homosexual or heterosexual, may occur at any time, and probably occurs throughout the process; and one may enter a relationship with another woman before, at the same time, or after identifying oneself as a lesbian. (Sophie, 1985/1986, pp. 49–50)

Cultural diversity in identity formation. Acquiring a gay male or lesbian identity takes place against a background of family and cultural tradition, values, and social networks. Furthermore, racial and ethnic groups in the United States experience prejudice and discrimination on the basis of minority group status, which places additional constraints on life options, relationships, and identity (Cazenave, 1979, 1984; Ericksen, 1980; Mays, 1985). Frequently, the dilemma for racial or ethnic minority lesbians and gay men becomes one of managing conflicting allegiances among different communities (Loiacano, 1989; Morales, 1989). They must participate in divergent social worlds, balancing demands and crossing boundaries of the different groups, including the gay male and lesbian community, one's ethnic culture, the majority culture, and for women, the women's or feminist community. Individuals with double and triple minority status may experience discrimination and prejudice as outsiders in each community (Kanuha, 1990; Mays & Cochran, 1986). Although the goal may be to identify with, or be part of, both the ethnic or racial and lesbian or gay male communities, typically the result is greater comfort in the gay male and lesbian community but a stronger identity with the ethnic or racial group (Chan, 1989; Espin, 1987; Icard, 1985/1986; Wooden, Kawasaki, & Mayeda, 1983).

> I would be extremely unhappy if all my Latin culture were taken out of my lesbian life. . . . I identify myself as a lesbian more intensely than as a Cuban/Latin. But it is a very painful question because I feel that I am both, and I don't want to have to choose. (Espin, 1987, p. 47)

In research with small samples, race and skin color more frequently contribute to childhood harassment than cross-gender behavior (Sears, 1989). Similarly, as adults, samples of Asian-American, Latina, and African-American lesbians reported that discrimination was more frequent because of their race; gender was second and their sexual orientation was third (Chan, 1989; Espin, 1987; Mays & Cochran, 1986). However, Chan (1989) found that Asian-American gay men reported more frequent discrimination by the majority culture because they were gay.

Cooperation, interdependence and strong commitment to one's extended family and ethnic community as a primary reference group are highly valued in many cultures. Thus, gay men and lesbians may be perceived as challenging or violating social expectations not only for their personal life-style but also because they are placing personal desires above the needs of their family or the community (Amaro, 1978; Kanuha, 1990). Moreover, some misperceive homosexuality as a "White Western" phenomenon that is alien to their own ethnic group.

> Even though there are a lot of black homosexuals, a lot of blacks
> do not want to accept that fact. A homosexual thing is a white thing.
> (Sears, 1989, p. 428)

Thus, lesbians and gay men often feel like outcasts within their ethnic or racial community, may remain closeted there, and avoid disclosure to their families (Espin, 1987; Loiacano, 1989; Tremble, Schneider, & Appathurai, 1989).

Within the gay male and lesbian community, ethnic and racial discrimination can lead to being unacknowledged, unaccepted, or perceived as exotic (Chan, 1989). Often, gender or sexual stereotypes become linked with racial stereotypes (Icard, 1985/1986; Wooden et al., 1983). As a result, it is often difficult to find a niche because of discrimination (C. Klein, 1986; Morales, 1989; Tremble et al., 1989) and because prevailing Anglo norms may conflict with norms from their own ethnic communities (de Monteflores, 1981; Zimmerman, 1984).

> Lionel was in love with black people but not in love with black
> individuals. He had an image that because I was black, I was a stud,
> and if I didn't continually portray that image, that would upset him.
> (Silverstein, 1981, p. 164)

In recent years, lesbians and gay men of color have formed groups and organizations specifically created to provide support and a kind of extended family (Hidalgo, 1984; Icard, 1985/1986). For example, Mays and Cochran (1986) found that the main source of social support for their sample of African-American lesbians was other African-American lesbians.

Despite some similarities of experience, considerable diversity exists among ethnic and racial groups on the basis of ancestral heritage, national origin, generation, language, and socioeconomic status. In the United States several different traditions can be identified. For example, many African Americans view homosexuality as a threat to the family and group survival in the face of racism. Although sexuality is viewed as a natural and positive part of life that leads to childbearing and continues the race despite forces that threaten its members (P. M. Wilson, 1986) and there is some flexibility in gender roles within the family (Cazenave, 1979, 1984; Ericksen, 1980; Greene, 1986), nonetheless, homosexuality and interracial marriage are perceived by some as racial genocide. As a result, lesbians and gay men are perceived as guilty for failing to promote group survival through propagation of the race and for not supporting the racial struggle against oppression (Greene, 1986; Icard, 1985/1986). Although many Black churches are intolerant of homosexuality, there is a movement toward the development of Black gay churches (Tinney, 1986).

> If Black lesbians and gay men are willing to check their sexuality at the door of the church, and come bearing gifts of talent, there are relatively few problems. . . . The development of Black gay churches will make it possible for Black gay Christians, for the first time, to hear the gospel in their own "language of the Spirit," respond to the gospel in their own ways, and reinterpret the gospel in their own cultural context—taking into account both race and sexual orientation at every step in this process. (Tinney, 1986, pp. 73, 76)

For some Latino men, it is not infrequent for sexual contacts to include same-gender behavior, beginning in adolescence (Carballo-Dieguez, 1989; Espin, 1984). Sexual behavior is defined by the "masculinity" of the act: Men who insert their penises are regarded as masculine; those who receive them are viewed as feminine and degraded (Paz, 1961). Thus, same-gender sexual contact is tolerated if it is seen as masculine, but gay men are perceived as feminine and are subjected to stigma, shame, and prejudice (Carrier, 1976, 1980, 1985). Latino communities are less aware of the existence of lesbians than of gay men within their culture. Generally, only the openly butch types (i.e., those violating gender roles) are recognized as lesbians (Espin, 1984; Tremble et al., 1989). Vasquez (1979) found that lesbians who were more acculturated into "American ways" were less likely to be involved in playing the husband–wife roles in their relationships. Furthermore, Latina lesbians challenge the well-defined role of women in these cultures. They are perceived as being too independent from the family and not sufficiently feminine. They violate the cultural norms of submissiveness, virtuousness, respectfulness toward elders, deference to men, interdependence, and the expectation to reside within their family until marriage. Therefore, many Latina lesbians hide their sexual orientation to avoid stigmatization within their own ethnic communities (Amaro, 1978; Espin, 1987; Hildalgo, 1984).

> Being a lesbian is by definition an act of treason against our cultural values. . . . To be a lesbian we have to leave the fold of our family, and seek support within the mainstream white lesbian community. (Romo-Carmona, 1987, p. xxvi)

Asian Americans often regard sex as a taboo topic that is not to be discussed and see homosexuality as a potential threat to marriage and carrying on the family line. Within Confucian tradition, men ᠈ carriers of the family name, kinship linkage, and family heritage (D. Lee & Saul, 1987). To fail to produce offspring is a serious matter, especially because sexuality cannot be discussed openly. Being gay may represent one's first serious violation of parental norms (Abramson, 1986; Aoki, 1983). Therefore, gay men must manage the loss of face for not carrying on the family name and for making an individual choice rather than giving unquestioning respect to their elders (Bradshaw, 1990; Gock, 1986; Wooden et al., 1983). Asian communities in the United States still emphasize sharply delineated gender roles and negate or deny the possibility of lesbian existence (Lin, 1978). If acknowledged, lesbians are perceived as tarnishing the family honor by not being dutiful daughters, by rejecting the role of wife and mother, and by rejecting the role of passive reliance and deference to men and the submersion of identity within the family structure (Chan, 1987; Pamela, 1989; Shon & Ja, 1982). In addition, there is strong community pressure to remain closeted and not to be open about being gay or lesbian (Chan, 1989).

> My family holds Western culture somehow responsible for off-beat youth. They think my being lesbian is my being young, and confused, and rebellious. They feel it has something to do with trying to fit into White culture. It's one aspect among many that they don't like abut me. . . . And they're waiting for me to stop rebelling and to be heterosexual, go out on dates, and come home early. (Tremble et al., 1989, p. 260)

Native-American cultures have strong historical traditions of acceptance of homosexuality for both men and women, but Anglo values and reservation life have modified those values to some extent. Traditional values of many Native-American tribes did not link physical anatomy to gender roles. Anthropological evidence documents that socially recognized cross-gender roles and third gender roles were widespread, including *berdache* for men and *women warriors* for women (Blackwood, 1984; Whitehead, 1981; Williams, 1985). Anglo culture eventually altered and suppressed this traditional view. As a result, contemporary Native Americans report greater stigmatization and great difficulty being open about their homosexuality (Owlfeather, 1988). In addition, many migrated to cities where they had to manage racism and were cut off from traditional values (Williams, 1986).

> In the old days, during life on the plains, the people respected each other's vision. Berdaches had an integral place in the rigors and lifestyle of the tribe. The way they were viewed was not the same as the contemporary Indian gay lifestyle and consciousness that we have now—they were not fighting for a place in society and to be

accepted by that society. They already had a place, a very special and sacred place. (Owlfeather, 1988, p. 100)

It would be expected that lesbians and gay men of color and those from ethnic or religious backgrounds with especially negative attitudes about homosexuality would find it difficult to come out and to develop a positive gay male or lesbian identity.

Time lag in sexual identity development. Heterosexual adolescents probably do not question their sexual orientation because other-gender sexual feelings, life-style, and identity are not inconsistent with social expectations (cf. Stein & Cohen, 1986). However, gay men and lesbians appear to require several years to move from their initial awareness of same-gender sexual feelings to self-identification and then to acceptance of and commitment to a positive gay male or lesbian identity (McDonald, 1982; Riddle & Morin, 1977; Vance & Green, 1984). The modal pattern is shown in Table 1. On the average, gay men are aware of same-gender sexual feelings and act on this awareness during early to midadolescence. Lesbians are aware of these feelings during mid- to late adolescence but do not act on them until early adulthood, on the average.

Several factors may contribute to the delay, or time lag, for lesbian and gay adolescents. First, gay men and lesbians learn about homosexuality before they know that they are part of that group (Fein & Nuehring, 1981); their identity process is thereby delayed because they feel they share little in common with homosexuals as a group as they are defined by conventional society (Troiden, 1979). Second, societal attitudes toward homosexuality—such as degree of openness and tolerance, avail-

Table 1
Modal Ages for Milestones of Lesbian and Gay Male Identity Development

	Age (in years)	
Identity development	Lesbians	Gay Men
Initial awareness of same-gender affectional-erotic feelings	14–16	12–13
Initial same-gender sexual experience	20–22	14–15
Self-identification as lesbian or gay	21–23	19–21
Initial same-gender sexual relationship	20–24	21–24
Positive gay or lesbian identity	24–29	22–26

Note. These data represent a summary of the following studies: Bell and Weinberg (1978), Jay and Young (1979), and Riddle and Morin (1977). Data from lesbians only: Chapman and Brannock (1987), Gramick (1984), Schaefer (1976), and Vance and Green (1984). Data from gay men only: Dank (1971), Harry and Duvall (1978), Lynch (1987), McDonald (1982), Remafedi (1987), Roesler and Deisher (1972), and T. S. Weinberg (1978).

ability of accurate information, significant others who share a positive view of lesbians and gay men, and legal protections to buffer discrimination and prejudice—have been found to be inversely related to the length of time it takes individuals to form a gay male or lesbian identity (Carrier, 1980; Harry & Duvall, 1978; McDonald, 1982; Troiden & Goode, 1980). For example, in a study of four cultures by Ross (1989), the more sexually restrictive and negative the attitudes were regarding homosexuality in the culture, the greater the suppression of the respondents' gay identity and the later the ages that the gay men discovered their homosexuality. Third, social assumptions about universal development of heterosexuality complicate and delay gay male and lesbian identity development (Herdt, 1989; Herek, 1986; Stein & Cohen, 1986). That is, the absence of social affirmation of homosexuality and lack of explicit roles means that lesbians and gay men must invent their own personal framework for identity and for maintenance of self-esteem (Brown, 1989). Fourth, because of heterosexist assumptions and social pressure, the vast majority of gay men and lesbians report both same-gender and other-gender sexual arousal and behavior during adolescence and early adulthood (Bell & Weinberg, 1978; Bell et al., 1981; Jay & Young, 1979; Remafedi, 1987). Engaging in other-gender sexual experiences (including marriage) may delay self-discovery as gay (Bozett, 1989; Gramick, 1984; Troiden & Goode, 1980). Thus, lesbians and gay men may misclassify themselves, their behavior, or experiences as heterosexual, which would interfere with the labeling process of homosexual identity development (Hencken, 1984).

This delay in sexual identity development appears to be more pronounced for women than for men, especially because sexual maturation occurs earlier in girls than in boys. There are several plausible reasons for this difference. Lesbians are more likely to be involved in other-gender sexual activity than gay men, less likely to have same-gender sexual contact, more likely to continue other-gender sexual activity after questioning their sexual identity and after having sexual contact with another woman, and more likely to get married than gay men (Bell & Weinberg, 1978; Chapman & Brannock, 1987). It may be that lesbians continue other-gender sexual activities because they are conforming to social norms that emphasize heterosexual dating (Gramick, 1984; Schaefer, 1976). One woman in Troiden's (1989) study stated a common theme:

> I thought my attraction to women was a passing phase and would go away once I started having intercourse with my boyfriend. (p. 57)

In contrast, during adolescence gay men are more likely than lesbians to engage in same-gender sexual behavior, fantasize about same-gender sex, and be sexually attracted to members of the same gender (Bell & Weinberg, 1978; Sears, 1989).

Other factors, such as geographic setting, may facilitate or hinder gay male and lesbian identity development. For example, gay men who live in proximity to urban centers arrive at a gay identity sooner than those living in outlying areas (D'Augelli, 1989; Troiden & Goode, 1980). In contrast, gay men living in suburban areas tend to be more circumspect in revealing their identity, have fewer same-gender sexual relationships, have less social involvement with other gay men and more social involvement with heterosexuals than do those living in urban areas (Lynch, 1987; M. S. Weinberg & Williams, 1974). Likewise, gay men and lesbians living in rural areas experience greater isolation and find it more difficult to make enduring friendships and relationships; rural social networks tend to be more inaccessible and exclusionary than in urban areas (D'Augelli, Collins, & Hart, 1987; Hollander, 1989; Moses & Buckner, 1980).

Recent social change regarding greater visibility of the gay male and lesbian community, as noted earlier, may have reduced the extent of this lag time in development. Moreover, it may have increased the willingness of lesbians and gay men to disclose their identity to others.

Identity Disclosure to Family, Friends, and Coworkers

Data strongly suggest that a prerequisite for the emergence of a positive gay male or lesbian identity is the communication of one's sexual orientation to others (Bell & Weinberg, 1978; Bradford & Ryan, 1987; Hammersmith & Weinberg, 1973; Miranda & Storms, 1989). Moreover, studies have demonstrated the psychological benefits of coming out to others: enhanced personal integrity (Rand, Graham, & Rawlings, 1982); increased self-affirmation (Wells & Kline, 1987); identity integration (Murphy, 1989); increased intimacy in relationships (Cramer & Roach, 1988; Wells & Kline, 1987); greater freedom from concealing, anticipating, and defending against rejection (Cramer & Roach, 1988; M. S. Weinberg & Williams, 1974); decreased feelings of isolation (Murphy, 1989); increased sense of public affirmation of sexual identity (Schneider, 1986); and greater acceptance from others (Olsen, 1987).

In deciding whether or not to tell, lesbians and gay men must weigh problems presented by their marginal status that reflect the social realities and risks of their environment (Bradford & Ryan, 1987). Gay men and lesbians expect and report experiences of negative reactions, discrimination, and prejudice on the basis of disclosures of their sexual identity in a variety of areas of life, including child custody (Actenberg, 1988; Falk, 1989), antigay hate crimes (Garnets et al., 1990; Herek, 1989), and discrimination or fear of discrimination in employment (Hall, 1989; Levine, 1979; Levine & Leonard, 1984).

Balancing the costs and benefits of identity disclosure is a multi-faceted, life-long process of decision making. The principle of *rational outness* is usually the pragmatic solution: "to be as open as possible, because it feels healthy to be honest, and as closed as necessary to protect against discrimination" (Bradford & Ryan, 1987, p. 77). Generally, gay men and lesbians disclose to close heterosexual friends and to siblings more often than to parents, coworkers, or employers.

Moreover, data have indicated that the recipient of the coming out message either is more positive to begin with or also benefits. That is, people who know someone who is lesbian or gay (even those from groups with generally antigay attitudes) tend to have more positive attitudes about gay men and lesbians compared with other members of their group (Herek, 1991).

Disclosure to parents and other significant relatives often precipitates a period of turmoil for the family frequently involving three initial reactions. First, parents feel guilt and personal responsibility for their child's homosexuality and experience a sense of failure as parents (Griffin, Wirth, & Wirth, 1986; Robinson, Walters, & Skeen, 1989). Second, parents may ignore their child's individuality and personal experience by applying negative values and misconceptions about homosexuality to their son or daughter; likewise, they may fear others will similarly apply stereotypes to them, leading to isolation and ostracism from their social network. Third, the "new" identity may create feelings of alienation and family members might react as if the person were unfamiliar and estranged; as a result family roles and relationships can be disrupted (Devine, 1984; Strommen, 1989). Often, parents' reactions are based on early psychological theories that attributed the cause of homosexuality to the parent–child relationship; these theories, which were based on studies with biased samples such as psychotherapy patients, have not been supported by more recent empirical research (e.g., Bell et al., 1981). A typical reaction is the following:

> Every book that I had seen said homosexuality was caused by a disturbance in the family. They said that there was usually an absent or rejecting father and a domineering, seductive, or binding kind of mother. I thought about how much Jack worked when the kids were small and the fact that I was the one who stayed home and took care of them. I twisted it all around and said "Yes, maybe we are like that. Maybe there was something really wrong with us." (Griffin et al., 1986, p. 7)

Resolution of the family issues that result from disclosure by a son or daughter is often a complex and lengthy process, sometimes aided by a peer support group known as Parents and Friends of Lesbians and Gays (Collins & Zimmerman, 1983; Griffin et al., 1986; Kleinberg, 1986; Robinson et al., 1989).

There are few data about coming out to other relatives, such as siblings or to grandparents. Often, disclosure may be made to relatives who are expected to be the most supportive, and sometimes the family protects the secret from members who are thought to be most unwilling to react positively.

Several studies have focused on married bisexual, gay, or lesbian individuals coming out to their heterosexual spouses. Disclosure of the wife's bisexuality or lesbianism seems almost always to lead to divorce; thus, most research has focused on bisexual or gay men who remain married (Coleman, 1985a). Disclosure of the husband's gay or bisexual orientation also often results in separation or divorce (Bozett, 1982; Miller, 1978, 1979). However, sometimes disclosure ends barriers to intimacy in marriage and helps to integrate homosexuality or bisexuality into restructured marital relationships such as open or semiopen marriages or asexual friendships (Brownfain, 1985; Coleman, 1985b; Gochros, 1989; Latham & White, 1978; Wolfe, 1985). In general, bisexual-identified men report greater contentment in marriages, more sexual activity with wives, and longer marriages than men who are gay identified (Brownfain, 1985). The most salient factors for the stabilization of mixed-orientation marriages appear to be that the bisexual orientation is disclosed by husbands early and acknowledged by spouses as a fact of the marriage and that the husbands show an ongoing ability to face their same-gender sexual desires realistically without losing empathy and concern for their wives' needs and rights (Gochros, 1989; Matteson, 1985, 1987). Wives have been found to react both to the homosexuality and to issues of isolation, lack of support, stigma, and loss (Auerback & Moser, 1987; Gochros, 1985; Hays & Samuels, 1989). Support groups for wives of gay and bisexual men have been found to be helpful in negotiating and adapting to the disclosure (Auerback & Moser, 1987; Gochros, 1989).

Researchers have noted that it rare to find women remain married or in sexually open relationships among bisexual samples (Coleman, 1985a); in one study 97% of the lesbian wives were divorced, compared with 78% of gay husbands (Wyers, 1987). The primary reasons lesbian and bisexual women give for ending their marriages relatively quickly are lack of sexual desire for the spouse, low tolerance for open marriages or for secretive extramarital relationships, and their husband's lack of tolerance of their bisexual life-style (Coleman, 1985a; Matteson, 1987).

> As in female homosexual relationships, bisexual women seem to be less able than bisexual males to tolerate multiple relationships. So in their marital relationships they might feel a greater need to end the relationship because of the basic incompatibility they perceive between their homosexual feelings and activities and their marriage. In addition, their husbands might not be able to tolerate their wives' homosexual activity, although, with the roles reversed, such a dou-

ble standard allows the males to tolerate their own outside homosexual interests and activities without much difficulty. (Coleman,
1985a, p. 97)

It should be noted that these differences in the marital adaptations of
bisexual and homosexual men and women may reflect gender differences
between women and men.

Coming out at work typically causes lesbians and gay men a great
deal of anxiety about both formal and informal employment discrimination (Levine & Leonard, 1984). For example, over two thirds of gay men
and lesbians reported in surveys conducted across a variety of occupational and work settings (Levine & Leonard, 1984; Winkelpleck & West-
field, 1982) that their disclosure would be a problem at work. Reports
of actual discrimination and related problems at work ranged from 20%
to 35% (Blumstein & Schwartz, 1983; Bradford & Ryan, 1987; Taylor,
1986). Lesbians appear to experience double jeopardy in the work setting
both as women and as lesbians (Hall, 1989; Schneider, 1986). Gay men
and lesbians in higher status occupations are less likely to disclose their
sexual identity at work than those in lower status occupations (Bradford
& Ryan, 1987; Harry & Duvall, 1978; Schneider, 1986). The most common
coping strategy reported is that gay men and lesbians tend to lead a
somewhat double life at work, putting a significant amount of energy
into monitoring a heterosexual facade through the use of managed
information, avoidance of leisure with coworkers, and separation of work
and home life (Hall, 1989; Shachar & Gilbert, 1983). Usually they come
out to coworkers more frequently than to employers and use a strategy
of partial and highly selective disclosure (Bell & Weinberg, 1978; Olsen,
1987; M. S. Weinberg & Williams, 1974). Often, lesbians and gay men
experience at work the greatest discrepancy between the extent to which
they would like to be out and the degree to which they actually are open
(cf. Kooden et al., 1979). Other solutions adopted include self-employ-
ment and forming support groups at work sites or within one's profession
or career (Bell & Weinberg, 1978; Levine & Leonard, 1984; Russo, 1982).

Some Differences Between Gay Men and Lesbians

Gender is a powerful organizer of sexual behavior, identity, and relationship patterns. In general, gay men are more similar to heterosexual
men, and lesbian women more similar to heterosexual women, than to
each other. For example, in an undergraduate course on the psychology
of the lesbian experience taught by Linda Garnets, the gay men and
lesbians initially are closely aligned. As the class progresses, however,
the alliances switch: The lesbian and heterosexual women feel they share
more in common, and the gay and heterosexual men experience greater

similarities. On one hand, lesbians and gay men experience the same social pressure to conform to gender expectations as is the case for others. Moreover, they share many gender-typed experiences and pre-dispositions with others of the same gender. On the other hand, they create patterns of behavior, identity, and relationships that neither mirror nor duplicate heterosexual patterns.

Gender Differences in Roles and Behavior

In the United States, what it means *not* to be heterosexual is different in many respects for lesbians and gay men. In particular, lesbians share with women the institutional oppression of sexism (which includes access to fewer material resources) and with gay men the denial of civil rights and the social stigma of homosexuality (Eldridge, 1987; Zimmerman, 1984). Moreover, women and men are unequally constrained from same-gender intimacy and from gender nonconformity (Blumstein & Schwartz, 1989; Henderson, 1984). In short, lesbians are not identical to gay men.

Heterosexual masculinity is an identity defined in terms both of what it is and what it is not: the absence of any trace of femininity or any interest in men that could be interpreted as potentially homosexual (Herek, 1986; Thompson & Pleck, 1986). Endorsement of traditional masculine roles is related to fear of femininity and homophobia (Herek, 1988; O'Neill, Helms, & Gable, 1986). In addition, men are socialized to be sexually active and initiating and to strive for immediate gratification. They receive greater social support than women for sexual experimentation, for separating sex and love, and for enjoying casual sex for its own sake without emotional involvement (Fracher & Kimmel, 1987; Gagnon & Simon, 1973).

Heterosexual femininity involves assuming social roles, specifically those of wife and mother. This is achieved by learning to attract a man and to define oneself in terms of psychological, emotional, and physical dependence on men. Part of the ideology of heterosexual femininity is experiencing male approval and love as central to self-esteem (Faraday, 1981). Women learn to be sexual in the contest of social relationships, to place constraints on exploration of their sexuality, to emphasize feelings, to minimize the importance of immediate sexual activity, to experience emotional involvement and commitment toward another person before sexual activity is initiated, and to be reactive to male sexual needs. As a result, female gender socialization may limit sexual expression for both heterosexual and lesbian women and inhibit discovery on one's unique sexuality (Blackwood, 1985; Faraday, 1981; Palladino & Stephenson, 1990).

Gay men tend to be sexually active with male partners before labeling themselves as gay and generally seek experiences in settings where they gather for sexual purposes to help define themselves as gay (Dank, 1971; Herdt, 1989; Larsen, 1982; T. S. Weinberg, 1978). For example, Paroski (1987), in a study of gay male and lesbian adolescents, found that 95% of males compared with 16% of females learned about homosexuality through sexual encounters; similarly, he reported that 81% of the males and 31% of the females visited locations thought or known to be gay or lesbian (many of these places, such as public restrooms, are used only by men for sexual purposes). Moreover, gay men are likely to have sexual experiences with a variety of partners before they focus on one special person (Bell & Weinberg, 1978; Sears, 1989; M. S. Weinberg & Williams, 1974). Sexual and erotic compatibility (e.g., physical appearance) appears to be more salient for gay men than for lesbians in selecting partners (Blumstein & Schwartz, 1983; Sergio & Cody, 1985). Gay men tend to develop affectional relationships out of sexual ones (Harry, 1983). These patterns parallel data on heterosexual men (V. Green, 1985; Hunt, 1974; Phillis & Gramko, 1985; G. D. Wilson, 1987).

Lesbians tend to experience sexual feelings in situations of romantic love and emotional attachment (Blumstein & Schwartz, 1989; Vetere, 1983). Several studies have shown that lesbians experience emotional attraction to another female several years before experiencing physical attraction—mean ages were 14.5 and 17.4 years, respectively (Gramick, 1984; Vance & Green, 1984; cf. Schaefer, 1977). Unlike gay men, lesbians are more likely to have sexual experiences in the context of emotional relationships with one woman or a series of "special women" (Hedblom, 1973; Ponse, 1978; Sears, 1989). Many lesbians have their first same-gender sexual experience with a peer or in a friendship context (Schaefer, 1977; Vetere, 1983). Moreover, women who identify as lesbian tend to do so primarily on the basis of a lesbian relationship and only secondarily on the basis of sexual contact. These findings parallel data on heterosexual women (Blumstein & Schwartz, 1989; G. D. Wilson, 1987).

In summary, gay men are similar to heterosexual men and lesbians are similar to heterosexual women. However, gay men and lesbians do not adhere rigidly to traditional gender roles (Kurdek, 1987; Kurdek & Schmitt, 1986a; Macklin, 1983). Frequently, gay men and lesbians adopt a nontraditional identity that *includes* nontraditional gender role norms. Thus, the experience of gay men and lesbians provides a unique opportunity to see the impact on identity, behavior, and relationships when the traditional patterns based on gender are reduced or removed.

Differences in Meaning of Sexual Feelings and Experiences

Gay men have been noted to emphasize erotic and genital meanings of their sexual relationships (Riddle & Morin, 1977; Sears, 1989). Moreover, gay men tend to believe that sexual orientation is discovered and to define *gay* in terms of sexual arousal and sexual behavior (Hencken,

1984). Lesbians are more likely than are gay men to define their sexual identity in terms of affectional preferences (emotional quality and love between partners), political choices (affirmation of solidarity with all women or breaking with certain traditional standards of behavior for women), and the idea that sexual orientation is chosen (Hunnisett, 1986; Peplau & Cochran, 1981; Ponse, 1984; Vetere, 1983). Moreover, lesbians are more likely than gay men to define themselves in terms of their total identity and not only by their sexual behavior (Faderman, 1984; Ponse, 1984). It has been suggested by Blumstein and Schwartz (1989) that if the Kinsey scale were to assess sexuality in women more accurately, it would have evaluated the "intensity and frequency of love relationships, some of which might have only incidental, overt erotic components" (p. 23). For example, a lesbian in Sears's (1989) study defined a homosexual as a person who "has intimate love for a person of the same sex." A gay man in this study defined a homosexual as "someone who has sex with the same sex."

Likewise, gay men and lesbians use different stigma-management strategies in order to avoid labeling themselves as gay or lesbian (de Monteflores & Schultz, 1978; Groves & Ventura, 1983; Hencken, 1984). Consistent with male role expectations, gay men tend to use strategies that deny affective involvement in order to minimize the importance of sexual experiences with men. For example, Hencken (1984) noted that gay men may neutralize emotions by emphasizing sexual gratification as a goal of sexuality ("It's just physical," "I was just horny") or by denying responsibilities for feelings or actions ("I was drunk"). Lesbians are more likely to avoid identifying as lesbian by emphasizing their feelings and minimizing the saliency of sexuality than are gay men. For example, lesbians more often report using the "special case" strategy to avoid identifying as gay; they romanticize sexual events and explain them in terms of intense love and feeling for a particular woman (de Monteflores & Schultz, 1978; Hencken, 1984).

> I never thought of my feelings and our lovemaking as lesbian. The whole experience was too beautiful for it to be something so ugly. I didn't think I could ever have those feelings for another woman. (Troiden, 1988, p. 49)

Sanctions for Violating Male and Female Gender Roles

In order to assume a gay male or lesbian identity, individuals must diverge from traditional gender norms regarding sexual behavior. As children both lesbians and gay men report a similar incidence of cross-gender behavior (60% in one study), but girls are much less likely to experience harassment for it (Sears, 1989). As a consequence, gay men may become sensitized sooner in childhood to being "different" (Bell &

Weinberg, 1978; Bell et al., 1981; Troiden, 1988). These data are consistent with those found for heterosexual boys and girls. That is, girls who act like boys receive fewer negative sanctions than boys who act like girls. Both mothers and fathers view cross-gender activities as being more strongly associated with homosexuality for boys than for girls (Block, 1983; Bolton & MacEachron, 1988). Similarly, same-gender intimacy and affection are permitted in Anglo-European families for girls and women but are highly suspect for boys and men (Henderson, 1984; R. Lewis, 1978). Likewise, homophobic attitudes are more prevalent among men than among women, at least in heterosexual samples (Herek, 1988; Kite, 1984).

> Proving one's manhood/womanhood is in the popular imagination bound up with the rejection of any fag or dyke characteristics. If this seems more obvious in the case of men, it is because women have traditionally been defined as inferior, and whereas there is some grudging respect accorded women with masculine qualities, none is given to "womanly" men. Even among children "tomboys" are more acceptable than "sissies." (Altman, 1971, pp. 69–70)

Fear of being labeled homosexual is an especially important socialization influence in American society. It is the most frequently selected as the "worst thing" a man can call another man (Preston & Stanley, 1987). Both women and men who manifest characteristics inconsistent with those prescribed by the culture are more likely to be labeled homosexual (Deaux & Lewis, 1984; Herek, 1984; Storms, Stivers, Lambers, & Hill, 1981). One significant function of this social stigma is to define limits of acceptable behavior for men and for women (Herek, 1986). Thus, gender roles are enforced through the stigma of homosexuality. Moreover, the content of antigay stereotypes is tied to gender nonconformity (Herek, 1991).

> Homophobia begins in elementary school when "girl," "sissy," "queer," "virgin," and "fag" are the worst put-downs boys can hear. . . . Then homophobia begins to play itself out in locker-room talk where "the guys" boast of "scoring." To be "cool," and to avoid being called "gay," boys forcibly push for intercourse with girls. . . . Even masturbation is affected by homophobia and misogyny. In the hallways, and in sexuality education classes, boys often say, "only fags masturbate" or "why masturbate, you can always find an ugly girl willing to have sex." Homophobia thus encourages boys to label people based on stereotypes; to compete with and distance themselves from other boys; and to objectify, and even rape, girls. (Friedman, 1989, p. 8)

It therefore may be suggested that homophobia is harmful to heterosexuals as well as to lesbians and gay men because it keeps everyone in their place by raising fears that deviation from traditional gender roles will lead to one being seen as a "fag" or "lezzie."

Gay and Lesbian Relationships

Same-gender sexual relationships develop within a social context of societal disapproval with an absence of social legitimization and support; families and other social institutions often stigmatize such relationships and there are no prescribed roles and behaviors to structure such relationships (Dailey, 1979; Kurdek & Schmitt, 1987a; Risman & Schwartz, 1988). In part because of the absence of prescribed patterns, lesbian and gay male relationships are diverse and do not conform to heterosexist role stereotypes (Peplau, 1991). In contrast, they tend to rely on innovative processes of creating idiosyncratic rules, expectations, and division of labor within the relationship (Peplau & Cochran, 1990). Moreover, same-gender sexual relationships tend to be as loving, committed, stable, and satisfying as heterosexual marriages (Kurdek & Schmitt, 1986c; Peplau & Gordon, 1983).

> Same-sex relationships seem to be a naturally occurring experiment in role-free relationships. (Harry, 1984, p. 3)

Researchers have investigated the experiences of gay men and lesbians and made comparisons across married, cohabiting heterosexual, gay male, and lesbian couples. The same-gender and cross-gender comparisons have provided an opportunity to assess varying influences of gender and sexual orientation on intimate relationships, the unique characteristics of gay male and lesbian relationships, and factors that characterize intimate relationships regardless of sexual orientation. Some of the major findings are the following:

1. Many similarities are found between heterosexual and homosexual couples, indicating commonality in dynamics within the relationship and a similar range of diversity among relationships (Dailey, 1979; Eldridge & Gilbert, 1990; Jones & DeCecco, 1982; Kurdek & Schmitt, 1987a). For example, homosexual and heterosexual couples matched on age, education, and length of relationship reported similar relationship values and level of relationship satisfaction (related to duration of the relationship), perceived the relationship as loving and satisfying, and sought similar characteristics in their partners (Cardell, Finn, & Marecek, 1981; Kurdek & Schmitt, 1986c; Harry, 1983; Peplau & Cochran, 1981; Peplau, Cochran, & Mays, 1986).

2. Gender roles appear to be more powerful than sexual orientation in influencing behaviors in intimate relationships. In general, gender roles exert stronger effects than biological sex; for example, relationships in which both partners were androgynous or feminine showed higher relationship quality than for masculine or undifferentiated partners (Kurdek, 1987). Psychological femininity has been associated with stability, security, and support for continuation of both heterosexual and homosexual relationships (Schullo & Alperson, 1984), intimacy among gay men (Harry, 1984), and constructive responses to dissatisfaction in close relationships (Rusbult, Zembrodt, & Iwaniszek, 1986).

3. Gay men and lesbians bring to love relationships many of the same expectations, values, and interests as heterosexuals of the same gender. That is, lesbians are more likely than gay men to live with their primary partner and be in a steady relationship (Bell & Weinberg, 1978; Duffy & Rusbult, 1986; Peplau & Amaro, 1982; Schaefer, 1977); prefer having sex only with partners they care about, view sexuality and love as closely linked, and desire sexual exclusivity (Bell & Weinberg, 1978; Cotton, 1974; Peplau & Amaro, 1982; Schaefer, 1977); place greater importance on emotional intimacy (Blumstein & Schwartz, 1983; Kurdek & Schmitt, 1986a; R. A. Lewis, Kozac, & Grosnick, 1981; Vetere, 1983); value and have equality of involvement and equality in power (Blumstein & Schwartz, 1983; Caldwell & Peplau, 1984; Lynch & Reilly, 1986); and find variations in dyadic attachment and personal autonomy values to be more relevant and important to lesbian relationship experiences (Eldridge & Gilbert, 1990; Peplau & Cochran, 1981; Peplau, Cochran, Rook, & Padesky, 1978). Gay men are more likely than lesbians to report an interest in sex, sexual variety, and for sexual openness to be the most frequent relationship pattern (Bell & Weinberg, 1978; Blasband & Peplau, 1985; Blumstein & Schwartz, 1983; Peplau & Cochran, 1981). A typical pattern is a progression from sexual exclusivity during the initial phase of the relationship toward greater sexual openness; gay male couples experiment with and modify sexually exclusive arrangements (Blasband & Peplau, 1985). Researchers who have compared gay men in open and closed relationships have found no significant differences in psychological adjustment (Blasband & Peplau, 1985; Harry, 1984; Kurdek & Schmitt, 1986b).

4. A gender-based division of labor is not necessary for relationships to function well. Traditional gender roles are less common in lesbian and gay couples than in heterosexual couples (Cardell et al., 1981; Howard, Blumstein, & Schwartz, 1986; Kurdek, 1987; Marecek, Finn, & Cardell, 1982). Partners in gay male and lesbian relationships show greater equality, reciprocity, and role flexibility than partners in heterosexual relationships (Blumstein & Schwartz, 1983; Kurdek & Schmitt, 1986c; Lynch & Reilly, 1986). Most gay male and lesbian couples value power equality and shared decision making as a goal for their relationships (Blumstein & Schwartz, 1983; Kurdek & Schmitt, 1986a; Peplau,

1983). In general, lesbian and gay male couples frequently adopt a peer-friendship model of intimate relationships; few incorporate elements of husband–wife roles into their relationship (Bell & Weinberg, 1978; Blumstein & Schwartz, 1983; Caldwell & Peplau, 1984; Harry, 1983).

5. Lesbians and gay men and heterosexuals receive similar amounts of emotional and social support, but from different sources; nonetheless, they report similar levels of satisfaction (Kurdek, 1988; Kurdek & Schmitt, 1986c, 1987b; Peplau, 1991). In general, married heterosexuals perceive greater levels of support from family of origin than do lesbians and gay men, whereas gay men and lesbians perceive greater support from friends and partners than do their heterosexual counterparts (Blumstein & Schwartz, 1983; Kurdek, 1988; Kurdek & Schmitt, 1987b; McWhirter & Mattison, 1984).

Lesbian and Gay Parenting

Gay men and lesbians become parents in several ways: by heterosexual contact, often during a marriage; by alternative (artificial) insemination, in which the donor may or may not be known; by mutual agreement to rear a child communally, perhaps between a gay male couple and a lesbian couple (parenthood may be known or may be randomly selected); and by foster parenthood, where allowed, or by adoption—in which case, race or cultural background may be discordant from the parents and other siblings. Each of these types of parenthood presents unique issues, potential problems, and opportunities for creative innovation.

> My younger son picked up a girl in a bar in Virginia Beach one summer who was grieving over her mother having come out to her. "My Mom is a Lesbian, too," he told her, and took her home to look through his photograph album at our pictures, our happy family. (MacPike, 1989, p. 37)

Considerable research attention has focused on lesbian and gay male parents, primarily because of custody and adoption issues. The findings have supported the conclusion that lesbian mothers are likely to be good parents and to have no ill effects on their children because of their sexual orientation (Falk, 1989; R. Green, Mandel, Hotvedt, Gray, & Smith, 1986; Hill, 1987). Likewise, R. Green et al. (1986) reported no differences between children from heterosexual and lesbian families in peer group relationships, popularity, or social adjustment. Moreover, there is considerable evidence that the sexual orientation of mothers has no detrimental effect on the child's gender role development and is not associated with the child's sexual orientation (Falk, 1989; Gibbs, 1989; R. Green, 1982; R. Green et al., 1986; Hoeffer, 1981). Because women-headed households tend to be economically disadvantaged, whether they are lesbian or heterosexual, socioeconomic factors are likely to override sexual orientation in terms of effects on children of lesbian mothers.

> They think . . . that instead of getting up/in the middle of the night/for a 2 AM and 6AM feeding/we rise up and chant/*you're gonna be a dyke/you're gonna be a dyke.* (Parker, 1987, p. 208)

Although research on the effects of gay fathers is scarce, it suggests that gay fathers are likely to be good parents, that the children can cope with this family arrangement satisfactorily, and that the father's openness about his sexual orientation is beneficial (Bozett, 1987, 1988, 1989; Miller, 1979, 1987).

Some research has examined the effects of the social stigma of having a gay or lesbian parent on the child. In general, although such stigma exists, its effects have tended to be no greater than for children from divorcing families and may be offset by the parents' efforts to prevent or counteract it (Bozett, 1987; Falk, 1989). Likewise, parental disclosures of their sexual orientation appears to have a positive effect on the parent–child relationship by strengthening the relationship between gay male and lesbian parents and their children and by reducing the psychological distance between the parents and their children (Auerback & Mosher, 1987; Bell & Weinberg, 1978; Miller, 1979). Moreover, parents often perceive benefits of disclosure for their children, such as learning to have empathy for others and an opportunity to be exposed to different viewpoints (Cramer, 1986; Harris & Turner, 1985).

> Rather than posing a menace to children, gays may actually facilitate important developmental learning. To offset the pressures of a heterosexual society toward adopting traditional sex-role behavior, gays often demonstrate a variety of alternative adaptations. . . . Presumably, an increased comfort with diversity could result in a greater ability to make personal choices independent of societal pressures to conform. Comfort with diversity appears crucial to effecting a reversal of present attitudes towards homosexualtiy. (Riddle, 1978, p. 53)

Additional research is clearly needed on the uniqueness of lesbian and gay parenting, especially focusing on the growing number of lesbians and gay men who are choosing to parent and the complex issues of the effects of coparenting.

Similarly, greater research attention needs to be given to the uniqueness of lesbian and gay male experiences of other other life span issues such as adolescence and aging.

Lesbians who are middle-aged today are a unique population. We constitute the "Bridge Generation." We were young and most of us "came out" before the women's movement or the gay liberation movement. Our midlife changes are occurring in a world which is substantially different from the world in which we learned "how to be a lesbian." (Sang, Warshow, & Smith, 1991)

Conclusions

The psychological study of lesbian and gay issues is an emerging field that has only begun to explore the ramifications of the social significance attributed to sexual orientation. Although homosexuality is no longer considered to be a form of mental illness, considerable attention has been given to a wide range of factors thought to predispose individuals to homosexuality. Nonetheless, today no more is known about the specific origins of sexual orientation than is known about the origins of other characteristics such as expertise in ballet, chess, or the violin. The best conclusion is that a complex set of factors interact, varying from individual to individual, to produce lesbian and gay adults. Likewise, the gay male and lesbian community is diverse and multiethnic and differs by gender, socioeconomic status, and few generalizations apply across cultural borders.

We have discussed the relevance of sexual orientation to the psychological understanding of people, the development of gay male and lesbian identity within a multicultural society, some differences between lesbians and gay men, and lesbian and gay male relationships and parenting. Throughout, we have noted the broader context of gender roles, social change, and the interrelation of these issues to the political arena. In concluding, we call attention to the salient issues for psychology in terms of practice and research.

Two waves of gay and lesbian affirmative practice have been noted (Gonsiorek, 1988). The first wave assisted gay men and lesbians in understanding and accepting their sexual orientation as a natural part of themselves, helped them develop srategies for coping and forming a positive sense of identity, and taugh them the effect of social attitudes, prejudice, discrimination and heterosexism on psychological functioning. A second wave has now emerged and four themes are evident: (a) using education, training, ethical and professional guidelines, and research to reduce bias in theories and practice; for example, a forthcoming issue of the *American Psychologist* will focus on the theme of removing the stigma—15 years later; (b) integrating gay affirmative concepts into current personality theories and therapy approaches; (c) promoting empirical testing of gay affirmative modes and theories; and (d) examining ways in which gay and lesbian paradigms help inform and reconceptualize issues of sexuality, gender roles, identity, intimacy, family relationships, and life span development.

> By defining norms and terms from within lesbian and gay realities, psychologists ask themselves how these new paradigms might broaden the understanding of heterosexual realities as well. (Brown, 1989, pp. 454–455)

Similarly, psychological research has shifted from removing the stigma of pathology from lesbians and gay men to examining issues of implicit concern to them. Five major themes have emerged: (a) Research on mental health has documented that as individuals, couples, and a social community, gay men and lesbians do not show lower levels of adjustment. Moreover, research has focused on the nature and impact of negative social attitudes toward lesbians and gay men and has documented the pervasive effects of heterosexist bias and homophobia within American society. (b) Research has shifted from viewing homosexuals as a group with definite characteristics to a recognition of the diversity that exists among lesbians and gay men. This view has led to an increased awareness of the similarity between heterosexuals and homosexuals on one hand; on the other hand, it has called attention to the effects of gender, ethnicity, race, age, socioeconomic status, geographic locale, and life-style on salient characteristics of gay men and lesbians. (c) Theoretical perspectives on homosexuality have shifted from attention to an illness model that emphasized origins and treatment to an affirmative model that examines how gay men and lesbians form and maintain their identity and manage ordinary problems of life span development. (d) The view that sexual orientation is an inherent characteristic of an individual has been broadened to include the role of social and historical influences in shaping the meaning and expression of homosexuality. (e) The relationship between gender roles and sexual orientation has received greater attention. Research has indicated that gender is a central organizing factor for heterosexuals, lesbians, and gay men in personal experiences, values, and relationship styles.

Finally, the importance of understanding sexual orientation for heterosexuals has become apparent. Social policy, legislative deliberations, and judicial decisions have increasingly recognized the legitimacy of gay male and lesbian issues, often encouraged by psychological research and perspectives (see Appendix B). Moreover, all people can benefit from acknowledging the restrictive constraint of heterosexist bias that limits behavior to rigid gender roles, requires 100% heterosexuality, and defines one's value as a man or woman by one's rejection of homosexuality. In particular, lesbians and gay men can make a contribution to greater appreciation of human diversity and the benefits that result from examining predetermined constraints that limit fulfillment of one's unique potential.

References

Abramson, P. R. (1986). The cultural context of Japanese sexuality: An American perspective. *Psychologia, 29*, 1–9.

Actenberg, R. (1988). Preserving and protecting the families of lesbians and gay men. In M. Shernoff & W. A. Scott (Eds.), *The sourcebook on lesbian/gay health care* (pp. 237–245). Washington, DC: National Lesbian and Gay Health Foundation.

Adam, B. D. (1978). Inferiorization and self-esteem. *Social Psychology, 41*, 47–57.

Adam, B. (1987). *The rise of a gay and lesbian movement*. Boston: Twayne.

Altman, D. (1971). *Homosexual oppression and liberation*. New York: Outerbridge & Dienstfrey.

Altman, D. (1981). *Coming out in the seventies*. Boston: Alyson.

Amaro, H. (1978, October 2). *"Coming out" conflicts for Hispanic lesbians*. Paper presented at the National Coalition of Hispanic Mental Health and Human Service Organizations (COSSMHO), Austin, TX.

Aoki, B. (1983, August). *Gay Asian Americans: Adapting within the family context*. Paper presented at the 91st Annual Convention of the American Psychological Association, Anaheim, CA.

Auerback, S., & Moser, C. (1987). Groups for the wives of gay and bisexual men. *Social Work, 32*, 321–325.

Backer, T. E., Batchelor, W. F., Jones, J. M., & Mays, V. M. (1988). Introduction to the special issue: Psychology and AIDS. *American Psychologist, 43*, 835–836.

Barrett, S. E. (1990). Paths toward diversity: An intrapsychic perspective. *Women and Therapy, 9*(1/2), 41–52.

Bayer, R. (1981). *Homosexuality and American psychiatry: The politics of diagnosis*. New York: Basic Books.

Bell, A. P., & Weinberg, M. S. (1978). *Homosexualities: A study of diversity among men and women*. New York: Simon & Schuster.

Bell, A. P., Weinberg, M. S., & Hammersmith, S. K. (1981). *Sexual preference: Its development in men and women*. Bloomington: Indiana University Press.

Bierly, M. M. (1985). Prejudice toward contemporary outgroups as a generalized attitude. *Journal of Applied Social Psychology, 15*, 189–199.

Blackwood, E. (1984). Sexuality and gender in certain Native American tribes: The case of cross-gender females. *Signs, 10*, 27–42.

Blackwood, E. (1985). Breaking the mirror: The construction of lesbianism and the anthropological discourse on homosexuality. *Journal of Homosexuality, 11*(3–4), 1–17.

Blasband, D., & Peplau, L. A. (1985). Sexual exclusivity versus openness in gay male couples. *Archives of Sexual Behavior, 14*, 395–412.

Block, J. H. (1983). Differential premises arising from differential socialization of the sexes: Some conjectures. *Child Development, 54*, 1335–1354.

Blumstein, P., & Schwartz, P. (1977). Bisexuality: Some social psychological issues. *Journal of Social Issues, 33*(2), 30–45.

Blumstein, P., & Schwartz, P. (1983). *American couples: Money, work, sex*. New York: Morrow.

Blumstein, P., & Schwartz, P. (1989). Intimate relationships and the creation of sexuality. In B. Risman & P. Schwartz (Eds.), *Gender in intimate relationships: A microstructural approach* (pp. 120–129). Belmont, CA: Wadsworth.

Bolton, F. G., & MacEachron, A. (1988). Adolescent male sexuality: A developmental perspective. *Journal of Adolescent Research, 3*, 259–273.

Boxer, A., & Cohler, B. (1989). The life course of gay and lesbian youth: An immodest proposal for the study of lives. *Journal of Homosexuality, 17*(1–2–3–4), 317–355.

Bozett, F. W. (1982). Heterogeneous couples in heterosexual marriages: Gay men and straight women. *Journal of Marital and Sexual Therapy, 8,* 81–89.

Bozett, F. W. (1987). Children of gay fathers. In F. W. Bozett (Ed.), *Gay and lesbian parents* (pp. 39–57). New York: Praeger.

Bozett, F. W. (1988). Social control of identity by children of gay fathers. *Western Journal of Nursing Research, 10,* 550–565.

Bozett, F. W. (1989). Gay fathers: A review of the literature. *Journal of Homosexuality, 18*(1–2), 137–162.

Bradford, J., & Ryan, C. (1987). *National Lesbian Health Care Survey: Mental health implications.* Washington, DC: National Lesbian and Gay Health Foundation.

Bradshaw, C. K. (1990). A Japanese view of dependency: What can Amae psychology contribute to feminist theory and therapy? *Women and Therapy, 9*(1–2), 67–86.

Brown, L. S. (1989). New voices, new visions: Toward a lesbian/gay paradigm for psychology. *Psychology of Women, 13,* 445–458.

Brownfain, J. J. (1985). A study of the married bisexual male: Paradox and resolution. *Journal of Homosexuality, 11*(1–2), 173–188.

Caldwell, M. A., & Peplau, L. A. (1984). The balance of power in lesbian relationships. *Sex Roles, 10,* 587–600.

Carballo-Dieguez, A. (1989). Hispanic culture, gay male culture and AIDS: Counseling implications. *Journal of Counseling and Development, 68,* 26–30.

Cardell, M., Finn, S., & Marecek, J. (1981). Sex-role identity, sex-role behavior, and satisfaction in heterosexual, lesbian, and gay male couples. *Psychology of Women Quarterly, 5,* 488–494.

Carrier, J. M. (1976). Cultural factors affecting urban Mexican male homosexual behavior. *Archives of Sexual Behavior, 5,* 103–124.

Carrier, J. M. (1980). Homosexual behavior in cross-cultural perspective. In J. Marmor (Ed.), *Homosexual behavior: A modern reappraisal* (pp. 100–122). New York: Basic Books.

Carrier, J. M. (1985). Mexican male bisexuality. *Journal of Homosexuality, 11*(1–2), 75–85.

Cass, V. C. (1979). Homosexual identity formation: A theoretical model. *Journal of Homosexuality, 4*(3), 219–235.

Cass, V. C. (1984). Homosexual identity formation: Testing a theoretical model. *Journal of Sex Research, 20,* 143–167.

Cazenave, N. A. (1979). Social structure and personal choice. Effects on intimacy, marriage and the family alternative lifestyle research. *Alternative Lifestyles, 2,* 331–358.

Cazenave, N. A. (1984). Race, socioeconomic status, and age: The social context of American masculinity. *Sex Roles, 11,* 639–656.

Chan, C. S. (1987). Asian lesbians: Psychological issues in the "coming out" process. *Asian American Psychological Association Journal, 12*(1), 16–18.

Chan, C. S. (1989). Issues of identity development among Asian American lesbians and gay men. *Journal of Counseling and Development, 68,* 16–20.

Chapman, B. E., & Brannock, J. C. (1987). A proposed model of lesbian identity development: An empirical investigation. *Journal of Homosexuality, 14*(3–4), 69–80.

Coleman E. (1981/1982). Developmental stages of the coming-out process, *Journal of Homosexuality, 7*, 31–43.

Coleman, E. (1985a). Bisexual women in marriages. *Journal of Homosexuality, 11*(1–2), 87–99.

Coleman, E. (1985b). Integration of male bisexuality and marriage. *Journal of Homosexuality, 11*(1–2), 189–207.

Coleman, E. (1987). Assessment of sexual orientation. *Journal of Homosexuality, 14*(1–2), 9–24.

Collins, L., & Zimmerman, N. (1983). Homosexual and bisexual issues. In J. C. Hansen, J. D. Woody, & R. H. Woody (Eds.), *Sexual issues in family therapy* (pp. 82–100). Rockville, MD: Aspen.

Committee on Lesbian and Gay Concerns. (1990). *Final Report of the Task Force on Bias in Psychotherapy With Lesbians and Gay Men*. Washington, DC: American Psychological Association.

Conger, J. J. (1975). Proceedings of the American Psychological Association, Incorporated, for the year 1974: Minutes of the annual meeting of the Council of Representatives. *American Psychologist, 30*, 620–651.

Cotton, W. L. (1974). Social and sexual relationships of lesbians. *Journal of Sex Research, 11*, 139–148.

Cramer, D. (1986). Gay parents and their children: A review of research and practical implications. *Journal of Counseling and Development, 64*, 504–507.

Cramer, D. W., & Roach, A. S. (1988). Coming out to mom and dad: A study of gay males and their relationships with their parents. *Journal of Homosexuality, 15*(3–4), 79–91.

Dailey, D. M. (1979). Adjustment of heterosexual and homosexual couples in pairing relationships: An exploratory study. *Journal of Sex Research, 15*, 143–157.

Dank, B. M. (1971). Coming out in the gay world. *Psychiatry, 34*, 180–197.

Deaux, K., & Lewis, L. L. (1984). Structure of gender stereotypes: Interrelationships among components and gender label. *Journal of Personality and Social Psychology, 46*, 991–1004.

D'Augelli, A. R. (1989). The development of a helping community for lesbians and gay men: A case study in community psychology. *Journal of Community Psychology, 17*, 18–29.

D'Augelli, A. R., Collins, C., & Hart, M. (1987). Social support patterns of lesbian women in a rural helping network. *Journal of Rural Community Psychology, 8*, 12–22.

de Monteflores, C. (1981). Conflicting allegiances: Therapy issues with Hispanic lesbians. *Catalyst, 12*, 31–36.

de Monteflores, C. (1986). Notes on the management of difference. In T. Stein & C. Cohen (Eds.), *Contemporary perspectives on psychotherapy with lesbians and gay men* (pp. 73–101). New York: Plenum Press.

de Monteflores, C., & Schultz, S. (1978). Coming out: Similarities and differences for lesbians and gay men. *Journal of Social Issues, 34*(3), 59–72.

D'Emilio, J. (1983). *Sexual politics, sexual communities: The making of a homosexual minority in the United States, 1940–1970*. Chicago: University of Chicago Press.

Devine, J. L. (1984). A systematic inspection of affectional preference orientation and the family of origin. *Journal of Social Work and Human Sexuality, 2*(2–3), 9–17.

Dixon, J. K. (1984). The commencement of bisexual activity in swinging married women over age thirty. *Journal of Sex Research, 20,* 71–90.

Dixon, J. K. (1985). Sexuality and relationship changes in married females following the commencement of bisexual activity. *Journal of Homosexuality, 11*(1–2), 115–133.

Duffy, S. M., & Rusbult, C. E. (1986). Satisfaction and commitment in homosexual and heterosexual relationships. *Journal of Homosexuality, 12*(2), 1–24.

Eldridge, N. S. (1987). Gender issues in counseling same-sex couples. *Professional Psychology: Research and Practice, 18,* 567–572.

Eldridge, N. S., & Gilbert, L. A. (1990). Correlates of relationship satisfaction in lesbian couples. *Psychology of Women Quarterly, 14,* 43–62.

Ericksen, J. A. (1980). Race, sex, and alternative lifestyle choices. *Alternative Lifestyles, 3,* 405–424.

Espin, O. M. (1984). Cultural and historical influences on sexuality in Hispanic/Latin women: Implications for psychotherapy. In C. Vance (Ed.), *Pleasure and danger: Exploring female sexuality* (pp. 149–163). London: Routledge & Kegan Paul.

Espin, O. M. (1987). Issues of identity in the psychology of Latina lesbians. In the Boston Lesbian Psychologies Collective (Eds.), *Lesbian psychologies: Explorations and challenges* (pp. 35–51). Urbana-Champaign: University of Illinois Press.

Faderman, L. (1984). The "new gay" lesbian. *Journal of Homosexuality, 10*(3–4), 85–95.

Falk, P. J. (1989). Lesbian mothers: Psychosocial assumptions in family law. *American Psychologist, 44,* 941–947.

Faraday, A. (1981). Liberating lesbian research. In K. Plummer (Ed.), *The making of the modern homosexual* (pp. 112–129). London: Hutchinson.

Fein, S. B., & Nuehring, E. M. (1981). Intrapsychic effects of stigma: A process of breakdown and reconstruction of social reality. *Journal of Homosexuality, 7*(1), 3–13.

Foucault, M. (1979). *The history of sexuality.* London: Allen Lane.

Ford, C. S., & Beach, F. (1951). *Patterns of sexual behavior.* New York: Harper.

Fracher, J. C., & Kimmel, M. S. (1987). Hard issues and soft spots: Counseling men about sexuality. In M. Scher, M. Stevens, G. Good, & G. A. Eichenfield (Eds.), *Handbook of counseling and psychotherapy with men* (pp. 83–96). Newbury Park, CA: Sage.

Friedman, J. (1989). The impact of homophobia on male sexual development. *Siecus Report, 17*(5), 8–9.

Gagnon, J. H., & Simon, W. (1973). *Sexual conduct: The social sources of human sexuality.* Chicago: Aldine.

Garnets, L., Herek, G. M., & Levy, B. (1990). Violence and victimization of lesbians and gay men: Mental health consequences. *Journal of Interpersonal Violence, 5,* 366–383.

Gibbs, E. D. (1989). Psychological development of children raised by lesbian mothers: A review of research. *Women and Therapy, 8*(1–2), 65–75.

Gillow, K. E., & Davis, L. L. (1987). Lesbian stress and coping methods. *Journal of Psychosocial Nursing, 25*(9), 28–32.

Gladue, B. A. (1987). Psychobiological contributions. In L. Diamant (Ed.), *Male and female homosexuality: Psychological approaches* (pp. 129–153). Washington, DC: Hemisphere.

Gladue, B. A., Green, R., & Hellman, R. E. (1984). Neuroendocrine response to estrogen and sexual orientation. *Science, 225*, 1496–1499.

Gochros, J. S. (1985). Wives' reactions to learning that their husbands are bisexual. *Journal of Homosexuality, 11*(1–2), 101–113.

Gochros, J. S. (1989). *When husbands come out of the closet.* New York: Haworth.

Gock, T. (1986, August). *Issues in gay affirmative psychotherapy with ethnically/culturally diverse populations.* Paper presented at the 94th Annual Convention of the American Psychological Association, Washington, DC.

Golden, C. (1987). Diversity and variability in women's sexual identities. In The Boston Lesbian Psychologies Collective (Eds.), *Lesbian psychologies: Explorations and challenges* (pp. 19–34). Urbana-Champaign: University of Illinois Press.

Gonsiorek, J. C. (1988). Current and future directions in gay/lesbian affirmative mental health practice. In M. Shernoff & W. A. Scott (Eds.), *The sourcebook on lesbian/gay health care* (pp. 107–113). Washington, DC: National Lesbian and Gay Health Foundation.

Gramick, J. (1984). Developing a lesbian identity. In T. Darty & S. Potter (Eds.), *Women-identified women* (pp. 31–44). Palo Alto, CA: Mayfield.

Green, R. (1982). The best interests of the child with a lesbian mother. *American Academy of Psychiatry and the Law Bulletin, 10*, 7–15.

Green, R., Mandel, J. B., Hotvedt, M. E., Gray, J., & Smith, L. (1986). Lesbian mothers and their children: A comparison with solo parent heterosexual mothers and their children. *Archives of Sexual Behavior, 15*, 167–184.

Green, V. (1985). Experimental factors in childhood and adolescent sexual behavior: Family interactions and previous sexual experiences. *Journal of Sex Research, 21*, 157–182.

Greenberg, D. F. (1988). *The construction of homosexuality.* Chicago, IL: University of Chicago Press.

Greene, B. (1986). When the therapist is White and the patient is Black: Considerations for psychotherapy in the feminist heterosexual and lesbian communities. In D. Howard (Ed.), *The dynamics of feminist therapy* (pp. 41–65). New York: Haworth.

Griffin, C., Wirth, M., & Wirth, A. (1986). *Beyond acceptance: Parents of lesbians and gays talk about their experiences.* Englewood Cliffs, NJ: Prentice-Hall.

Groves, P., & Ventura, L. (1983). The lesbian coming out process: Therapeutic considerations. *Personnel and Guidance Journal, 61*, 146–149.

Hall, M. (1989). Private experiences in the public domain: Lesbians in organizations. In J. Hearn, D. L. Sheppard, P. Tancred-Sheriff, & G. Burrell (Eds.), *The sexuality of organization* (pp. 125–138). Newbury Park, CA: Sage.

Hammersmith, S. K., & Weinberg, M. S. (1973). Homosexual identity: Commitment, adjustments, and significant others. *Sociometry, 36*(1), 56–78.

Hanley-Hackenbruck, P. (1988). Psychotherapy and the "coming out" process. *Journal of Gay and Lesbian Psychotherapy, 1*(1), 21–39.

Harris, M. B., & Turner, P. H. (1985). Gay and lesbian parents. *Journal of Homosexuality, 12*(2), 101–113.

Harry, J. (1983). Gay male and lesbian relationships. In E. Macklin & R. Rubin (Eds.), *Contemporary families and alternative lifestyles: Handbook on research and theory* (pp. 216–234). Beverly Hills, CA: Sage.

Harry, J. (1984). *Gay couples.* New York: Praeger.

Harry, J., & Duvall, W. B. (1978). *The social organization of gay males*. New York: Praeger.

Hart, J., & Richardson, D. (Eds.). (1981). *The theory and practice of homosexuality.* London: Routledge & Kegan Paul.

Hay, H. (1990, April 22–28). Identifying as gay—there's the key. *Gay Community News*, p. 5.

Hays, D., & Samuels, A. (1989). Heterosexual women's perceptions of their marriage to bisexual or homosexual men. *Journal of Homosexuality, 18*(1–2), 81–100.

Hedblom, J. H. (1973). Dimensions of lesbian sexual experience. *Archives of Sexual Behavior, 2*, 329–341.

Hencken, J. (1984). Conceptualizations of homosexual behavior which preclude homosexual self-labeling. *Journal of Homosexuality, 9*(4), 53–63.

Hencken, J., & O'Dowd, W. (1977). Coming out as an aspect of identity formation. *Gai Saber, 1*(1), 18–22.

Henderson, A. I. (1984). Homosexuality in the college years: Developmental differences between men and women. *Journal of American College Health, 32*, 216–219.

Hendricks, S. E., Graber, B., & Rodriguez-Sierra, J. F. (1989). Neuroendocrine responses to exogenous estrogen: No differences between heterosexual and homosexual men. *Psychoneuroendocrinology, 14*, 177–185.

Herdt, G. (1989). Gay and lesbian youth, emergent identities, and cultural scenes at home and abroad. *Journal of Homosexuality, 17*(1–2–3–4), 1–42.

Herek, G. M. (1984). Attitudes toward lesbians and gay men: A factor-analytic study. *Journal of Homosexuality, 10*(1–2), 39–52.

Herek, G. M. (1985). On doing, being, and not being: Prejudice and the social construction of sexuality. *Journal of Homosexuality, 12*(1), 135–151.

Herek, G. M. (1986). On heterosexual masculinity: Some psychical consequences of the social construction of gender and sexuality. *American Behavioral Scientist, 29*, 563–577.

Herek, G. M. (1988). Heterosexuals' attitudes toward lesbians and gay men: Correlates and gender differences. *Journal of Sex Research, 25*, 451–477.

Herek, G. M. (1989). Hate crimes against lesbians and gay men: Issues for research and policy. *American Psychologist, 44*, 948–955.

Herek, G. M. (1990a). Gay people and government security clearances: A social science perspective. *American Psychologist, 45*, 1035–1042.

Herek, G. M. (1990b). Illness, stigma, and AIDS. In G. R. VandenBos & P. T. Costa (Eds.), *Psychological aspects of serious illness* (pp. 107–150). Washington, DC: American Psychological Association.

Herek, G. M. (1991). Stigma, prejudice, and violence against lesbians and gay men. In J. C. Gonriorek & J. D. Weinrich (Eds.), *Homosexuality: Research findings for public policy* (pp. 60–80). Newbury Park, CA: Sage.

Hidalgo, H. A. (1984). The Puerto Rican lesbian in the United States. In T. Darty & S. Potter (Eds.), *Women-identified women* (pp. 105–115). Palo Alto, CA: Mayfield.

Hill, M. (1987). Child-rearing attitudes of Black lesbian mothers. In the Boston Lesbian Psychologies Collective (Ed.), *Lesbian psychologies: Explorations and challenges* (pp. 215–226). Urbana-Champaign: University of Illinois Press.

Hoeffer, B. (1981). Children's acquisition of sex-role behavior in lesbian-mother families. *American Journal of Orthopsychiatry, 51*, 536–544.

Hollander, J. P. (1989). Restructuring lesbian social networks: Evaluation of an intervention. *Journal of Gay and Lesbian Psychotherapy, 1*, 63–71.

Hooker, E. (1957). The adjustment of the male overt homosexual. *Journal of Projective Techniques, 21*, 18–31.

Howard, J. A., Blumstein, P., & Schwartz, P. (1986). Sex, power, and influence tactics in intimate relationships. *Journal of Personality and Social Psychology, 51*, 102–109.

Hunnisett, R. (1986). Developing phenomenological method for researching lesbian existence. *Canadian Journal of Counseling, 20*, 255–286.

Hunt, M. (1974). *Sexual behavior in the 1970s*. Chicago: Playboy Press.

Icard, L. (1985/1986). Black gay men and conflicting social identities: Sexual orientation versus racial identity. *Journal of Social Work and Human Sexuality, 4*, 83–92.

Jay, K., & Young, A. (1979). *The gay report*. New York: Summit.

Jones, R. W., & DeCecco, J. P. (1982). The femininity and masculinity of partners in heterosexual and homosexual relationships. *Journal of Homosexuality, 8*(2), 37–44.

Kanuha, V. (1990). Compounding the triple jeopardy: Battering in lesbian of color relationships. *Women and Therapy, 9*, 169–184.

Kimmel, D. C. (1978). Adult development and aging: A gay perspective. *Journal of Social Issues, 34*, 113–130.

Kinsey, A. C., Pomeroy, W. B., & Martin, C. E. (1948). *Sexual behavior in the human male*. Philadelphia: W. B. Saunders.

Kinsey, A. C., Pomeroy, W. B., Martin, C. E., & Gebhard, P. H. (1953). *Sexual behavior in the human female*. Philadelphia: W. B. Saunders.

Kite, M. E. (1984). Sex differences in attitudes towards homosexuals: A meta-analytic review. *Journal of Homosexuality, 10*(1–2), 69–81.

Kitzinger, C. (1987). *The social construction of lesbianism*. London: Sage.

Klein, C. (1986). *Counseling our own*. Seattle, WA: Consultant Services Northwest.

Klein, F., Sepekoff, B., & Wolf, T. J. (1986). Sexual orientation: A multi-variable dynamic process. *Journal of Homosexuality, 11*(1–2), 35–49.

Kleinberg, L. (1986). Coming home to self, going home to parents: Lesbian identity disclosure (The Stone Center Work in Progress Series, No. 24). Wellesley, MA: Wellesley College.

Kolodny, R. C., Masters, W. H., Hendryx, J., & Toro, G. (1971). Plasma testosterone and semen analysis in male homosexuals. *New England Journal of Medicine, 285*, 1170–1174.

Kooden, H. D., Morin, S. F., Riddle, D. I., Rogers, M., Sang, B. E., Strassburger, F. (1979). *Removing the stigma: Final report of the Board of Social and Ethical Responsibility for Psychology's Task Force on the Status of Lesbian and Gay Male Psychologists*. Washington, DC: American Psychological Association.

Krieger, S. (1982). Lesbian identity and community: Recent social science literature. *Signs, 8*, 91–108.

Kurdek, L. A. (1987). Sex role self-schema and psychological adjustment in coupled homosexual and heterosexual men and women. *Sex Roles, 17*, 549–562.

Kurdek, L. A. (1988). Perceived social support in gays and lesbians in cohabiting relationships. *Journal of Personality and Social Psychology, 54*, 504–509.

Kurdek, L. A., & Schmitt, J. P. (1986a). Interaction of sex role self concept with relationship quality and relationship beliefs in married, heterosexual cohabiting, gay and lesbian relationships. *Journal of Personality and Social Psychology, 51*, 365–370.

Kurdek, L. A., & Schmitt, J. P. (1986b). Relationship quality of gay men in closed or open relationships. *Journal of Homosexuality, 12*(2), 85–99.

Kurdek, L. A., & Schmitt, J. P. (1986c). Relationship quality of partners in heterosexual married, heterosexual cohabiting, and gay and lesbian relationships. *Journal of Personality and Social Psychology, 51*, 711–720.

Kurdek, L. A., & Schmitt, J. P. (1987a). Partner homogamy in married, heterosexual cohabiting, gay, and lesbian couples. *Journal of Sex Research, 23*, 212–232.

Kurdek, L. A., & Schmitt, J. P. (1987b). Perceived emotional support from family and friends in members of gay, lesbian, and heterosexual cohabiting couples. *Journal of Homosexuality, 14*(3–4), 57–68.

Larsen, P. C. (1981). Sexual identity and self-concept. *Journal of Homosexuality, 7*(1), 15–32.

Larsen, P. C. (1982). Gay male relationships. In W. Paul, J. D. Weinrich, J. C. Gonsiorek, & M. E. Hotvedt (Eds.), *Homosexuality: Social, psychological, and biological issues* (pp. 219–232). Beverly Hills, CA: Sage.

Latham, J. D., & White, G. D. (1978). Coping with homosexual expression within heterosexual marriages: Five case studies. *Journal of Sex and Marital Therapy, 4*, 198–212.

LaTorre, R. A., & Wedenberg, K. (1983). Psychological characteristics of bisexual, heterosexual, and homosexual women. *Journal of Homosexuality, 9*(1), 87–97.

Leavy, R., & Adams, E. (1986). Feminism as a correlate of self-esteem, self-acceptance, and social support among lesbians. *Psychology of Women Quarterly, 10*, 321–326.

Lee, J. A. (1977). Going public: A study in the sociology of homosexual liberation. *Journal of Homosexuality, 3*(1), 49–78.

Lee, D. B., & Saul, T. T. (1987). Counseling Asian men. In M. Scher, M. Stevens, G. Good, & G. A. Eichenfield (Eds.), *Handbook of counseling and psychotherapy with men* (pp. 180–191). Newbury Park, CA: Sage.

Levine, M. P. (1979). Employment discrimination against gay men. *International Review of Modern Sociology, 9*(5–7), 151–163.

Levine, M. P., & Leonard, R. (1984). Discrimination against lesbians in the workforce. *Signs, 9*, 700–710.

Lewis, L. A. (1984). The coming out process for lesbians: Integrating a stable identity. *Social Work, 29*, 464–469.

Lewis, R. (1978). Emotional intimacy among men. *Journal of Social Issues, 34*(1), 108–121.

Lewis, R. A., Kozac, E. B., & Grosnick, W. A. (1981). Commitment in same-sex love relationships. *Alternative Lifestyles, 4*, 22–42.

Lin, Y. (1978). The spectrum of lesbian experience: Personal testimony. In G. Vida (Ed.), *Our right to love: A lesbian resource book* (pp. 227–229). Englewood Cliffs, NJ: Prentice-Hall.

Lockard, D. (1985). The lesbian community: An anthropological approach. *Journal of Homosexuality, 11*(3–4), 83–95.

Loiacano, D. K. (1989). Gay identity issues among Black Americans: Racism, homophobia, and the need for validation. *Journal of Counseling and Development, 68*, 21–25.

Lowenstein, S. F. (1985). On the diversity of love object orientations among women. *Journal of Social Work and Human Sexuality, 3*(2/3), 7–24.

Lynch, F. R. (1987). Non-ghetto gays: A sociological study of suburban homosexuals. *Journal of Homosexuality, 13*(4), 13–42.

Lynch, J. M., & Reilly, M. E. (1986). Role relationships: Lesbian perspectives. *Journal of Homosexuality, 12*(2), 53–69.

MacDonald, A. P., Jr. (1983). A little bit of lavender goes a long way: A critique of research on sexual orientation. *Journal of Sex Research, 19*, 94–100.

Macklin, E. D. (1983). Effect of changing sex roles on the intimate relationships of men and women. *Marriage and Family Review, 6*(3–4), 97–113.

MacPike, L. (Ed.) (1989). *There's something I've been meaning to tell you.* Tallahassee, FL: Naiad Press.

Malyon, A. K. (1982). Psychotherapeutic implications of internalized homophobia in gay men. *Journal of Homosexuality, 7*(2–3), 59–69.

Marecek, J., Finn, S. E., & Cardell, M. (1982). Gender roles in the relationships of lesbians and gay men. *Journal of Homosexuality, 8*(2), 45–49.

Masters, W. H., & Johnson, V. E. (1979). *Homosexuality in perspective.* Boston: Little, Brown.

Matteson, D. R. (1985). Bisexual men in marriage: Is a positive homosexual identity and stable marriage possible? *Journal of Homosexuality, 11*(1–2), 149–173.

Matteson, D. R. (1987). The heterosexually married gay and lesbian parent. In F. W. Bozett (Ed.), *Gay and lesbian parents* (pp. 138–161). New York: Praeger.

Mays, V. M. (1985). Black women working together: Diversity in same sex relationships. *Women's Studies International Forum, 8*, 67–71.

Mays, V. M., & Cochran, S. D. (1986, August). *The Black lesbian relationship project: Relationship experiences and the perception of discrimination.* Paper presented at the 94th Annual Convention of the American Psychological Association, Washington, DC.

McDonald, G. J. (1982). Individual differences in the coming out process of gay men: Implications for theoretical models. *Journal of Homosexuality, 8*(1), 47–60.

McWhirter, D. P., & Mattison, A. M. (1984). *The male couple.* Englewood Cliffs, NJ: Prentice-Hall.

Miller, B. (1978). Adult sexual resocialization: Adjustments towards a stigmatized identity. *Alternative Lifestyles, 1*, 207–234.

Miller, B. (1979). Gay fathers and their children. *Family Coordinator, 28*, 544–552.

Miller, B. (1987). Counseling gay husbands and fathers. In F. W. Bozett (Ed.), *Gay and lesbian parents* (pp. 175–187). New York: Praeger.

Minton, H. L., & McDonald, G. J. (1983/1984). Homosexual identity formation as a developmental process. *Journal of Homosexuality, 9*(2–3), 91–104.

Miranda, J., & Storms, M. (1989). Psychological adjustment of lesbians and gay men. *Journal of Counseling and Development, 68*, 41–45.

Money, J. (1987). Sin, sickness, or status? Homosexual gender identity and psychoneuroendocrinology. *American Psychologist, 42*, 384–399.

Money, J. (1988). *Gay, straight, and in-between: The sexology of erotic orientation.* New York: Oxford University Press.

Morales, E. S. (1989). Ethnic minority families and minority gays and lesbians. *Marriage and Family Review, 14,* 217–239.

Morin, S. (1977). Heterosexual bias in psychological research on lesbianism and male homosexuality. *American Psychologist, 32,* 629–637.

Moses, A. E., & Buckner, J. A. (1980). The special problems of rural gay clients. In A. E. Moses & R. O. Hawkins, Jr. (Eds.), *Counseling lesbian women and men: A life issues approach* (pp. 173–180). St. Louis, MO: C. V. Mosby.

Murphy, B. (1989). Lesbian couples and their parents: The effects of perceived parental attitudes on the couple. *Journal of Counseling and Development, 68,* 46–51.

Olsen, M. R. (1987). A study of gay and lesbian teachers. *Journal of Homosexuality, 13*(4), 73–81.

O'Neill, J. M., Helms, B. J., & Gable, R. K. (1986). Gender-Role Conflict Scale: College men's fear of femininity. *Sex Roles, 14,* 335–350.

Owlfeather, M. (1988). Children of grandmother moon. In W. Roscoe (Ed.), *Living the spirit: A gay American Indian anthology* (pp. 97–105). New York: St. Martin's Press.

Palladino, D., & Stephenson, Y. (1990). Perceptions of the sexual self: Their impact on relationships between lesbian and heterosexual women. *Women and Therapy, 9,* 231–253.

Pamela, H. (1989). Asian American lesbians: An emerging voice in the Asian American community. In Asian Women United of California (Eds.), *Making waves: An anthology of writings by and about Asian American women* (pp. 282–290). Boston: Beacon Press.

Paroski, P. (1987). Healthcare delivery and the concerns of gay and lesbian adolescents. *Journal of Adolescent Health Care, 8,* 188–192.

Parker, P. (1987). Legacy. In S. Pollack & J. Vaughn (Eds.), *Politics of the heart: A lesbian parenting anthology* (pp. 208–212). Ithaca, NY: Firebrand Books.

Paul, W. (1982). Minority status for gay people: Majority reactions and social context. In W. Paul, J. D. Weinrich, J. C. Gonsiorek, & M. E. Hotvedt (Eds.), *Homosexuality: Social, psychological, and biological issues* (pp. 351–369). Beverly Hills, CA: Sage.

Paz, O. (1961). *The labyrinth of solitude: Life and thought in Mexico.* New York: Grove Press.

Peplau, L. A. (1983). Roles and gender. In H. H. Kelley, E. Berscheid, A. Christensen, J. H. Harvey, T. L. Huston, G. Levinger, E. McClintock, L. A. Peplau, & D. R. Peterson (Eds.), *Close Relationships* (pp. 220–264). San Francisco: Freeman.

Peplau, L. A. (1991). Lesbian and gay relationships. In J. C. Gonsiorek & J. D. Weinrich (Eds.), *Homosexuality: Research findings for public policy* (pp. 177–196). Newbury Park, CA: Sage.

Peplau, L. A., & Amaro, H. (1982). Understanding lesbian relationships. In W. Paul, J. D. Weinrich, J. C. Gonsiorek, & M. E. Hotvedt (Eds.), *Homosexuality: Social, psychological, and biological issues* (pp. 233–248). Beverly Hills, CA: Sage.

Peplau, L. A., & Cochran, S. D. (1981). Value orientations in the intimate relationships of gay men. *Journal of Homosexuality, 6*(3), 1–19.

Peplau, L. A., & Cochran, S. D. (1990). A relationship perspective on homosexuality. In D. P. McWhirter, S. A. Sanders, & J. M. Reinisch (Eds.), *Homosexuality/heterosexuality: The Kinsey scale and current research* (pp. 321–349). New York: Oxford University Press.

Peplau, L. A., Cochran, S. D., & Mays, V. M. (1986, August). *Satisfaction in the intimate relationships of Black lesbians*. Paper presented at the 94th Annual Convention of the American Psychological Association, Washington, DC.

Peplau, L. A., Cochran, S. D., Rook, K., & Padesky, C. (1978). Women in love: Attachment and autonomy in lesbian relationships. *Journal of Social Issues, 34*(3), 7–27.

Peplau, L. A., & Gordon, S. L. (1983). The intimate relationships of lesbians and gay men. In E. R. Allgeier & N. B. McCormick (Eds.), *The changing boundaries: Gender roles and sexual behavior* (pp. 226–244). Palo Alto, CA: Mayfield.

Petrow, S. (1990, May). Together wherever we go. *The Advocate*, pp. 42–44.

Phillis, D. E., & Gramko, M. H. (1985). Sex differences in sexual activity: Reality or illusion. *Journal of Sex Research, 21*, 437–448.

Plummer, K. (1975). *Sexual stigma: An interactionist account*. London: Routledge & Kegan Paul.

Plummer, K. (1981). Going gay: Identities, life cycles, and lifestyles in the male gay world. In J. Hart & D. Richardson (Eds.), *The theory and practice of homosexuality* (pp. 93–110). London: Routledge & Kegan Paul.

Ponse, B. (1978). *Identities in the lesbian world: The social construction of self*. Westport, CT: Greenwood Press.

Ponse, B. (1984). The problematic meanings of "lesbian." In J. D. Douglas (Ed.), *The sociology of deviance* (pp. 25–33). Boston: Allyn & Bacon.

Preston, K., & Stanley, K. (1987). "What's the worst thing . . .?" Gender-directed insults. *Sex Roles, 17*, 209–219.

Radicalesbians. (1973). Women-identified women. In A. Koedt, E. Levine, & A. Rapone (Eds.), *Radical feminism* (pp. 240–245). New York: Quadrangle Books.

Rand, C., Graham, D. L., & Rawlings, E. (1982). Psychological health and factors the court seeks to control in lesbian mother custody trials. *Journal of Homosexuality, 8*(1), 27–39.

Remafedi, G. (1987). Male homosexuality: The adolescent's perspective. *Pediatrics, 79*, 326–330.

Rich, A. (1980). Compulsory heterosexuality and lesbian existence. *Signs, 5*, 631–660.

Richardson, D. (1987). Recent challenges to traditional assumptions about homosexuality: Some implications for practice. *Journal of Homosexuality, 13*(4), 1–12.

Riddle, D. I. (1978). Relating to children: Gays as role models. *Journal of Social Issues, 34*, 38–58.

Riddle, D. I., & Morin, S. F. (1977, November). Removing the stigma: Data from individuals. *APA Monitor*, pp. 16, 28.

Risman, B., & Schwartz, P. (1988). Sociological research on male and female homosexuality. *Annual Review of Sociology, 14*, 125–147.

Robinson, B. E., Walters, L. H., & Skeen, P. (1989). Response of parents to learning that their child is homosexual and concern over AIDS: A national study. *Journal of Homosexuality, 18*(1–2), 59–80.

Roesler, J., & Deisher, R. W. (1972). Youthful male homosexuality. *Journal of the American Medical Association, 219*, 1018–1023.

Romo-Carmona, M. (1987). In J. Ramos (Ed.), *Compañeras: Latina lesbians* (pp. xx–xxix). New York: Latina Lesbian History Project.

Ross, M. W. (1987). A theory of normal homosexuality. In L. Diamant (Ed.), *Male and female homosexuality: Psychological approaches* (pp. 237–259). Washington, DC: Hemisphere.

Ross, M. W. (1989). Gay youth in four cultures: A comparative study. *Journal of Homosexuality, 17*(1–2–3–4), 299–314.

Rusbult, C. E., Zembrodt, I. M., & Iwaniszek, J. (1986). The impact of gender and sex-role orientation on responses to dissatisfaction in close relationships. *Sex Roles, 15*, 1–20.

Russo, A. J. (1982). Power and influence in the homosexual community: A study of three California cities. *Dissertation Abstracts International, 43*, 561B. (University Microfilms No. DA8215211.)

Sanders, R. M., Bain, J., & Langevin, R. (1985). Peripheral sex hormones, homosexuality, and gender identity. In R. Langevin (Ed.), *Erotic preference, gender identity, and aggression in men: New research studies* (pp. 227–247). Hillsdale, NJ: Erlbaum.

Sang, B., Warshow, J., & Smith, A. (Eds.). (1991). *Lesbians at midlife: The creative transition*. San Francisco: CA: Spinsters.

Savin-Williams, R. C. (1989). Coming out to parents and self-esteem among gay and lesbian youth. *Journal of Homosexuality, 18*(1–2), 1–35.

Schaefer, S. (1976). Sexual and social problems of lesbians. *Journal of Sex Research, 12*, 50–69.

Schaefer, S. (1977). Sociosexual behavior in male and female homosexuals. *Archives of Sexual Behavior, 6*, 355–364.

Schmitt, J. P., & Kurdek, L. A. (1987). Personality correlates of positive identity and relationship involvement in gay men. *Journal of Homosexuality, 13*(4), 101–109.

Schneider, B. (1986). Coming out at work: Bridging the private/public gap. *Work and Occupations, 13*, 463–487.

Schullo, S. A., & Alperson, B. L. (1984). Interpersonal phenomenology as a function of sexual orientation, sex, sentiment, and trait categories in long-term dyadic relationships. *Journal of Personality and Social Psychology, 47*, 983–1002.

Sears, J. T. (1989). The impact of gender and race on growing up lesbian and gay in the South. *National Women's Studies Association Journal, 1*, 422–457.

Sergio, P. A., & Cody, J. (1985). Physical attractiveness and social assertiveness skills in male homosexual dating behavior and partner selection. *Journal of Social Psychology, 125*, 505–514.

Shachar, S. A., & Gilbert, L. A. (1983). Working lesbians: Role conflicts and coping strategies. *Psychology of Women Quarterly, 7*, 244–256.

Shon, S. P., & Ja, D. Y. (1982). Asian families. In M. McGoldrick, J. K. Pearce, & J. Giordano (Eds.), *Ethnicity and family therapy* (pp. 208–229). New York: Guilford Press.

Shively, M. G., & DeCecco, J. P. (1977). Components of sexual identity. *Journal of Homosexuality, 3*, 41–48.

Shneidman, E. (1989). The indian summer of life: A preliminary study of septuagenarians. *American Psychologist, 44*, 684–694.

Silverstein, C. (1981). *Man to man: Gay couples in America*. New York: William Morrow.

Sophie, J. (1985/1986). A critical examination of stage theories of lesbian identity development. *Journal of Homosexuality, 12*(2), 39–51.

Stein, T. S., & Cohen, C. J. (Eds.). (1986). *Psychotherapy with lesbians and gay men.* New York: Plenum Press.

Storms, M. D., Stivers, M. L., Lambers, S. M., & Hill, C. A. (1981). Sexual scripts for women. *Sex Roles, 3,* 257–263.

Strommen, E. F. (1989). "You're a what?": Family members' reactions to the disclosure of homosexuality. *Journal of Homosexuality, 18*(1–2), 37–58.

Swaab, D. F., & Hofman, M. A. (1988). Sexual differentiation of the human hypothalamus: Ontogeny of the sexually dimorphic nucleus of the preoptic area. *Developmental Brain Research, 44,* 314–318.

Taylor, N. (Ed.). (1986). *All in a day's work: A report on anti-lesbian discrimination in employment and unemployment in London.* London: Lesbian Employment Rights.

Thompson, E. H., & Pleck, J. H. (1986). The structure of male role norms. *American Behavioral Scientists, 29,* 531–543.

Tiefer, L. (1987). Social constructionism and the study of human sexuality. In P. Shaver & C. Hendrick (Eds.), *Review of social and personality psychology* (pp. 70–94). Beverly Hills, CA: Sage.

Tinney, J. S. (1986). Why a Black gay church? In J. Beam (Ed.), *In the life: A Black gay anthology* (pp. 70–86). Boston: Alyson.

Tremble, B., Schneider, M., & Appathurai, C. (1989). Growing up gay or lesbian in a multicultural context. *Journal of Homosexuality, 17*(1–2–3–4), 253–267.

Troiden, R. R. (1979). Becoming homosexual: A model of gay identity acquisition. *Psychiatry, 42,* 362–373.

Troiden, R. R. (1988). *Gay and lesbian identity: A sociological analysis.* New York: General Hall.

Troiden, R. R. (1989). The formation of homosexual identities. *Journal of Homosexuality, 17*(1–2–3–4), 43–73.

Troiden, R. R., & Goode, E. (1980). Variables related to the acquisition of a gay identity. *Journal of Homosexuality, 5*(4), 383–392.

Vance, B. K., & Green, V. (1984). Lesbian identities: An examination of sexual behavior and sex role acquisition as related to age of initial same-sex encounter. *Psychology of Women Quarterly, 8,* 293–307.

Vasquez, E. (1979). Homosexuality in the context of the Mexican-American culture. In D. Kuhnel (Ed.), *Sexual issues in social work: Emerging concerns in education and practice* (pp. 131–147). Honolulu: University of Hawaii School of Social Work.

Vetere, V. A. (1983). The role of friendship in the development and maintenance of lesbian love relationships. *Journal of Homosexuality, 8*(2), 51–65.

Watters, A. T. (1986). Heterosexual bias in psychological research on lesbianism and male homosexuality (1979–1983), utilizing the bibliographic and taxonomic system of Morin (1977). *Journal of Homosexuality, 13*(1), 35–58.

Weeks, J. (1977). *Coming out: Homosexual politics in Britain from the nineteenth century to the present.* London: Quartet.

Weeks, J. (1981). Discourse, desire and sexual deviance: Some problems in a history of homosexuality. In K. Plummer (Ed.), *The making of the modern homosexual* (pp. 76–111). London: Hutchinson.

Weinberg, M. S., & Williams, C. (1974). *Male homosexuals: Their problems and adaptations.* New York: Oxford University Press.

Weinberg, T. S. (1978). On "doing" and "being" gay: Sexual behavior and homosexual male self-identity. *Journal of Homosexuality, 4*(2), 143–156.

Weinberg, T. S. (1983). *Gay men, gay selves: The social construction of homosexual identities*. New York: Irvington.

Weinrich, J., & Williams, W. L. (1991). Strange customs, familiar lives: Homosexualities in other cultures. In J. C. Gonsiorek & J. D. Weinrich (Eds.), *Homosexuality: Research findings for public policy* (pp. 44–59). Newbury Park, CA: Sage.

Wells, J. W., & Kline, W. B. (1987). Self-disclosure of homosexual orientation. *Journal of Social Psychology, 127*, 191–197.

Whitehead, H. (1981). The bow and the burden strap: A new look at institutionalized homosexuality in native North America. In S. B. Ortner, & H. Whitehead (Eds.), *Sexual meanings: The culture construction of gender and sexuality* (pp. 80–115). New York: Cambridge University Press.

Williams, W. L. (1985). Persistence and change in the Berdache tradition among contemporary Lakota Indians. *Journal of Homosexuality, 11*(3–4), 191–200.

Williams W. L. (1986). *The spirit and the flesh: Sexual diversity in American Indian culture*. Boston: Beacon Press.

Williams, W. L. (1987). Women, men, and others. Beyond ethnocentrism in gender theory. *American Behavioral Scientist, 31*, 135–141.

Wilson, G. D. (1987). Male-female differences in sexual activity, enjoyment and fantasies. *Personality and Individual Differences, 8*, 125–127.

Wilson, P. M. (1986). Black culture and sexuality. *Journal of Social Work and Human Sexuality, 4*(3), 29–46.

Winkelpleck, J. M., & Westfeld, J. S. (1982). Counseling considerations with gay couples. *Personnel and Guidance Journal, 60*, 294–296.

Wolf, T. J. (1985). Marriages of bisexual men. *Journal of Homosexuality, 11*(1–2), 135–148.

Wooden, W. S., Kawasaki, H., & Mayeda, R. (1983). Lifestyles and identity maintenance among gay Japanese-American males. *Alternative Lifestyles, 5*, 236–243.

Wyers, N. L. (1987). Homosexuality in the family: Lesbian and gay spouses. *Social Work, 32*, 143–148.

Yearwood, L., & Weinberg, T. (1979). Black organizations, gay organizations: Sociological parallels. In M. Levine (Ed.), *Gay men: The sociology of male homosexuality* (pp. 301–316). New York: Harper & Row.

Zimmerman, B. (1984). The politics of transliteration: Lesbian personal narratives. *Signs, 9*, 663–682.

Zuger, B. (1988). Is early effeminate behavior in boys early homosexuality? *Comprehensive Psychiatry, 29*, 509–519.

Appendix A: Definitions of Key Terms[1]

Androgynophila Emotional attraction and sexual desire in which love and lust are attached to both a man and a woman serially or simultaneously by a person of either gender (from Greek *andros* man + *gyne* woman + *philia* love).

Bisexual Sexual contacts with people of the same gender and people of the other gender, either concurrently or sequentially; it may involve either genital acts or a long-term affectional–erotic status. It is also a term for people whose affectional–erotic status or life-style reflects androgynophilia; sometimes termed *ambisexual.*

Coming Out The sequence of events through which individuals recognize their same-gender sexual orientation and disclose it to others.

Gay Term for a person whose affectional–erotic status and life-style reflect homophilia; it often refers to men but may include both women and men.

Heterophilia A type of emotional attraction and sexual desire in which love and lust are attached to people of the other gender (from Greek *hetero* other + *philia* love).

Heterosexual Sexual contacts with people of the other gender; it may involve either genital acts or a long-term affectional–erotic status.

Heterosexism The belief that heterophilia and heterosexual affectional–erotic status are better or more natural than homophilia or homosexual affectional–erotic status.

Homophilia A type of emotional attraction and sexual desire in which love and lust are attached to those of the same gender (from Greek *homos* same + *philia* love).

Homophobia A term that has commonly come to refer to prejudice against people who are homophilic (from Greek *homos* same + *phobos* fear or fright). It should not be considered a clinical phobia.

Homosexual Sexual contacts with people of the same gender; it may involve either genital acts or a long-term affectional–erotic status. (Because the term has multiple meanings, its use as an adjective is often unclear; e.g., homosexual rape, homosexual spokesperson, homosexual partner.)

Lesbian Term for a woman whose affectional–erotic status and life-style reflect homophilia.

Sexual Orientation The relative balance between an individual's homophilia and heterophilia, viewed as separate parallel dimensions. It reflects one's affectional–erotic attraction to the same gender, other gender, or to both women and men.

---

[1]Several of these definitions are based on those proposed by Money (1988).

Appendix B

Resources Available From the American Psychological Association

The following American Psychological Association amicus briefs are available from the Public Interest Directorate, American Psychological Association, 1200 17th Street, NW, Washington, DC 20036:

Bersoff, D. N., & Ogden, D. W. (1989). *In the United States Court of Appeals for the Seventh Circuit: Miriam BenShalom v. John O. Marsh, Jr., Secretary of the U.S. Army. Brief of amicus curiae. American Psychological Association. In support of plaintiff/appellee* (Nos. 88-2771 & 89-1213).

Bersoff, D. N., Ogden, D. W., & Dunlap, M. C. (1988). *In the United States Court of Appeals for the Ninth Circuit: Sergeant Perry J. Watkins v. United States Army, et al. Brief of amicus curiae. American Psychological Association. In support of plaintiff-appellant* (No. 85-4006). (Reprinted in G. B. Melton, 1989. Public policy and private prejudice: Psychology and law on gay rights. *American Psychologist, 44*, 933–940.)

Ewing, M. F., Ennis, B. J., & Bersoff, D. N. (1983). *In the Supreme Court of the United States: State of New York v. Robert Uplinger and Susan Butler. Brief of amici curiae. American Psychological Association, American Psychiatric Association, and American Public Health Association. In support of respondents* (No. 82-1724).

Ogden, D. W., Ewing, M. F., & Bersoff, D. N. (1986). *In the Supreme Court of the United States: Michael J. Bowers, Attorney General of Georgia v. Michael Hardwick, and John and Mary Doe. Brief of amici curiae. American Psychological Association and American Public Health Association. In support of respondents* (No. 85-140).

The following American Psychological Association Committee on Lesbian and Gay Concerns documents are available from the Committee on Lesbian and Gay Concerns, American Psychological Association, 1200 17th Street, NW, Washington, DC 20036:

American Psychological Association. (1988). *American Psychological Association policy statements on lesbian and gay issues.* Washington, DC: Author.

American Psychological Association. (1991). *Graduate faculty in psychology interested in gay and lesbian issues 1990.* Washington, DC: Author.

American Psychological Association Committee on Lesbian and Gay Concerns. (1990). *A selected bibliography of lesbian and gay concerns in psychology: An affirmative perspective.* Washington, DC: American Psychological Association.

Task Force on Bias in Psychotherapy With Lesbians and Gay Men. (1990). *Final report.* Washington, DC: American Psychological Association.

Additional Resources

Bradford, J., & Ryan, C. (1987). *National Lesbian Health Care Survey: Mental health implications.* Washington, DC: National Lesbian and Gay Health Foundation. (P.O. Box 65472, Washington, DC 20035)

Curry, H., & Clifford, D. (1989). *A legal guide for lesbian and gay couples.* Berkeley, CA: Nolo Press. (950 Parker Street, Berkeley, CA 94710)

Gartrell, N., & Hamilton, J. *Lesbian mother study.* A multicity 20-year longitudinal study of lesbian families (in progress). (Institute for Research on Women's Health, 1616 18th Street, NW, #109-B, Washington, DC 20009)

Haldeman, D. C. (1991). Sexual orientation conversion therapy for gay men and lesbians: A scientific examination. In J. Gonsiorek & J. Weinrich (Eds.), *Homosexuality: Research findings for public policy* (pp. 149–160). Newbury Park, CA: Sage.

Hidalgo, H., Peterson, T. L., & Woodman, N. J. (Eds.). (1985). *Lesbian and gay issues: A resource manual for social workers.* Silver Spring, MD: National Association of Social Workers. (7981 Eastern Avenue, Silver Spring, MD 20910)

Human Rights Foundation, Inc. (1984). *Demystifying homosexuality: A teaching guide about lesbians and gay men.* New York: Irvington.

National Association for Lesbian and Gay Gerontology. (1989). *Resource guide: Lesbian and gay aging.* San Francisco, CA: Author. (1853 Market Street, San Francisco, CA 94103)

National Center for Lesbian Rights. (1987). *Lesbian and gay parenting: A psychological and legal perspective.* San Francisco, CA: Author. (1663 Mission Street, 5th floor, San Francisco, CA 94013)

National Gay and Lesbian Task Force. (1986). *Dealing with violence: A guide for gay and lesbian people.* Washington, DC: Author. (NGLTF, 1517 U Street, NW, Washington, DC 20009)

Shernoff, M., & Scott, W. A. (1988). *The sourcebook on lesbian/gay health care.* Washington, DC: National Lesbian and Gay Health Foundation. (P.O. Box 65472, Washington, DC 20035)

Whitlock, K. (1989). *Bridges of respect: Creating support for lesbian and gay youth.* Philadelphia: American Friends Service Committee. (1501 Cherry Street, Philadelphia, PA 19102)